Survival
of the Black Family

Survival of the Black Family

The Institutional Impact of U.S. Social Policy

K. Sue Jewell

PRAEGER

New York
Westport, Connecticut
London

Library of Congress Cataloging-in-Publication Data

Jewell, K. Sue.
  Survival of the black family.

  Bibliography: p.
  Includes index.
  1. Family policy—United States. 2. Afro-American
families. I. Title.
HQ536.J48   1988   306.8′5′08996073   88–2338
ISBN 0–275–92985–X (alk. paper)

Library of Congress Catalog Card Number: 88–2338
ISBN: 0–275–92985–X

First published in 1988

Praeger Publishers, One Madison Avenue, New York, NY   10010
A division of Greenwood Press, Inc.

Printed in the United States of America

∞

The paper used in this book complies with the
Permanent Paper Standard issued by the National
Information Standards Organization (Z39.48–1984).

10   9   8   7   6   5   4   3   2   1

FOR
SISI
AND
CURTIS

CONTENTS

PREFACE

The central thesis of *Survival of the Black Family: The Institutional Impact of U. S. Social Policy* is that policies, procedures, and assumptions underlying social and economic programs in the 1960s and 1970s contributed to the disintegration of black two-parent and extended families and to an increase in black families headed by women. In addition, these factors are related to the decline of other important institutions.

The primary reason for the failure of liberal social policy to enhance the status of black families was that social and economic programs and civil rights legislation could not effectively remove social barriers, which prevent black families from participating fully in mainstream American society.

While it is not the intent of the author to minimize the important role that economic factors play in contributing to upward mobility and economic independence for both black and white families, it is the case that social policy can determine the overall impact of social and economic conditions on society members. This is particularly true for families that occupy an economically depressed status. Furthermore, in the absence of policies and practices that guarantee that all individuals will be permitted equal access to societal institutions, the most optimal economic climate will not afford blacks and other disenfranchised groups opportunities to achieve at a level comparable to that of majority group members. Therefore, an examination of social policy is essential to a thorough understanding of the economic status of extant black families.

Although I argue that social policies and their absence have strongly influenced the emergence and decline of diverse black family structures, liberal social policy, as implemented in the United States, has had an adverse effect on black two-parent families. Of equal importance are myths emanating from this period, which suggest that:

1. Substantial social and economic gains were made by black families.
2. Social institutions now offer blacks and other racial and ethnic minorities unlimited opportunities, as a direct consequence of the policies and practices of this era.
3. Extant black families that are economically depressed have only themselves to blame for their failure to successfully compete for societal rewards.

In refuting the myths of significant black family progress and the omnipresence of social equity in major societal institutions (both attributed largely to liberal social policy) attention is focused on the extent to which black families have been adversely affected by a process of assimilation, which was socio-psychological rather than economic. Moreover, efforts designed to bring about integration resulted in the systematic exposure of blacks, through educational institutions, the workplace, and the media, to competing socializing agents. Understandably, the compelling nature of such forces has served to undermine values, beliefs, and other black cultural systems that had ensured the survival and progress of black families.

In addition to examining the impact of social and economic programs on black institutions in general and the family in particular, I present a discussion of how neoconservatism in the 1980s has affected the status of black families.

I conclude that liberal social policy, despite claims to the contrary, resulted in modest rather than substantial gains for black families. Further, I contend that the illusion that institutions have been permanently altered, thereby affording black families equal access, has led to the perpetuation of the belief that the failure of black families to overcome social and economic obstacles is a function of individual rather than institutional shortcomings.

Finally, I offer guidelines that are not exhaustive, but rather essential to the formulation of a social policy that could enhance the status of black families in the United States. Such a social policy would demonstrate its effectiveness through the inclusion of black families in all levels of major institutions within American society.

ACKNOWLEDGMENTS

I wish to acknowledge the support and assistance of those who contributed to the completion of this book. The final preparation of the manuscript was supported, in part, by a small grant from the College of Humanities of the Ohio State University.

I am grateful for the collegial support I received from Okey Onyejekwe. A special thanks to Susan Toliver, Florence Bonner, John Stanfield, and Robert Hill, and other reviewers who provided me with valuable feedback.

The technical assistance and instruction in the use of word processors were graciously provided by Pat Lowe, Connie Dantuono, and Jackie Hosley. In addition, my thanks to Rose Smith, who typed the tables with diligence and patience. The advice and suggestions on preparing the manuscript from the staff at Praeger were extremely helpful.

Finally, I would like to express my sincere gratitude to Henry Warren, Valerie Warren, Kathy Warren, Michael Warren, SiSi Jewell, Curtis Taylor Jewell II, and Curtis Taylor Jewell for their sacrifices and unconditional moral support during the entire preparation of the manuscript.

Survival
of the Black Family

1 INTRODUCTION

LIBERAL SOCIAL POLICY DEFINED

Social policy is a topic which in contemporary society has joined the ranks of religion and politics in being able to polemicize discussions among seemingly homogeneous, congenial segments of the population. Perhaps one reason for the volatility that is apt to be generated by discussions of social policy, which on the surface appears to be an innocuous issue, is the direction it took in the 1960s and the constituency for which it became intended. Because blacks petitioned the government to develop mechanisms to eliminate the barriers that prevented their participation in societal institutions, the government became involved in formulating, funding, and monitoring social and economic programs. In effect, a major goal of liberal social policy was to elevate the status of black families in the United States. The scope of social and economic programs was not limited to blacks, but was extended to poor families irrespective of race or ethnic background. However, since an inordinate number of black families were represented among the nation's poor, liberal social policy was by design intended to meet their needs.

While definitions of *liberalism* vary, here defined, it is a belief system that embraces the precepts that the federal government has a responsibility to do all within its power to ensure that all its people receive equitable treatment and are given equal opportunities to participate fully in social, political, and economic institutions. Moreover, *liberalism* refers to the federal government's attempt to effect social justice for historically disenfranchised groups (such as blacks, the poor, women, and other racial and ethnic minorities) by implementing and expanding social service programs, passing civil rights legislation, and exercising rigorous enforcement powers. Liberal social policy, which is commonly associated with the period ranging from 1960 to the late 1970s but more accurately reflects a more expansive era, beginning in the mid 1950s is generally credited/ faulted with having brought about major progress or major problems for black families.

Heated debates that revolve around social policy surround efforts in the 1980s to rescind liberal policies and practices. The social conservatism characteristic of the 1980s has set the climate for discussions regarding the effectiveness of liberal social policy, the benefits, and the costs.

This book examines the impact of liberal social policy on black families in America. In so doing, I accept the premise that black families have always been affected by the social policy, even though, until the 1960s (with the exception of a brief period following emancipation), they had never been the intended recipients of a national social policy in this country. It is obvious that black families, as well as families with membership in other racial and ethnic groups, are affected to some degree by any form of domestic policy. Due to their economically depressed status and inextricably related to their systematic exclusion from traditional institutions, black families have been especially vulnerable to public policy changes, as well as to fluctuations in other social, economic and political events. Furthermore, social policy affects not only the structure of black families, but the dynamics as well. Just as social systems on a macro level are sustained and perpetuated by their interdependent relationships, institutions within the black community are also mutually dependent. What affects one institution will surely impact to some extent on another. For example, when social policy impacts upon the black family, one can be relatively sure that other institutions in the black community (such as the black church, black-owned businesses, etc.) are also affected. In addition to altering the structure of black families, social policy also has had a profound effect on the dynamics of these institutions. An elaborate and complex series of adaptive mechanisms has evolved for the purpose of ensuring the survival and progress of black families. Many of these systems and patterns of interaction emerged in response to the absence of a national social policy that would have provided essential goods and services to black families. Mutual aid networks, which represent a mechanism for the exchange of valuable commodities are an example of one such process that has been responsible for the ability of black families to function largely without support from sources external to the black community.[1]

In discussions of liberal social policy, there is a tendency to confuse social welfare policy with more global social policy initiatives. Furthermore, as with the stereotyped image of social welfare programs, the misconception that black people have been the sole beneficiaries of liberal social and economic programs is quite pervasive. In this examination of liberal social policy I am referring to those programs that include social welfare services, but that are not limited to public assistance alone. In the main, I am exploring those social and economic programs that were developed and expanded during the 1960s and 1970s. While I recognize that some of these programs were first developed in the 1930s, and that others were created in the decade preceding 1960, the primary focus is on the 1960s and 1970s because of the infusion of relatively large amounts of government funds into these programs during these two decades. Further, this period, unlike others, was marked by a more liberal pattern of administration, policies, and practices, which resulted in services being extended to larger numbers of individuals. It is important to note that although the period under consideration was, on balance, characterized by liberal policies, the entire time span was not. The Nixon and Ford administrations contained elements of both liberalism and conservatism, with emphasis on the latter. However, despite the interlude of the Nixon and Ford administrations, this new thrust in monetary allocations, innovative policy initiatives, and extended benefits encompass our definition of liberal social policy. Further, the scope of my analysis of the impact of social policy on black families includes the passage of laws that were also designed to give disenfranchised groups access to institutions that had, prior to the 1960s, maintained a position of exclusivity and rigidity, thereby limiting the participation of blacks, women, Hispanics, and other racial and ethnic minorities. Legislation that falls within this realm includes: affirmative action; the Voting Rights Act; fair housing legislation; *Brown versus the Board of Education*, which made school segregation unconstitutional; and other laws passed to guarantee that all U. S. citizens are accorded the same opportunities for institutional participation.

When in this work reference is made to government involvement being "great" or "massive," it is done with an historical perspective in mind. While there is disagreement over what constitutes "great" or "massive" with respect to monetary allocations and total governmental involvement, the sheer magnitude of the investment made by the federal government during the 1960s and 1970s was unprecedented. It is with this knowledge that I use these descriptive terms. In this same vein, I remain cognizant of the fact that the percentages of moneys spent for federal programs must be viewed relative to other government expenditures during the period under consideration. It is not within the purview of this book to examine social policy within the context of its effectiveness or capacity to fulfill a social obligation based on monetary appropriations alone. This is not to suggest that the government's commitment to eradicate social injustices and to enable black families to reach economic parity with white families is somehow unrelated to the amounts of money committed for such an endeavor. However, the ability of liberal social policy to effect necessary changes in the status of black families and their members extends beyond the funds which the federal government has committed. In fact, the allocation of monies to social and economic programs is but one manifestation of the government's perception of its obligation.

The problem addressed in this book is: Why did liberal social policy in the United States fail? If, as I believe, liberal social policy *was* ineffective, the questions I seek to answer are: Why? and What evidence is there to substantiate this claim? Another question I shall attempt to answer is: What has been the overall effect of liberal social policy on the status of black families? Finally, I explore those conditions that must be present if a social policy is to effectively enhance the status and functioning capacity of black families and their members.

My premise that liberal social policy, as enacted in the United States, was unsuccessful is not intended to mean that liberal social policy enacted in parts of Europe, or that which may emerge in other forms in the United States, is or will be ineffective. As such, inferences to that effect are unacceptable and not representative of my position. What I propose is that liberal social policy initiated in the 1950s and expanded during the 1960s and 1970s did not accomplish the mission for which it was intended. Succinctly stated, social and economic programs that evolved from liberal social policy in the United States have failed to eventuate in full participation for black and poor families in mainstream institutions. Although these programs had a broader-based constituency, the focus will be placed on the effects of these programs on black families. My rationale for focusing on black families is that inherent in my thesis is the belief that race was and continues to be a salient factor in determining an individual's life chances in America. Consequently, a holistic or generic perspective, designed to explain why social policy failed to prevent the perpetuation and growth of underclass families in general, would not sufficiently address racially based factors, which have systematically precluded blacks from gaining equal access to opportunity structures. And to do so would be, in theory, to ignore a major purpose for which liberal social policy was designed. Before the twenty-year period was over, a number of other disenfranchised groups, including Hispanics, American Indians, and white women, also became contenders for the redistribution of power and wealth initially sought by blacks in the civil rights movement. Although these groups share a commonality of interests with blacks in that they have all experienced systematic forms of social inequities, there are distinct historical experiences that have resulted in coping strategies that are somewhat unique to each group. It is these adaptive strategies developed by black families, which encompass family structure and dynamics, that have been a response to social policy; as social policy has changed, the strategies have been changed as well.

THE GOVERNMENT'S ROLE IN SOCIAL POLICY

By explaining the effect that liberal social policy has had on black families in America, I do not argue for the divestment of the federal government or any other levels of government in the funding, development, and supervision of social and economic programs. In fact, I maintain that government participation in the development, funding, and enforcement of social and economic programs is not only important but essential if black families are to substantially increase their level of participation in societal institutions throughout the United States.

Accordingly, the issue is not whether the government has a responsibility for ensuring that black families—and all families—have an equal opportunity to participate fully in social institutions. Rather, the issue is identifying the most expedient way in which the government should fulfill its obligation to guarantee that all groups, irrespective of race, gender, or ethnicity are granted fundamental civil rights.

The neoconservatives, who have vociferously attacked the government's involvement in social policy, have done so for the purpose of eliminating social and economic programs. Members of this political interest group offer diverse reasons for the failure of liberal social policy to result in economic independence for black and poor families. Diverse as they are, these arguments are designed with one goal in mind; the radical revision of social policy in general and social welfare policy in particular. This "either-or" approach to social policy is an approach of no utility to the government, the recipients of such programs, or society at large. Few enterprises conduct business in this fashion; to do so would undoubtedly have devastating consequences. Instead, the goal of a well-run business is to enhance function to an optimal level through carefully calculated change. Accordingly, functional features or system components should remain, and those that do not function properly must be either modified and retained or defined as possessing little value and discarded. Rarely is a total system that has salvageable components defined as being of no utility and completely eliminated. Yet, in the 1980s conservatives proposed that liberal social policy was detrimental to recipients, as well as to the general population whose tax dollars supported social and economic programs. Blaming liberal social policy for a high federal deficit and an inadequate national security, conservatives pushed for a drastic reduction in funding and the complete elimination of social and economic programs.

THE BLACK FAMILY AND SOCIAL POLICY: ASCRIBING RESPONSIBILITY

Clearly, the factors identified as causing the failure of liberal social policy dictate the nature of the solution. For those who see the government as too permissive and black families as the problem, understandably the solution is the elimination of such programs. Conversely, when the failure of liberal social policy is more correctly attributed to misconceptions regarding the recipients of social and economic programs, faulty planning, poor administration, ineffective enforcement, and the inability to develop mechanisms for overcoming institutional resistance, appropriate solutions focus on modifying the programs and identifying strategies that will make social policies and practices more efficacious.

Irrespective of factors which militated against social and economic programs achieving their desired ends, little benefit can be derived from ascribing blame for their failures. As such, what I offer in this discussion is a form of social criticism, not condemnation. Though the latter approach may be feasible for partisan politics, it is of no utility to those who are committed to developing strategies that will ameliorate social and economic conditions for black families in the United States. In fact, a nonpartisan effort is a requisite for the formulation of a social policy that will possess the capacity for the ongoing formation, implementation and assessment of social and economic programs.

Perhaps one of the most rudimentary steps toward establishing an effective social policy is the reassessment of the positive and negative consequences of past social and economic programs. Before one can effectively develop a social policy designed to assure that black families and their members are able to participate fully in social institutions, the plethora of data generated by past social and economic programs must be analyzed. Interestingly, those who oppose liberal social policy on the grounds that the government's involvement was tantamount to intrusion in the open market have been eager to conduct inquiries to determine the outcomes of such programs. While their findings are likely to be similar to those of liberals who advocate government involvement in social service delivery, the interpretation and recommendations are generally quite different.

While polarization exists among various segments of the population regarding the role of government toward improving the plight of black and poor families, there is a surfeit of individuals who have not yet established a firm position and for whom no answer is readily available. It has been argued that historically the masses have remained ambivalent regarding social policy and the plight of the less economically advantaged.[2] Much of this uncertainty is related to the adversarial nature of social policy. To a great extent, the proliferation of diametrically opposed views has confused the issue for the public. However, since the inception of liberal social policy, uncertainty over what should be done to improve the economic position of black families has shifted to who is responsible for doing so. In some quarters, the federal government is considered the entity that should assume this responsibility. Others maintain that black families must resolve their own problems. And still there is the position that the problem cannot be adequately improved in light of available resources and the magnitude and institutionalization of the problem, and without the collaborative efforts of the government, black families, and micro and macro institutions. It is the last position that is set forth in this book.

THE ROLE OF ACADEME

In seeking solutions to social problems, policy-makers have relied on academic scholarship. Although academic scholarship is intended to influence public policy, the converse is not without precedent. Thus, social policy has also served as the impetus for research, which tends to corroborate a priori social-policy decisions. It is difficult to conceive how those who utilize this approach can consider it a reliable method for formulating social policy. Though academicians use scientific methods and instruments to gather data, pertinent to social-policy decision-making, the extreme divergence in interpretation of this data is reflected in contradictory findings and policy recommendations. While it is not realistic to assume that social scientists should agree on all or even most policy issues, the degree of disparity is far too great in general policy issues as well as in areas of specificity. This pronounced lack of agreement among academicians regarding social policy tends to be exacerbated when the unit of analysis is social policy within the black community. While polarization is understandable within the larger society, where there is overt and conscious variability in terms of political interests, the role of objectivity and adherence to scientific rigor should result in more uniformity in the academy. Regrettably, such is not the case.

There appear to be two major perspectives in academe, which mirror those within the larger society. As such, academicians tend to be proponents of either the liberal or conservative persuasion. Those who subscribe to the former generally express unswerving support for social and economic programs implemented in the 1960s and 1970s. In the other school of thought are conservatives, who oppose liberal social policy and believe that it is decidedly perilous to tamper with the open market system. Split along these same lines are academicians who differentially assign responsibility for improving the economically dependent status of black families: liberals expect societal institutions to improve conditions for blacks while conservatives insist that blacks must reach parity with whites through their own efforts, without government support. A careful analysis of the literature is likely to reveal considerable disagreement among scholars regarding the functions of various structures and dynamics within institutions in the black community and the larger society. Clearly, if academic scholarship is to influence social policy within the black community, it must overcome this impasse. To do so, however, means that academicians must become less vulnerable to the political pressures that exist within both the larger society and the academy. As such, those who are exponents of the liberal persuasion should have little difficulty identifying policy recommendations that entail the use of blacks' assets, regardless of how infinitesimal. Moreover, scholars who adhere to the conservative viewpoint must be ready to concede that government involvement in the open-market system is sometimes imperative if other means of increasing private sector participation have met with limited success. From this vantage point comes the recognition that academic scholarship should play a salient role in the formulation of social policy, rather than social policy affecting academic scholarship.

Academic scholarship relative to the study of any problem is dynamic and not static. The evolutionary nature of academic scholarship is rarely questioned when scientific investigation in the physical sciences leads to policy decisions that later undergo modification, as improved measurement techniques are developed and new data are generated. But academic scholarship that results in policy decisions in the arena of social policy is, oftentimes, expected to be absolute, firm, and unchanging. Whether in the physical or social sciences, academic scholarship should operate within the same parameters. Accordingly, when changes occur that warrant new social policy recommendations, researchers should willingly make changes without reluctance.

SOCIAL POLICY BY DEFAULT: ANOTHER BASIS FOR FAILURE

Social policy and the black family are topics which have received considerable attention over the last twenty-five years. A significant portion of these discussions focused on the necessity for liberal social policy, which would reduce black family dependency and enhance stabilization. As problems became apparent and the structure of black families and other institutions in the black community began to reflect the negative impact of liberal social policy, academicians and nonacademicains increased their examination of these phenomena. However, because liberal social policy evolved out of protests and demands of the 1960s, its proponents—whether academicians, policy-makers, administrators, or recipients—have been placed in a position of defensiveness. Therefore, criticisms of liberal social policy by its advocates were generally considered self-defeating. Liberals refrained from criticizing social policies and practices fearing that their opponents would consider such self-criticism a justification to eradicate social and economic programs and to eliminate government involvement. Equally important is the fact that those aspects of liberal social policy that were damaging to black institutions, including the black family, remained virtually unchanged.

The precariousness of this situation, whereby any criticism of liberal social policy was likely to be interpreted as total program failure, is evident in the appearance of problems that, with intervention, could have been prevented. Trepidation on the part of advocates of liberal social policy to enunciate the emergence of problems and the need for policy and administrative change represents an inherent flaw in liberal social policy in the United States. For this reason alone, it is unlikely that liberal social policy could have achieved the goals for which it was designed. This is not to imply that changes did not occur in the policies and administration of social and economic programs. But the belief, on the part of administrators, academicians, and supporters of liberal social policy, that the identification of problems in social and economic programs would have jeopardized components in need of modification or elimination and have imperiled social and economic programs in their entirety militated against the success of these endeavors.

The fact that liberal social policy was not able to elevate black families to a position of economic independence is an issue that all too often is overlooked. Moreover, problems that have increased for black families during the era of liberal social policy are not spuriously but highly correlated with the nature of programs developed and their administration. To continue to ignore the debilitating effects of these programs is likely to be even more devastating to the future of black families and other black institutions.

Thus, I undertake the task of dispelling the misconception that liberal social policy, in general, was beneficial to black families. Associated with the myth that liberal social policy has been advantageous to black families is the myth that institutions within American society are no longer exclusive, but offer to blacks, women, and members of all racial and ethnic groups equal opportunities to compete for societal rewards. Though changes were made in the practices of major institutions to afford access to minority groups, discriminatory practices, which continue to limit the participation of blacks as a cultural group, remain. At the same time, there are blacks who experienced individual success.[3] Ostensibly, upward mobility for those individuals and families was also mitigated. Because an image of institutional cooperation emerged from government efforts to ensure social equity, black families that are poor continue to be blamed for their social and economic status. Similarly, this sentiment is applied to black families across all socioeconomic levels. Coupled with the fact that government efforts were devoted to seeking and implementing forms of redress for past racial injustices, some people feel that black families have received special favors or opportunities denied to others. The combined effect attributes failure to blacks for not taking advantage of these opportunities, but does not recognize that liberal social policy failed to accomplish its objectives. Moreover, this notion of institutional cooperation belies the underrepresentation of blacks in high-level occupations, business ownership, and other positions of power and wealth throughout the United States.

A PLURALISTIC APPROACH

Although most analyses of this kind focus almost exclusively on the economic consequences of social policy, it is important that the social–psychological implications of social policy also be examined. It is far too simplistic to limit an assessment of the impact of liberal social policy on black families to one dimension alone. And to a large extent, the assumptions upon which social policy are based are sociological. To be sure, perceptions of black families as structurally and functionally dysfunctional have been at the basis of both conservative and liberal social policy. While the failure of social and economic programs to overcome structural barriers has had a devastating impact on black families, the perception of their social inadequacy also contributed significantly to the destablizing effect of liberal social policy. Clearly, an effective social policy must eliminate societal barriers, and do so by acknowledging the strengths of black families.

NOTES

1. Andrew Billingsley, *Children of the Storm: Black Children and American Child Welfare* (New York: Harcourt Brace Jovanovich, 1972), p. 46; Robert Hill, *The Strengths of Black Families* (New York: National Urban League, 1972), p. 56; Robert Hill, *Eco-*

nomic Policies and Black Progress: Myths and Realities (Washington, D. C.: National Urban League, 1981), p. 79; Robert Hill, *Self-help Groups in the African-American Community: Current Organization and Service* (North Carolina: University of North Carolina School of Social Work, 1987), pp. 4–5; Carol Stack, *All Our Kin: Strategies for Survival in a Black Community* (New York: Harper & Row, 1974), p. 28; Herbert Gutman, *The Black Family in Slavery and Freedom: 1750–1925* (New York: Vintage, 1976), pp. 213–214; Harriette Pipes McAdoo, "Black Mothers and the Extended Family Support Network" in La Frances Rodgers-Rose, ed., *The Black Woman* (Beverly Hills, California: Sage, 1980), pp. 125–127; Carrie Allen McCray, "The Black Woman and Family Roles" in La Frances Rodgers-Rose, ed., *The Black Woman* (Beverly Hills, California: Sage, 1980), pp. 70–73; K. Sue Jewell, "Use of Social Welfare Programs and the Disintegration of the Black Nuclear Family," *The Western Journal of Black Studies* 8 (Winter, 1984), pp. 193–195.

2. "Reagan's Polarized America," Newsweek (April 5, 1982), p. 19.

3. Derrick A. Bell, Jr., *Race, Racism and American Law* (Boston: Little Brown and Company, 1980), p. 43.

2 SOCIAL POLICY AND BLACK FAMILY STRUCTURE

A discussion of the effects of social policy on the formation, maintenance, and dissolution of black family structures can best be understood through a historical analysis of black family patterns. Although U. S. liberal social policy contributed to the erosion of black two-parent and extended families, conservative social policy and the absence of a national public policy, that addressed the needs of blacks have been responsible for the emergence and disintegration of other types of black family arrangements.[1] Unquestionably, the absence of a national social policy resulted in the development of structures among black families that influence their many configurations today. Interestingly, there exists a considerable lack of agreement among scholars regarding the origins and causes of black family structures. Essentially two major perspectives relative to etiology and causation of black family structures have been advanced.

THEORETICAL PERSPECTIVES ON BLACK FAMILY STRUCTURE

According to Herskovits (1958) and Nobles (1974), the contemporary black American family is predicated on precolonial African culture, with its emphasis on the clan.[2] Conversely, Frazier (1932, 1939), Elkins (1963), Moynihan (1965), and Rainwater and Yancey (1967), argued that the vicissitudes of slavery destroyed African familial structures and gave rise to a multiplicity of black family constellations that continue to exist today.[3] Accordingly, the matrifocal character of black families is offered as evidence that the patriarchal nature of traditional African families was submerged during slavery. Related to this perspective is the thesis of matriarchy as the primary cause of intergenerational poverty, crime, and other forms of social disorganization among black families. Popularized in 1965 by Daniel P. Moynihan, then the Secretary of Labor, the analysis of black family structures as a determinant of economic dependence served as a buttress for the reformulation of social policy. The myriad social welfare programs that ensued were based on Moynihan's research, which polemicized the issue of societal versus matriarchal culpability for the depressed economic status of black Americans. Although social programs were developed and expanded in direct response to the belief in black family disorganization, there has never been any consensus regarding black family structure, its origins, causes, or the ability of black families to perform the functions to which they have been assigned. In fact, the debate over whether black families are matriarchal and the extent to which they conform to the traditional nuclear family continues more than twenty years later.

In sum, two major disparate theoretical formulations have been proffered. One one hand, black families are perceived as deviations from the normative family arrangment—that is, the nuclear family—because slavery destroyed the traditional African family. The opposing view holds that in general black families are primarily nuclear. And that black nuclear families represent variations brought about due to harsh social and economic conditions. Sudarkasa cites the validity in both models and suggests that a thorough study of black family organizations be undertaken.[4]

In either case, the controversy surrounding black family structure is related to the inordinate proportion of black families with female heads. The fact that black families have always had a larger percentage of females maintaining households than white families has raised numerous questions regarding its functioning capability, particularly in the area of socializing male children.[5] Yet, concern over the ability of black families to function at a level comparable to white middle-class families has not been limited to black families maintained by females. Augmented, extended, and other variations of black families have also been characterized by some social scientists as being incapable of performing at a level par with the traditional nuclear family.[6]

Over the last two decades, a considerable amount of time and energy has been devoted to arguments and counter-arguments as to whether black family structure is deviant, variant, or congruent with the idealized nuclear family. Even more alarming is the recognition that social policy has been predicated on these apparent inconsistencies and misconceptions, which plague black family studies. Whatever their theoretical perspective, social scientists representing both schools of though have attempted to verify or refute the matriarchal culpability theory. In the past, many liberal sociologists who challenged the matriarchal culpability theory, which placed the onus for black deprivation on female-controlled black families, accurately repudiated the prevalence of matriarchy.[7]

Frequently, efforts to confirm or deny the prevalence of the black matriarchy has led to the systematic comparing of black families to white families, for the purpose of establishing gross similarities or differences in terms of structure and functioning. Still, a thorough analysis of the structure and dynamics of black families has yet to be conducted. Clearly, scholars who have developed elaborate paradigms in defense of black family structures, comparing them to white families and explaining variability as solely due to economic factors, are as guilty of proliferating misconceptions about black family structure as are those who attribute social ills confronting blacks to black families alone. Whether one subscribes to the belief that black family structures are matriarchal, predicated on African cultural tradition, or hybrids of white American familial structures, it is difficult to refute that black families are unique and do not conform to the traditional nuclear model.

The failure on the part of social scientists to develop a conceptual model that explains the causes and nature of black family structures and the dynamics that affect the maintenance of black families is due largely to continuous efforts to analyze black families using the normative paradigm. Theoreticians, those in the cultural deviance and relativism schools, continue to examine black families using a middle-class, nuclear model as the barometer. But not all factors that affect white family structures impact similarly upon the structures of black families. The primary difference is that black families, because of social and economic hardships, developed unique family arrangements.[8] Hence, black families became dependent upon external informal support systems to a greater extent than did their white counterparts.[9] Even the most progressive and upwardly mobile black families have achieved success due to social support systems, which are outside their immediate families. In other words, black families have not been autonomous units; rather they have historically relied on informal social support systems for survival. Thus, to compare black families to white families, either to confirm or rebut theories purporting deviance or relativism, is akin to comparing apples to oranges.

Clearly, social policy dictates the availability of fundamental resources and strongly mediates the provision of goods and services by institutional and noninstitutional service providers. Because black famiies, like white families, are dependent on external sources for survival, the survival of all families is to a greater or lesser degree inextricably related to social policy. However, because race is a salient factor, which determines differential access to economic opportunity structures, social policy is likely to have a greater impact on black families. Whether social policy is conservative or liberal, black families must rely on entities outside of their primary familial unit for essential goods and services. But social policy can and does alter the nature of the exchange relationship between the black family and institutional and informal social support systems. In the case of liberal social policy, in which numerous social and economic programs were developed and entitlement was liberalized, government social welfare programs replaced mutual aid networks, transferring dependency from noninstitutional support systems to institutional ones. In theory, governmental agencies were neither intended nor designed to supplant these informal support sytems but were developed as emergency measures to bring about economic independence by supplementing existing informal social support systems.

In addition to their failure to bring about social and economic parity, social welfare programs drastically altered noninstitutional support systems and modified value and belief systems, thereby accelerating the demise of black two-parent and extended families and the growth of black female-headed families. Moreover, the introduction of a plethora of social programs did more than modify the structure of black families. It radically changed the life cycle of black families.

Before explaining the process by which the structure and life cycle of the black family adversely underwent modification, it is necessary to dispel two common myths regarding black families. First is the myth that black and white families are similar in terms of structure and dynamics. This notion came about largely as a means of refuting the thesis of the matriarchal character of black families. Still, there is no empirical evidence to support this contention. As early as 1932, when E. Franklin Frazier criticized lower-class black families for the disproportionate number of female-maintained families, scholars were quick to note that the majority of black families, like white families, were nuclear.[10] Later, when Moynihan advanced his thesis on the matriarchal character of black families, a number of sociologists hastily pointed to the majority of black families which, they argued, were like white families relative to their nuclear structural arrangment. Gutman added further corroboration to the argument that black families should not be labeled social anomalies and pathological, based on the fact that many were headed by females; he used census data to establish that as early as 1890, 90 percent of all black families were of the nuclear type. Unlike many social scientists, Gutman's use of the concept ''nuclear type'' also implied that black and white family structures must be considered in relative and not absolute terms.[11]

Although some researchers have gone to great lengths to establish that the black family is typically structured like the white family, in many instances subfamilies and variable forms are mentioned. For example, Billingsley developed an extensive composite of familial constellations that exist as autonomous units or within black families.[12] For instance, female-headed families have been found to coexist within a nuclear or extended structure. When subfamilies are found to coexist with nuclear families, the entire structure is redefined, becoming an extended or augmented nuclear family. In fact, the various types of black familial arrangements that are found independently or within another family arrangement are too numerous to mention. The issue is not that these structures are not found among whites, for they are. Instead, the controversy is over the prevalence of diverse structural arrangements within the black community. According to traditionalists, the larger the percentage of families of the simple nuclear type the greater is conformity to societal expectations. Conversely, the lower the percentage of nuclear families, the greater is the use of the deviance label in describing these families.[13] Understandably, the desire to identify black family structure with that of white families is related to eliminating the deviance label assigned to black families. If black families do not differ significantly from white families, then social scientists, policy-makers and society at large would have difficulty maintaining negative labels and stereotypes, which affect the treatment of blacks in society.

There is a surfeit of evidence suggesting that black families are unique, and while they may approximate those of white families, they are different in composition, structure, and dynamics over the life cycle of the family unit. In addition to Gutman, researchers including Billingsley, Hill, and Staples recognized that while black families were largely nuclear in type, their structures did not strictly conform to that of the traditional white nuclear family.[14] Ostensibly, occupants of a socially and economically disadvantaged status are not in a position to maintain an autonomous structural arrangement such as the nuclear family ad infinitum. Therefore, although husband and wife may be present in the home, black families in general have not conformed to the ideal "nuclear" type of familial structure. Perhaps one major reason for the unique qualities of black nuclear-type families has been their willingnesss to modify their structure based on the needs of their consanguine and fictive kin. Thus, referring to black families with both husband and wife present as nuclear generally requires qualification. Until recently, white families defined as nuclear were more likely to contain a husband, wife, and children over a longer period of the family life cycle than corresponding black families.

The second misconception about black families is that their structures are static. Heretofore, black families have been viewed as static. While it is true that white families, until the 1970s, have been relatively static; black family structures have been transitory. Over the black family life cycle, a variety of changes are likely to occur within the family structure. While the frequency of structural change is related to socioeconomic status, black families are characterized by changing structures across all social classes. Hence, a developmental approach is a necessity for analyzing black family structure.

According to Billingsley and Hill, the diversity of black family structures represents adaptations that are necessary to ensure survival.[15] Thus, it is important to note that black families, with their flexible and dynamic structures, have manifested optimal levels of functioning. Despite adverse social and economic forces, the flexibility of the black family has ensured its stability and perpetuation. Failure to understand black families and the propensity among policy makers and social practitioners to mold black families into an ideal nuclear model through liberal social and economic programs contributed to the deterioration of viable black family structures.

When the federal government began massive intervention into social-service delivery to ensure equity and equal access to opportunities for blacks and the poor, there was little agreement on or understanding of the social forces that had created black family structures. Policy-makers and human-service administrators did not understand that the absence of social policy and later the trend toward conservative policy, in conjunction with limited opportunities for blacks to achieve economic independence, had created black families that were malleable and mutually dependent on informal support systems for survival and progress. In the case of the majority of black families that were labeled "nuclear," there was also a failure to recognize that these families, while appearing on the surface to be structured according to the idealized family model, were more likely to undergo structural change over time. And they, like other black families, were held intact by dependence on noninstitutional support systems. In effect, the thread that kept black families together was a social-exchange network embedded in a value and belief system based on the norm of reciprocity. It was also this commitment to collective cooperativism that eventuated in the unique structures and dynamics characteristic of black families. Taking in new members and permitting the coexistence of subfamilies is evidence of the interdependent relationships of black families and members of informal support systems.[16]

The foregoing myths, along with the misconception of the matriarchal character of black families, became firmly entrenched in social policy in the 1960s and served as the basis for government expansion of social programs. Thus liberalization of social policy was designed to bring about economic independence by transforming matriarchal black families into patriarchal structures, with black males legitimately ursurping power from black women through economic privilege. Regrettably, social programs, while based on the need to destroy what was purported to be the black matriarchy, ironically created it. In so doing, black insitutions and cultural value systems, which were responsible for keeping black two-parent families intact, were undermined.

DEVELOPMENTAL CHANGES IN BLACK FAMILY STRUCTURES

In 1960, before the liberalization of social policy, 74 percent of all black families were maintained by a husband and wife, 22 percent were headed by women, and the remaining 4 percent were families maintained by black males.[17] By 1980, approximately two decades after the introduction and expansion of social programs, black families had undergone considerable change. A dramatic increase in the rate of marital dissolutions through separation and divorce resulted in the decline of black husband-wife families and the growth of black families headed by women. The percentage of black families maintained by married couples had declined to 55 percent in 1982, while the number of black women heading families rose to 41 percent in this same period. In roughly ten years following the implementation of a plethora of social programs (designed to stabilize black and poor families), the divorce rates for black couples escalated from 104 per 1,000 in 1970 to 220 divorces per 1,000 married couples in 1982. By 1980, divorce had become endemic to black couples, with black college-educated women being the most likely to occupy a divorced status.[18] The alarming increase in divorce among black men and women was not the only reason that the structure of black families began undergoing change. Separation, the most common method of marital dissolution among low-income blacks, and out-of-wedlock births also had a significant impact on black family structure, as evidenced by the growing number of female-maintained families. Despite the fact that black women who give birth to children out of wedlock eventually marry, the percentage choosing to remain single and maintain families independent of a husband has increased drastically. Of black families with a female head, 12 percent of the female heads of household had never married in 1960; however, the proportion of black families headed by a women who had never married reached 32 percent by 1982.[19]

Between 1960 and 1980 other changes in black families became apparent, suggesting that the life cycle of black families had been seriously altered.

Restructuring

Gutman in his examination of black family structures from 1750 to 1925 alludes to the necessity for social scientists to explore the changing nature of black families.[20] However, social scientists have identified numerous patterns of black families, considering each as static and independent of all others. When researchers have attempted to scientifically investigate variations in black family structure over the family life cycle, there has been little theoretical basis for doing so.[21] Specifically, Billingsley, in refuting the generalizability of deviance to all black families, enumerated a number of black family structures. He argued that these familial constellations reflected the resiliency of black families, which were able to adapt and survive in the face of inexorable social and economic conditions. In testing Billingsley's model, Williams and Stockton found there were still other family structures not encompassed in this elaborate model.[22] The notion of the fluidity and malleability of black family structures serves to enlighten these discussions. While there is an abundance of evidence giving credence to the existence of a multiplicity of family structures, constant changes in black families have received little attention.

Moreover, before the 1960s, black families that conformed somewhat to the definition of the simple nuclear family were still likely to undergo more structural changes during the family life cycle than were similarly situated white families. In either case this occurs by the addition or loss of a member to the family structure.

Structural changes in existing families, caused by modifying the composition of family and nonfamily members, are not peculiar to black families. Indeed, white families also undergo change during the family life cycle. What is unique to black families is the frequency and causes of restructuring or modifying the original family structure. Allowing new members to become a part of the family unit and later depart is due to economic exigency, more so for black families than for white families. In general, the most common reason for altering an existing family structure is maturation. At this point in the family life cycle, children leave to establish independent living arrangements, or a family member is lost through death. Historically, black families restructured for economic expediency as well as maturation of its members. Essentially, white family restructuring has been characterized more by the latter than by financial exigency.

Restructuring families is not a recent phenomenon for blacks. Gutman found the existence of subfamilies, extended families, and various other forms of black families existing following slavery.[23] In many instances, these variant family units reflected the modification of existing family structures.

One common reason for family restructuring is the proportion of black females with children born out of wedlock. Hill and Gutman argue that black women, while having a relatively high rate of births outside the legal confines of marriage, generally do marry.[24] When the out-of-wedlock child is born, the existing family is modified to accommodate the new child. During the interim between out-of-wedlock births and marriage, many black women and their children remain in their preexisting family, family of orientation, thereby creating subfamilies. Thus, from the original family structure emerges a new family constellation. Following marriage, the black female and her offspring leave her family of orientation, and the structure once again undergoes modification.

Other causes for restructuring include taking in relatives (extended), nonrelatives (augmented), marital dissolution (incipient nuclear), maturation of children, and death. Fluctuations in family structures are indeed normative for black families.

The creation and expansion of social-welfare programs has definitely altered the causes, frequently, and tenure of black family restructuring. Prior to 1960, a larger proportion of the black elderly lived in extended families. But in the 1950s social security was amended to cover a broader range of occupations in which blacks were employed, and federally subsidized housing for the elderly was increased; therefore, there was no longer a great need for black families to provide living accommodations for older relatives.

In addition, public welfare provides various types of public assistance to female single parents. In effect, this assistance decreases dependence on relatives and promotes autonomous living, thereby reducing the period of time a female single parent and her offspring must reside with her family of orientation. The temporal nature of black family restructuring has also undergone modification. In the absence of social-welfare programs, when black families were restructured the length of time the modified structure remained stable was generally determined by the black female becoming economically independent of her family due to marriage or employment. In general, these were the dynamics that were likely to restore the family of origin to its status. In general, restructuring of black families typically resulted in members adapting to a new family constellation for an indefinite period of time.

Of equal importance is the acceleration of changes in the black family life cycle. Because of the relatively high number of births to unmarried black adolescents, the process of restructuring has been accelerated. In 1983, 55 percent of all black children were born out of wedlock. Fifty-seven percent of these children were born to females under the age of 17, and one-third of these births were to black teens 15 to 17 years of age. Moreover, 36 percent were first births.[25]

Undoubtedly, large numbers of black families undergo restructuring to accept related children. The actual duration of such living arrangements, with the mother and her children living within an established family, is an area that requires empirical research. Although a large percentage of out-of-wedlock births are teenage mothers, the availability of social-welfare programs serves to lessen the period of time during which the black female and her children must be dependent on her family of orientation.[26]

Once we recognize the changing nature of black families, it becomes clear that comparing black family structures to those of white families is of little utility. This was especially true before the 1970s, when white families were primarily restructuring due to marriage, maturation of children, and death of family members. Today, as in black families, marital dissolution is increasingly becoming a frequent cause of restructuring among white families. Conditions that give rise to family restructuring for blacks, while including the reasons that white families restructure, continue to be closely related to economic factors. Restructuring out of economic necessity as well as for maturation has been a salient characteristic of black families. Moreover, the economically depressed status of black families, linked with the absence of a national social policy designed to promote economic independence, has served to facilitate the establishment of a complex social exchange system. Thus, the formation of self-help networks led ultimately to the malleability of black family structures. The black family's readiness to absorb individuals in need of food, clothing, shelter, and the like, set the stage for the continuous reshaping of black families. It is important to note that prior to liberal social policy, black families were restructured to ensure stability. After the enactment and expansion of liberal social policy, black families have increasingly undergone restructuring as a result of marital instability. Furthermore, since the inception of liberal social policy, black families have rarely needed to accommodate elderly relatives and nonrelatives, so family restructuring began to occur almost exclusively to accommodate women and children.

Serial Families

The movement from one family structure to another, or serial families, is also common along the black population. Historically, family mobility among blacks has occurred because of economic hardships and to maintain marital stability. More recently, serial families, like restructuring for blacks, tends to be related to marital instability. Since two out of three marriages among black couples end in divorce, and a larger number of lower-income black families prefer separation as a method of resolving marital inharmony, the maritally disrupted black female and her children frequently become displaced.[27] Typically, when marriages are dissolved, the black female and her children return to her family of orientation. There she receives the emotional and financial support necessary to reduce stresses associated with uncoupling. Once the black female is financially and emotionally capable of social reintegration, she leaves with her children to establish an independent living arrangement. Because of the tenuous nature of employment, lower wages for black women, inflationary costs of living, and noncompliance with child support payments, independent living for the separated or divorced black female with children is precarious at best. Thus, it is understandable that black female single parents are forced to move between family structures, establishing and reestablishing a temporary residence within their families of orientation. Moreover, since health insurance is not universally available, unexpected medical expenses can also trigger serial families forcing, black women and their children to resume dependence on relatives and friends for shelter and other basic physiological needs.

The phenomenon of moving from one family structure to another among black families is not new. Shortly after emancipation and throughout the mass migration of blacks to the North, prior to World War I and again at the time of World War II, entire black families in search of employment and improved living conditions established a pattern of serial families.

Billingsley and Billingsley state that black men and women wandered from town to town establishing temporary living arrangements with various black families.[28] These contacts were made possible by social networking. When a friend or relative in the South recommended an individual to a family in the North it was highly probable that the family would "put the individual up" until he or she could secure employment.

A resurgence of serial family structuring has parallelled the increase in the rate of marital dissolution among blacks. Once separated or divorced, black female single parents discover their standard of living decreases substantially, making it necessary for them to return to their families of orientation until they can financially afford independent living. Because of occupational segregation and lack of salable job skills, black female single parents have financial difficulties that affect the maintenance of independent households. Consequently, for some black single women and their children, particularly unwed adolescents, serial families are an integral part of life.

ABSENCE OF SOCIAL POLICY AND THE VARIABILITY OF BLACK FAMILY STRUCTURES

Aside from a brief time during Reconstruction, when the Freedmen's Bureau provided goods and services to black men, women, and children, black families received a modicum of institutional support until the 1960s.[29] Because of strong public opposition to the federal government providing aid to the needy, the Freedman's Bureau was disbanded in 1872, seven years after its inception.

With the exception of short periods of high employment, black men in the

United States have experienced unusually high rates of unemployment. Faced with joblessness, underemployment, and limited job skills, black men, women, and children were compelled to modify existing family structures and to move often between families. Unquestionably, restructuring and serial families enabled black families to remain intact and to cope with dire social and economic conditions.

Because social welfare services were unavailable to augment subsistence-level incomes, black families relied almost exclusively on informal social-support systems for their survival. During the period following Emancipation and throughout the 1940s, black families expanded and contracted as members, both relatives and nonrelatives, arrived and departed. Augmenting families with new members to consolidate and preserve resources proved to be an efficacious adaptive mechanism and served to preserve the basic two-parent structure of the black family.

FEDERALIZING SOCIAL POLICY

It was not until 1935 that the federal government was forced to formulate a national social policy to relieve economic pressures brought about by the Depression. The passage of the Social Security Act in 1935 marked the federal government's first attempt since Emancipation to address the needs of the economically disadvantaged on a massive scale. Until then, states and voluntary organizations had provided fragmented social welfare services to the poor. Because of racial discrimination in the administration of social services, black families had difficulty receiving public assistance.[30] By creating social insurance, public assistance, and health and welfare services under the Social Security Act, the federal government temporarily restored productivity necessary for consumption. The government's action helped restore the people's confidence in the private enterprise system. This thrust toward providing for the "deserving poor" and ensuring economic well-being for the masses was directly related to social unrest.[31] To take the drastic measure of enacting a national policy to provide assistance to individuals who were unable to care for themselves represented a radical shift in public policy. Indeed, the federal government's posture at that time corroborates the supposition advanced by Piven and Cloward, that social policy is formulated on the basis of interest group politics, and when the populace demonstrates unrest, social programs are created.[32] Conversely, when social order is restored, social programs are rescinded.

In effect, the federal government had moved from the absence of social policy—a laissez-faire attitude—to liberal social policy. Despite the far-reaching effects of these social programs, black families benefitted little from the federal government's involvement in social-welfare programs at this time.

Benefits derived from social security were not extended to individuals employed in service industries and agricultural occupations, thereby excluding the majority of black men and women. When the social insurance program was first instituted, only workers in industry and commerce were entitled to benefits. At that time, 34 percent of all black workers were employed in service jobs and another one-third were farm workers.[33]

Similarly, the Aid to Dependent Children Program (ADC) did not significantly affect the stability of black two-parent families, including those with unemployed male heads. Initially, since the beneficiaries of ADC were children, both husbands and wives were excluded from obtaining monetary benefits. Therefore, there was no exclusion of the father. Hence, there was no social-welfare policy that excluded males, thereby disrupting the family. To support this contention, at the end of the decade, there was even a slight increase in the percentage of black families with both husband and wife present. In 1940, 77 percent of all black families contained two parents, compared to 77.7 percent in 1950. Besides, the administration of social welfare programs remained decentralized at the state level, where differential administration continued to result in the exclusion of blacks.[34]

A decrease in the proportion of black families headed by women is further evidence that the new Aid to Dependent Children Program had virtually no effect on black family stability. In 1940, 17.9 percent of black families had female heads, compared to 1950 when black women maintaining families accounted for 17.6 percent of all black families.

Black unemployment rose to 50 percent in the peak of the Depression, while the corresponding rate was 25 percent for whites. Although blacks suffered significantly higher rates of joblessness and poverty than whites, in 1933 only 18 percent of black family heads of households and 15 percent in 1935 had been certified by the government for relief.[35] Moreover, in 1940 three out of four blacks lived in the rural South, where racial discrimination was more pronounced in the administration of social welfare programs. As a consequence, the formulation of a national social policy to provide assistance to the old and new poor had little effect on the socioeconomic status or structure of the black family. In essence, the initial consequences of early social welfare programs for black families, was tantamount to the earlier period, when a national social policy was nonexistent.

With a commitment to the free enterprise system, the federal government had little interest in maintaining or expanding social welfare services. Most efforts designed to bring about economic independence for poor families were considered emergency measures, and by the mid 1940s many federal appropriations to social programs created under the New Deal had been reduced.[36] Black families derived few benefits from these innovative social programs, for attached to these temporary emergency measures was the nineteenth-century philosophy that poverty was inextricably related to character flaws and personal turpitude.[37] Racial stereotypes categorizing blacks as lazy and shiftless created negative sentiments toward black families as recipients of public assistance. Further, these beliefs prevented many black families from receiving services that they needed and to which they were entitled. Consequently, black families' dependence on informal social-support sytems accelerated during the Depression years, as did their needs.

QUASI CONSERVATISM

Social scientists have characterized the period from the mid 1940s throughout the 1950s as one of political conservatism and economic growth.[38] During this period, there were no catastrophic changes in social-welfare policy or in the structure of black families. In general, changes in policy and black family structures were incremental in nature. Major social welfare programs legislated in the 1940s and 1950s were the National School Lunch Program in 1946, the Hill-Burton Hospital Construction Bill in 1946, and a special Milk Program in 1954. Moreover, Congress legislated the incorporation of disability insurance in social security programs, a new category of public assistance for the disabled, medical assistance to families receiving public assistance, and the expansion of the Aid to Dependent Children Program to include a relative with whom the child was living (Aid to Families with Dependent Children).

The 1950s brought legislation that increased the number of potential beneficiaries and liberalized benefit payments through modifications in benefit formulas. Although several new welfare programs were instituted, this era represented economic growth and an attitude of social complacency.[39] Despite the institution and expansion of social-welfare programs, administration of these programs was conservative, if not reactionary. Nowhere was this more noticeable than in the public disaffection with public assistance, particularly the Aid to Families with Dependent Children program. Throughout the country, states implemented punitive policies and procedures for limiting welfare rolls. Only social policies intended to enhance the lives of the middle class met with public approval.

"Man-in-the-house," "suitable home," and residency policies were adopted by numerous states to remove welfare recipients from the rolls. Of all the policies, the one used most effectively to eliminate blacks as welfare recipients was the requirement that welfare recipients be a resident of the state. By enforcing residency policies, states were able to prevent black migrants who moved from the South to the North from acquiring public assistance.

Midnight raids to determine if welfare mothers were ineligible for aid by virtue of living with a related or non-related man, occurred with frequency. Despite the intended deterrent effect of these policies, the number of beneficiaries of public assistance grew 13 percent between 1950 and 1960. Much of this growth occurred in the Aid to Families with Dependent Children program. The proportion of AFDC families that were black, according to Handel, increased from 36 percent in 1953 to 43 percent in 1961.[40] The elderly and widows with children received aid from Social Security, and the AFDC program became widely associated with mothers and children with absent fathers. Although white females and their children constituted a numerical majority of recipients, the program was viewed as one for black families deserted by husbands and for black women with illegitimate children. This labeling occurred because two-thirds of black welfare families resided in central cities of metropolitan areas, while white families were dispersed throughout small towns and were less visible.[41]

The first real indication that a relationship existed between social welfare programs and the stabiity of black families became apparent in the 1950s. Gradually, observable changes in black family structures began to take place. For most of the decade, black male employment was unusually high. During the Korean War, between 1951 and 1953, the jobless rates for blacks were the lowest (ranging approximately 4.5 percent to 5.4 percent).[42] Still, the proportion of welfare recipents who were black mothers and children increased. This growth was largely due to a drastic increase in the ratio of black children born out of wedlock, which climbed from 71.2 per 1,000 in 1950 to 98.3 per 1,000 unmarried women in 1960.

Earlier changes in social policy, and those legislated during this decade, set the trend for major changes in black family structure.

The black extended family also began to undergo structural changes. As more and more black males experienced a shift in occupation from farm worker to unskilled laborer, a larger number of blacks were entitled to Social Security benefits. Furthermore, Congress moved to extend coverage to occupations that had initially been excluded. This had a definite impact on enabling the elderly to become less dependent on their children and permitted the establishment of independent living arrangements. Throughout the general population, the number of related subfamilies declined from 2.5 million in 1950 to 1.5 million in 1960. Likewise, unrelated subfamilies decreased from 465,000 to 207,000 during the same ten-year period. Moreover, the number of subfamilies continued to decline until the mid 1970s.[43] Equally important was the amendment to the Social Security Act, entitling relatives of dependent children to receive public assistance.

Together these new laws were responsible for altering the black family structure and life cycle. These policies resulted in the attenuation of extended and augmented families and subfamiies. Also, amendements to Social Security, increasing benefits to the disabled, had an impact on the structure of black families. Hence, a decline in black extended and augmented famiies and subfamilies took place.

Although liberal social welfare legislation created economic independence for the elderly, conservative administration of social welfare programs, especially in the Aid to Families with Dependent Children program, promoted marital conflict, as welfare policies and practices required male absence as a condition for eligibility. Hence, through overt and covert practices, social welfare agencies, not black wives, forced men out of the home. Thus, the black female-headed household, created through separation, divorce, or nonmarriage, has been system-precipitated. Thus, one could expect an escalation in the dissolution of marriages among blacks and an increase in the number of black women with children who choose to permanently forego marriage. The trends in both of these areas was initiated in the 1950s and became firmly established by the 1980s. By excluding black males through the institution of the "man-in-the-house" policy in the 1950s and maintaining this policy in the 1960s and 1970s and by systematically entitling women, and not their husbands, to benefits, black two-parent families were undermined.

Overall, the decade of the 1950s, while defined as a period of social conservatism, had manifestations of liberalism. As further evidence of the quasi-conservative nature of this era was the *Brown vs. the Board of Education* Supreme Court decision, in which the court ruled that "separate but equal" in educational institutions was unconstitutional. Although this decision was liberal for the time, the court assumed a conservative stance relative to enforcing compliance.[44] Taylor states that it was not until more than fifteen years later, in 1971, that the court determined that mandatory desegregation (including busing, if necessary) was the only way to end segregation.[45] This aura of conservatism belies the passage of liberal social-welfare policies and the expanded role of the federal government in social-service delivery. Despite moderate to high rates of employment for black males, black family structure began reflecting the adverse impact of liberal social policy. Although the black elderly began acquiring economic independence because of policy initiatives, underclass black women with children began to transfer their dependence from informal social-support systems and their spouses to social welfare agencies. What this suggests is that extreme measures to deter potential recipients were essentially ineffective. For black families, restructuring and serial families took on new dimensions.

EXPANSION OF LIBERAL SOCIAL POLICY: A SOCIAL EXPERIMENT THAT FAILED

As William Graham Sumner said, It is dangerous to tinker with societies in the same way we carry out experiments in the medical field. When you experiment on an individual the worst that can happen is that the person will die. But society is an eternal organism. When you experiment on it, whatever the results, it is going to live on.[46]

The experiment that took place encompassed far more than the "great experiment" examined by Charles Murray.[47] Murray limits his discussion to an actual study, the Negative Income Tax Experiment (NIT), which failed to prove that a guaranteed income would not adversely affect adult family members' desire to work. Nor am I referring to the plethora of scientific investigations on the relationship between social welfare programs and family stability.[48]

The "social experiment" to which I refer was poorly conceptualized, had conflicting hypotheses, and had numerous uncontrolled variables, not to mention diverse methodologies. The purpose of this experiment was to explain, predict, and control poverty and its adverse effect on the dynamics and structure of families in America. Different underlying assumptions regarding the etiology of poverty, formulated on the basis of socioeconomic class, political persuasion, and other social and economic factors, led to the social experiment, more commonly known as liberal social policy.

The gradual expansion in the 1950s of the federal government's role in social service delivery set the stage for major changes that took place throughout the 1960s and 1970s. Responding to the demands of the Civil Rights movement and other social activists, the federal government developed public policies (initiated in the Kennedy administration and expanded under President Johnson's War on Poverty) that made it the focal point for funding, developing, and monitoring social-welfare services. Moreover, the liberalization of eligibility, which was legislated in the 1950s, was further revised to enable even larger numbers of persons to benefit from social programs. Civil disorders, protest movements, black population growth, and a sharp increase in black unemployment rates between 1958 and 1963 contributed to the drastic reformulation of social policy. Unlike the policies of the New Deal, social policy enacted during this twenty-year period was designed for the "old" poor, in which black families were overrepresented. For the second time in the history of this country, policy-makers, heavily influenced by the Johnson administration and the vociferous black populace, made monetary allocations and proposals for the express purpose of creating stability among poor and black families. The basis for the specific agenda of social and economic programs, proposed and implemented, was a report reflecting the status of black families conducted by Moynihan. In effect, the Johnson administration, relying heavily on Moynihan's findings, set out to change the structure of black families to make them conform to the middle-class nuclear model. At the time, the probability and consequences of failure of this experiment were not considered. Although the details of these programs will be explored in a later chapter, a preliminary discussion is presented here. Moreover, blacks, the largest single minority recipient class, were not integral to the planning, implementing, or evaluating of these programs.

According to Alexander and Weber, the period beginning in the early 1960s marked the most comprehensive revision of social welfare programs since 1935.[49] Many social programs, while designed to aid poor families irrespective of race or ethnicity, were developed specifically to improve the social and economic plight of black families by remedying past social injustices. These programs included financial assistance, housing subsidies, food stamps, child development centers, medical care, youth programs, work-training opportunities, and numerous other programs. In addition, civil rights legislation such as affirmative action laws, the voting rights act, and fair housing legislation were designed to bring about social and economic parity for blacks.

As social programs were instituted and expanded, the hopes and aspirations of black men and women were raised. But they were not alone in expecting that social and economic programs would be cost-effective and ultimately elevate the socioeconomic status of black families. That expanded liberal social policy would contribute to the disintegration of black two-parent families and the creation of a permanent underclass was neither intended nor projected.[50] It is extremely important to note that although many liberal social policies were designed to elevate the status of black and poor families, there were numerous unintended effects. The fact that social policies can and do have such consequences was recognized by Robert Merton, a sociologist, as early as 1936, and more recently by Walter Williams, a black economist.[51] While many lauded the inventive, comprehensive planning and administration of social and economic programs, others cautioned that the government's increased involvement in social-service delivery could have fissiparous consequences for the black family. In this vein, McCray warned of the potential threat to the mutual aid network's ability to continue to influence the maintenance of the black two-parent family. She stated, "For black families and black people, there is but one danger, if these informal adaptive and coping mechanisms are pulled into the bureaucratic structure, the informal nature of the network and the network itself could be destroyed."[52]

Liberal social policy, expanded in the 1960s and continued throughout the 1970s, did create divisiveness within black institutions and noninstitutional support systems. In spite of oppressive social and economic conditions, high rates of unemployment, inadequate housing, and racial discrimination, black two-parent families in various forms had remained intact prior to the 1950s. Until the expansion of liberal social policy, informal social-support systems, led by the black church, espoused the importance of sharing and caring among black families. Keeping black two-parent families intact was the primary objective of these self-help networks. However, the government through the sponsorship of social-welfare agencies created the following conditions, which contributed to the disintegration of black two-parent families:

1. Traditional black institutions were replaced by white institutions (e.g., schools, colleges, businesses).
2. The influence of the black church and mutual-aid network was usurped by the federal government.
3. The black family's value orientation was transformed from cooperative collectivism to competitive individualism.
4. The valuation of an individual's worth was based on the acquisition and possession of material wealth, rather than traditional criteria, whereby personal worth and esteem were predicated on helping others.
5. The transformation of overt discriminatory practices to covert forms of racial inequities led to institutional racial discrimination.

In addition to contributing to the decline of mutual-aid networks, liberal social programs designed to effect racial integration served to facilitate the decline of black institutions. These institutions had assumed prominence and viability by functioning as secondary socializing agents. Before the 1960s, black students who were enrolled in colleges and universities generally attended predominantly black institutions. In addition, public schools that were highly segregated provided moral support as well as academic preparation for black children. These social systems served as buffers. They shielded black youth from social injustices while providing them with valuable information on how to interact effectively in dual worlds. One other important function of traditional black institutions was to inculcate black children with a sense of cultural pride and self-worth. Traditional black institutions, as agents of socialization, imbued black children with self-esteem through positive reinforcement and black adult role models. Since most individuals employed by these institutions were black, they acted as positive and constructive role models for black children to emulate. The advent of liberal social policy should have enhanced such systems rather than establishing substitutes for them. One of the most devastating consequences of liberal social policy is that it attempted to recreate black culture in terms of both structure and dynamics. In effect, black colleges—which had historically depended on blacks for support, mainly because blacks had few alternatives—lost that support as black youth began to transfer en masse to predominately white public schools and colleges. Now, black institutions and black families are not as mutually supportive as in the past. In this case, the black family, which relied heavily on educational institutions to help socialize their offspring was placed at a disadvantage. However, this problem should come as little surprise; W. E. B. Dubois warned of this possibility some years ago. He cautioned that integration alone would result in an environment which was likely to impede the educational process for black youth.[53]

Moreover, the black church and mutual-aid network, which prescribed behavior for black family members, began to lose its influence on black two-parent families, as the government became the chief service provider. Added to the declining influence of these systems was the societal imperative that blacks become more culturally integrated, thereby abandoning traditional black values and accepting majority cultural values and norms. Thus, the government acquired control over black family structure and dynamics. Unlike the black church and mutual-aid network, the government mandated that the husband be absent as a condition for recipiency. Given what appeared to be a surfeit of educational, training, and employment opportunities generated by increased federal money to social programs, black families expected to derive enormous benefits and elevate their socioeconomic status. As a result, black families began to incorporate competitive individualism—a value characteristic of the larger society—into their own value orientation. It was believed that this mainstream ideology was necessary if blacks were to transform their families into autonomous nuclear family units.

Equally devastating to black families was the acceptance by blacks of a new set of criteria for measuring an individual's worth. Before the liberalization of social welfare services, black families ascribed status to individuals based on their willingness to help others.[54] In many ways, this method of determining a person's worth conflicted with capitalism, with its emphasis on competition as the means of acquiring wealth. On the basis of the capitalistic value orientation, the worth of an individual is commensurate with the amount of wealth that he or she possesses. Since black families were often extended or augmented or consisted of subfamilies, material possessions were important to the extent that they were shared with others.[55] Thus, family members who shared their resources were accorded status and esteem.

Competitive individualism as a value system had greater applicability to white families with a male head, since he was the most likely family member to be involved in competition in the labor force. Hence, resources were initially acquired and mediated by the male head of the household and later shared with members of his nuclear family. Because black two-parent families, for the most part, have been characterized by dual wage earners, and extended, augmented, and subfamilies, sharing and merging resources took precedence over a monopoly of resources by any one family member. In effect, structural barriers resulted in black families subscribing to cooperative collectivism for the purpose of survival and advancement. Operating under the premise that social obstacles were being removed, black families began to embrace values inherent in the larger society.

Differential progress of black females and black males in educational and occupational arenas between 1960 and 1980 led to the further devaluation of black males. In effect, a greater number of black women than men received college degrees. Further, more black women moved into white-collar occupations than did their male counterparts. The higher rate of occupational mobility among black women versus black men added to the belief that black males who were unable to acquire wealth were to blame, not society. The message that was propagated throughout society, as a result of the new social and economic programs, was that those who did not experience economic mobility had simply failed to take advantage of these opportunities.

Among the conditions that led in the 1960s to the social revolution and liberal social policy were blatant discriminatory practices, to which blacks were subjected throughout the country. Although these practices varied from region to region and were more pronounced in the South, the fact that blacks were victims of social injustices could not be denied. Because the federal government incorporated a fairly rigorous system for monitoring and enforcing affirmative action programs and the fair administration of all social programs, efforts to deny blacks, women, and other minorities equal access to opportunities became insidious and difficult for any external monitoring agent to prove. What has yet to occur is a systematic method by which these groups can efficiently substantiate claims of institutional discrimination.

Ostensibly, liberal social policy did not bring about economic independence for black families. In light of this unanticipated outcome, black families more than ever needed the support of black institutions and informal support systems. Since the government had replaced the black church and facilitated the decline of mutual-aid networks, black families had little choice but to increase their dependency on the government. Thus, the continuous, yet invidious, exclusion of blacks from full and equal participation in the economic system and the black families' acceptance of a new value system has resulted in the deterioration of black two-parent families and other salient institutions in the black community.

Not all black families are recipients of social welfare, yet middle-class blacks also failed to experience the economic gains that should have been forthcoming.

Unfortunately, black families, regardless of socioeconomic status, did not experience the economic growth that had been projected. Raised expectations caused by liberal social policy remained unfulfilled. In general, underclass black families did not move to the middle class, and middle-class black families did not become members of the upper class. Although some families did experience upward mobility and become members of the middle class, it is also the case that some black families descended the socioeconomic ladder, as the economy became inflationary and old-line industries declined.[56] The failure to meet these expectations was equally devastating to black middle-class families. In spite of affirmative action programs and educational loans and grants, black working-class and middle-class families made modest gains. And while many solidified their economic status, there is little evidence to suggest that a substantial percentage of black families were elevated to a higher stratum. In the aftermath of liberalism, the failure to convert underclass black families to stable and viable economic units is still attributed, by many, to the black family.[57]

One of the greatest tragedies during the era of liberal social policy was the failure of scholars, policy-makers, and practitioners to recognize the adverse effects of social programs on black family structure. Instead, there were arguments for the defensibility of these programs, despite growing evidence of their debilitating impact. Perhaps the conviction that social programs were long overdue and that something was better than nothing, as well as the fear that criticism would bring about the elimination of social and economic programs, clouded the signs of the deterioration of the black family and other microcultural institutions, and silenced individuals who would have otherwise raised these issues. A number of social, economic, and political processes prevented the necessary revision of social and economic programs but leaving these programs basically unaltered has contributed to the demise of black two-parent and extended families, as well as other black institutions.

What happened to black family structures in the 1980s, when the country entered a true period of social conservatism, both in terms of legislation and administration of social programs, is examined in Chapter 7.

NOTES

1. K. Sue Jewell. "Use of Social Welfare Programs and the Disintegration of the Black Nuclear Family," *The Western Journal of Black Studies* 8 (Winter, 1984), p. 196.

2. Melville Herskovits, *The Myth of the Negro Past* (Boston: Beacon, 1958), pp. 182–184; Wade Nobles, "Africanity: Its Role in Black Families," *The Black Scholar* 9 (June, 1974): 10–17.

3. Stanley Elkins, *Slavery: A Problem in American Institutional and Intellectual Life* (New York: Grosset and Dunlap, 1963); E. Franklin Frazier, *The Free Negro Family* (Nashville: Fisk University Press, 1932); E. Franklin Frazier, *The Negro Family in Chicago* (Chicago, University of Chicago Press, 1932); E. Franklin Frazier, *The Negro Family in the United States* (Chicago: University of Chicago Press, 1939); Daniel P. Moynihan, *The Negro Family: The Case for National Action* (Washington, D. C.: U. S. Government Printing Office, 1965); Lee Rainwater and William Yancey, *The Moynihan Report and the Politics of Controversy* (Cambridge, Massachusetts: M. I. T. Press, 1967).

4. Niara Sudarkasa, "Interpreting the African Heritage in Afro-American Family Organization," in Harriette Pipes McAdoo, ed., *Black Families*. (Beverly Hills, California: Sage Publications, 1981), pp. 37–40.

5. Robert Staples, "The Myth of the Black Matriarchy," *The Black Scholar* (June, 1970): pp. 12–13; Herbert Gutman, *The Black Family in Slavery and Freedom: 1750–1925* (New York: Vintage Books, 1976), p. 633.

6. J. Allen Williams, Jr. and Robert Stockton, "Black Family Structures and Functions: An Empirical Examination of Some Suggestions Made by Billingsley," *Journal of Marriage and the Family*, 35 (February, 1973), p. 48.

7. Staples, "The Myth of the Black Matriarchy," p. 8; Robert Hill, *The Strengths of Black Families* (New York: Emerson Hall, 1972), p. 18.

8. Andrew Billingsley, *Black Families in White America* (Englewood Cliffs, New Jersey: Prentice-Hall, 1968); Hill, *The Strengths of Black Families*, p. 5.

9. Carol Stack, *All Our Kin: Strategies for Survival in a Black Community* (New York: Harper and Row, 1974), p. 25; Carrie Allen McCray, "The Black Woman and Family Roles," in La Frances Rodgers-Rose, ed., *The Black Women* (Beverly Hills, California: Sage Publications, 1980), p. 70.

10. E. Franklin Frazier, *The Negro Family In Chicago*; E. Franklin Frazier, *The Free Negro Family*.

11. Gutman, *The Black Family in Slavery and Freedom, 1750–1925*, pp. 432–460.

12. Billingsley, *Black Families in White America*.

13. Talcott Parsons, "Age and Sex in the Structure of the United States," *American Sociological Review* 7 (1942): 604; Talcott Parsons and Robert F. Bales, *Family, Socialization and the Interaction Process* (Glencoe, Illinois: The Free Press, 1955), p. 10.

14. Billingsley, *Black Families in White America*; Hill, *The Strengths of Black Families*, p. 5; Staples, "The Myth of the Black Matriarchy," pp. 9–10.

15. Billingsley, *Black Families in White America*; Hill, *The Strengths of Black Families*, p. 5.

16. Hill, *The Strengths of Black Families*, pp. 5–8.

17. United States Bureau of the Census, *The Social and Economic Status of the Black Population in the United States: An Historical Overview, 1790–1978*. Series P–23, No. 80 (Washington, D. C.: U. S. Government Printing Office, June 1979), p. 103.

18. United States Bureau of the Census, *America's Black Population, 1970 to 1982: A Statistical View*. Series P–10/POP 82–1 (Washington, D. C.: U. S. Government Printing Office, July, 1983), p. 18.

19. Ibid, pp. 17–18.

20. Gutman, *The Black Family in Slavery and Freedom, 1750–1925*, pp. 432–460.

21. Ann Fischer, Joseph Beasley, and Carl Harter, "The Occurrence of the Extended Family of Procreation: A Developmental Approach to Negro Family Structure," *Journal of Marriage and the Family* (May, 1968): 291.

22. Williams and Stockton, "Black Family Structures and Functions," p. 47.

23. Gutman, *The Black Family in Slavery and Freedom, 1750–1925*, pp. 1–44.

24. Gutman, *The Black Family in Slavery and Freedom, 1750–1925*, pp. 363–460; Hill, *The Strengths of Black Families*, pp. 17–26.

25. "What Must Be Done About Children Having Children?" *Ebony* (March, 1985), p. 76.

26. Ibid., p. 78.

27. Robert Staples, *The World of Black Singles: Changing Patterns of Male-Female Relations* (Westport, Connecticut: Greenwood Press) p. 8. James McGhee, "The Black Family Today and Tomorrow," in The National Urban League, ed., *The State of Black America, 1985* (New York: National Urban League).

28. Andrew Billingsley and Amy Billingsley, "The Negro Family Life in America," *Social Service Review* 39 (September, 1965): 310.

29. Andrew Billingsley and Jeanne Giovannoni, *Children of the Storm* (New York: Harcourt, Brace-Jovanovich), pp. 1–18, 41–43.

30. June Axinn and Herman Levin, *Social Welfare* (New York: Dodd, Mead and Company, 1975).

31. Carolyn Shaw Bell, *The Economics of the Ghetto* (New York: Pegasus, 1970).

32. Frances Piven and Richard Cloward, *Regulating the Poor: The Functions of Public Welfare* (New York: Vintage, 1971), pp. 3–41.

33. United States of the Census, *The Social and Economic Status of the Black Population* (1979), p. 62.

34. Axinn and Levin, *Social Welfare*.

35. Ibid.

36. Robert McElvaine, *The Great Depression: America, 1929–1941* (New York: Times Books, 1984), pp. 306–332.

37. Gerald Handel, *Social Welfare in Western Society* (New York: Random House, 1982), pp. 41–73.

38. McElvaine, *The Great Depression*, pp. 323–349.

39. Axinn and Levin, *Social Welfare*.

40. Ibid.

41. Ibid.

42. United States Bureau of the Census, *The Social and Economic Status of the Black Population* (1979), p. 61.

43. United States Bureau of the Census, *Statistical Abstract of the United States: National Data Book and Guide to Sources*, 106th Edition (Washington, D. C.: U. S. Government Printing Office, 1986), p. 39.

44. William. L. Taylor, "Access to Economic Opportunity: Lessons Since Brown," in Leslie W. Dunbar, ed., *Minority Report: What Has Happened to Blacks, Hispanics, American Indians and Other Minorities in the Eighties* (New York: Pantheon Books, 1984), pp. 36–37.

45. Ibid.

46. William Tucker, "Kindness is Killing the Black Family," *This World* (January, 1985): 7.

47. Charles Murray, *Losing Ground: American Social Policy, 1950–1980* (New York: Basic Books, 1984), pp. 147–153.

48. Marjorie Honig, "AFDC Income, Recipient Rates and Family Dissolution" *Journal of Human Resources* 9 (Summer, 1974): 302; Mary Jo Bane, *Economic Influence on*

Divorce and Remarriage (Cambridge, Massachusetts: Center for the Study of Public Policy, 1975); Heather L. Ross and Isabel V. Sawhill, *Time of Transition: The Growth of Families Headed by Women* (Washington, D. C., The Urban Institute, 1975); Oliver C. Moles, "Marital Dissolution and Public Assistance Payments: Variation among American States," *Journal of Social Issues* 32 (Winter, 1976): 87; and Stephen Bahr, "The Effects of Welfare on Marital Stability and Remarriage" *Journal of Marriage and the Family* 41 (1979): 553.

49. Chauncey A. Alexander and David N. Weber, "Social Welfare: Historical Dates," *Encyclopedia of Social Work*, 17th Issue (Washington, D. C.: National Association of Social Workers, 1977), pp. 1487–1503.

50. Douglas Glasgow, *The Black Underclass* (New York: Vintage Books, 1981), pp. 3–4.

51. Robert K. Merton, "The Unanticipated Consequences of Purposive Social Action," *American Sociological Review* 1 (1936): pp. 894–904; Walter. E. Williams, *The State Against Blacks* (New York: McGraw-Hill, 1982), pp. 67–73.

52. McCray, "The Black Woman and Family Roles," p. 77.

53. Meyer Weinberg, *A Chance to Learn* (Cambridge, England: Cambridge University Press, 1977), p. 87.

54. Robert Staples, *Introduction to Black Sociology* (New York: McGraw-Hill, 1976), pp. 77–78.

55. Ibid.

56. "America's Underclass, Broken Lives: A Nation Apart," *U. S. News and World Report* (March 17, 1986), p. 20; Robert B. Hill, *Economic Policies and Black Progress: Myths and Realities* (Washington, D. C.: National Urban League, 1981), pp. 22–26.

57. George Gilder, Wealth and Poverty (New York: Basic Books, 1981); Murray, *Losing Ground: American Social Policy, 1950–1980; Lawrence Mead, Beyond Entitlement* (New York: Free Press, 1986).

3 INFORMAL SOCIAL-SUPPORT SYSTEMS

Although we live in a society that stresses individual and familial autonomy, few families are able to function without external support. Despite a societal philosophy of individualism and an emphasis on the nuclear family as an ideal prototype, white families, like their black counterparts, have had to rely on social-support systems for their survival. One major difference has been the source and nature of support available to black and white families. Until the 1960s, black families depended almost exclusively on informal social-support systems or mutual-aid networks for primary and secondary goods and services. Conversely, white families have had both institutional and noninstitutional support systems as providers of essential goods and services. While black and white families have relied to a greater or lesser extent on these external sources for assistance, formal agencies have tended to systematically exclude black families. As a result, an interdependent relationship was established between black families and members of informal helping networks.

The black family's ability to make positive contributions to society and to successfully socialize its offspring, while confronted with social barriers, has necessitated its dependence on sources outside the two-parent family unit. For years, the great demand and need for goods and services and the relative absence of aid from formal social-service agencies prevented black families from embracing the precepts of social isolation and independence, which had gained widespread acceptance, as large numbers of black families gravitated to urban areas, during and after the American industrial revolution. According to McCray, it was this "sense of caring and social responsibility in the Black community, plus strong kinship bonds and other reinforcements that kept black families together and strengthened their functioning.''[1]

Interestingly, even for white families, the notion of autonomy, privacy and the use of institutional and noninstitutional support systems have frequently undergone modification. Clearly, a cyclical pattern, representing varying degrees of familial dependence on formal and informal agencies, has evolved throughout American society.[2] Many consider the passage of the Elizabethan Poor Laws in 1601 to be the historical event that had the most profound influence on the formulation of American ideology regarding social welfare policy.[3] The initial shift from informal to formal social-support systems, designating responsibility to the government, was inextricably related to the passage of this legislation. Specifically, by mandating that towns and localities assume responsibility for their poor and creating institutions (almhouses) to care for the indigent, the Elizabethan Poor Laws set a precedent for government involvement in social-service delivery that continues today. Followed by a series of laws passed during the eighteenth, nineteenth, and twentieth centuries, institutions were further obligated to provide social services. Of equal importance, the government's expanded role in social-service delivery during the Great Depression of the 1930s firmly positioned federal, state, and local governments in the role of social-service providers.

Nevertheless, before the 1960s black families, unlike white families, were seldom given the option of receiving diverse goods and services on an ongoing basis from formal social-service agencies. Thus, the emergence of massive governmental involvement in the provision of social services during the 1960s and early 1970s resulted in an increase in the percentage of black families who could rely on formal social-service agencies to meet their needs. Indeed, the advent of this phenomenon was revolutionary for black families.

ORIGINS OF BLACK MUTUAL AID NETWORKS

For some, it is difficult to conceive an informal self-help network for black families that predates emancipation. Accordingly, references to black mutual-aid networks tend to focus on informal social support-systems following slavery. Nevertheless, historians allude to mutually dependent relationships among slave families. Evidence of the existence of mutual-aid networks during slavery can be found in communal cooking, child care, sewing, and other cooperative activities, which occurred in and around slave quarters. Moreover, collective responsibilities assumed by black families, during slavery, transcended the boundaries of the plantation to create what Sudarkasa refers to as "transresidential cooperation."[4] Seemingly, the exchange of goods and services involved the young and old, house slaves and field slaves, as well as black freedmen and women. Oftentimes they exchanged intangible as well as tangible goods, such as valuable information that facilitated the flight of runaway slaves. Hence, the survival of black families in America has always been predicated to some extent on the interdependence of members of the black community.

In spite of this collective sharing, black families were forced to rely on the slave owner as their primary source of goods and services. Even though the quantity, quality, and frequency of exchange of fundamental goods and services differed from plantation to plantation, the provision of life-sustaining commodities rested ultimately with the slave owner. As such, it is fair to say that although informal social-support sytems existed, slaves depended primarily on an institutional support system, that institution being what John Hope Franklin termed the "peculiar institution of slavery."[5] However, the degree to which slave families received basic commodities from their masters depended in large measure on the slave owner's resources and sense of moral obligation.[6]

Following slavery, the abrupt change in the dependent status of blacks warranted and resulted in massive govenmental assistance to black families. Established and administered by the federal government, the Freedmen's Bureau aided newly freed black men, women, and children by providing food, clothing, shelter, and vital information about consumerism, land acquisition, labor contracts, and so on. By and large, the limited governmental assistance blacks received during Reconstruction represented the only form of generic institutional support that blacks would receive for an extended period of time. More unfortunate than the modicum of support the government provided to black families was the fact that these services were offered for a mere seven years, from 1865 to 1872, before the Freedmen's Bureau was dismantled. Both before and after government services were offered, mutual-aid networks were mandatory for black family survival.

In the absence of social institutions designed to address the needs of black family members, informal mutual-aid networks were established. These networks provided basic goods and services such as food, shelter, clothing, and the like. In addition to providing goods and services for physical survival, they also offered guidance and counseling regarding personal and family matters. Mutual-aid networks enabled black men and women to identify strategies for ensuring the survival of the two-parent family. Billingsley states that following the period after slavery, when the Freedmen's Bureau was disbanded, social services were not provided by the larger society. And the black community, through "informal neighbor to neighbor" systems, had to provide resources for the care of children.[7] This ability of mutual-aid networks to provide the necessary elements for keeping black families intact, during unusually stressful conditions, is cogently documented by Gutman. He states that approximately 90 percent of all black families following slavery were intact two-parent families.[8]

Essentially, the mutual aid networks' positive impact on the black family can be attributed to the composition of the network, nature of the commodities exchanged, conditions for exchanging goods and services, and the limited availabiity of alternative sources of support for black families.

MUTUAL-AID NETWORKS: COMPOSITION AND COMMODITIES

Despite copious research in the area of networking, "mutual aid networks" and "self-help groups" are concepts that continue to be elusive. Factors that distinguish one form of networking from another are ambiguous and overlapping. In addition, sophisticated and complex networking designs have yet to result in an agreed upon definition of "social support."[9] Maguire suggests that social support is

"a feeling and attitude, as well as an act of concern and compassion. It is what friends, good neighbors, and relatives provide. When these kith and kin link together for the purpose of helping, they form a social support network."[10]

In general, informal social support systems may be comprised of any number of individuals. Not only do the number of members vary in any given self-help network, there are also differences in the relationships of individual members to each other and differences in their giving behavior.[11] Ideally, mutual-aid networks contain family members, as well as friends, neighbors, relatives, and fellow church members. Among the many factors that determine the effectiveness of informal social-support systems are size, basis of the relationship, capabilities, resources, and level of willingness of the network's members.[12] Moreover, attrition based on geographic and social mobility can have a decisive impact on the viability of social support systems. That is, when individuals move from one community to another, they are likely to establish new relationships, which alter the original structure of the network. In addition, upward mobility can result in new friendships and organizational affiliations that also serve to modify the initial components of the mutual-aid network. Consequently, physical and social mobility have a definite effect on informal social-support systems. Another common quality of mutual-aid networks is that they tend to be homogeneous on the basis of race, ethnicity, and social class. Other factors which affect the structure of mutual aid networks are age and marital status.[13]

The systematic exclusion of blacks from major societal institutions has limited the resources that the members of black mutual-aid networks have to exchange. This is particularly important, as limited information and contacts with key members of networks within the majority society would undoubtedly facilitate economic progress for black families and their members. Until a larger number of blacks are placed in authority positions within the larger society, members of black mutual-aid networks will not have enough inside knowledge needed to access social systems. Blacks will continue to be excluded from larger informal networks, which are essential for the upward mobility of black families. In effect, the systematic exclusion of blacks from mainstream participation, which is manifested as institutional segregation, continues to inhibit the effectiveness of black mutual-aid networks. For example, in 1982 only 13 percent of black males and females held baccalaureate degrees, compared to 25 percent of white males and females.[14] This alone is limiting in terms of the proportion of blacks who possess the knowledge necessary for accessing institutions of higher learning. Thus, a black youth seeking information, through his or her informal social-support system, regarding college admission policies, financial aid, and other nuances of matriculating in a college or university, will find a dearth of members available to provide this vital information. Further, the likelihood that such an individual is a member of any given mutual-aid network is even slighter when one considers geographic residence and social class. For instance, if this same youth resides in the inner city, it is even more improbable that valuable information about colleges and universities will be obtained from the individual's mutual-aid network. This is particularly true, since ascension to a higher social class, or success in general, is typically accompanied by the acquisition of certain status symbols. Generally, these include relocating from urban to suburban areas and interacting socially with others whose educational and occupational experiences are similar. As a consequence, informal social-support systems for black urban dwellers are likely to be devoid of middle-class members who possess invaluable information on accessing social systems.

In addition, a hierarchical system for the informal exchange of goods and services characterizes white mutual-aid networks more than black ones. The exclusivity and control that white males maintain over educational, economic, political, and religious institutions results in white males' possessing copious resources—the old-boy network. This has been and continues to be an issue of great concern in our society. In fact, one of the most ardent positions assumed by blacks, feminists, and other contenders for social power has been their disaffection with the old-boy network. Such a structural arrangement, with men controlling material and monetary resources and women and minorities mediating a modicum of such commodities, has clearly been to the detriment of black families and other minorities, whose race and gender inhibit their full participation in American institutions. Undoubtedly, there is a strong relationship between formal and informal social-support systems. Control over informal social-support sytems is certainly correlated with power and authority in social, economic, and political systems. Moreover, it is widely accepted that decisions that appear to have been made in the board room were arrived at on the golf course or at some other informal gathering attended by members of a mutal-aid network.

Historically, black women have occupied a key role in exchanging monetary, material, and other goods and services in mutual-aid networks.[15] Following Emancipation, when black women secured employment as domestics, and black males were systematically excluded from full-labor market participation, black women were invaluable to the mutual-aid network.[16] During this era, black women participated in self-help networks to perform the critical service of child care, which enabled them to secure and retain employment at a time when jobs for black men were virtually nonexistent. In all, the black mutual-aid network had the capacity for meeting the holistic needs of black families.

ROLE OF THE BLACK CHURCH

The entity most responsible for keeping the mutual-aid network intact and functioning properly was the black church. The black church has been in the vanguard of mutual-aid networks, as one of the chief providers of goods and services. Accordingly, schools, job training programs, credit unions, and related economic and educational institutions have been founded and administered by black churches. In addition to making food, shelter, and clothing available to black families, the black church has encouraged black families to engage in cooperative sharing and mutual responsibility. Functioning as one of the network's chief service providers, the black church prescribed certain behaviors to be followed by black families and other members of the network. In total, the black church has been instrumental in social-service delivery.[17]

The black church's commitment to ensuring the survival and progress of black families, in conjunction with the strong religious orientation of black families, gave the black church a position of prominence and influence over black men, women, and children.[18] However, this close affiliation with and dependency on the black church allowed the church to exercise considerable control over the lives of black families and their members. In effect, the black church used religious meetings, the mutual-aid network, and its own resources as a means of establishing and reinforcing values, beliefs, and behaviors. Similar to other social institutions, the black church became a mechanism for cultural transmission and social control. Blassingame substantiates the historic significance of the black church when he states that the black church served as an agency of social orientation, providing encouragement, guidelines, and reinforcement for the traditional values of marriage, family, morality, and spirituality in the face of the devastating effects of slavery.[19]

Since the black church occupied an honored position in the black community, black families adhered to its tenets of family cohesiveness and unity. With its high degree of integration in the black church, the mutual-aid network reinforced values, beliefs, and behaviors governing social interaction between husbands, wives, and children. These beliefs were grounded in theological principles that stressed traditional male and female roles.[20] Thus, black family members received positive or negative sanctions, depending on their willingness to exhibit prescribed behaviors. Nonconformity to established norms could result in the withholding of goods and services, or some other form of social sanctioning. With the ultimate goal being the maintenance of black two-parent families, it is little wonder that husbands and wives confronted with family or marital problems sought and utilized strategies for problem resolution that seldom included separation or divorce.

Later, as the government began to provide massive social services, the black church began to lose its authority. Furthermore, the mutual-aid network began to decline. At that time, black families were faced with weighing the latent, as well as the material and monetary, advantages and disadvantages of relying almost entirely on mutual-aid networks versus receiving support from the government. On one hand, the black mutual-aid network espoused philosophical issues inextricably related to the religious doctrine of the black church, such as mutual dependence, collective responsibility, and cooperation. By contrast, the government, like other institutions in the larger society, embraced an ideology of autonomy, social isolation, and individualism. The black family's decision to utilize formal social-support systems was largely based on monetary and material supply and demand. Ostensibly, the government's resources, to which blacks were entitled, were far more abundant than those possessed by informal social-support systems. However, a greater reliance on the government to meet fundamental needs had implicit ideological implications.

DYNAMICS OF EXCHANGE

To some extent, when examining black mutual aid networks I am forced to speak in the past tense. As was mentioned in the previous chapter, changes have occurred in the functioning of these complex informal social-support systems. Some changes were due to structural forces and others to the assimilation of black Americans into the larger society. Basically, the "mainstreaming" of blacks resulted in the acquisition of a new value system, which has brought about changes in the dynamics of mutual-aid networks. These changes necessitate that distinctions be made in mutual-aid networks that existed before the 1960s and those that functioned afterwards.

One important aspect of mutual-aid networks is the nature and quantity of the resources possessed by individual members. Figuratively, in terms of monetary and material resources, black mutual-aid networks have not had an inexhaustive supply to distribute to black families. In spite of this fact, the support black families received and gave to each other enabled the mutual-aid network to fulfill its mission of keeping black families together. Over time, the resources of the mutual-aid network became insufficient to meet the growing demands of black families. This condition was brought on by the mass migration of black families to the North, the higher cost of urban living, and the impersonal nature of city dwelling, and it put a strain on the functioning capacity of black mutual-aid networks. Increasingly, to give to others meant the depletion of one's own resources. Furthermore, obtaining resources from the mutual-aid network had always been a highly capricious endeavor. Frequently, it meant soliciting assistance from several members before obtaining needed goods and services. As Stack indicated in her study of the urban poor, the black mutual-aid network is extremely complex.[21] Like other informal social-support systems, the linkages and actual networking relative to primary and secondary networks is sophisticated and intricate.[22]

In traditional and contemporary black mutual-aid networks, members change roles frequently. Black men and women move with fluidity in assuming the role of provider and recipient. Individuals discharge their indebtedness as a recipient by becoming a provider. Indeed, the norm of reciprocity governs the entire exchange process.[23] Giving invokes an automatic system of exchange. This form of informal social support did more than promote black family stability, it also generated a collective sense of responsibility, which Herskovits, Staples, Blassingame, Sudarkasa, and others attribute to precolonial African culture.[24] It is this sense of mutual responsibility that extends beyond consanguineal boundaries, which black scholars have labeled an important African value.[25]

Though mutual aid networks were designed primarily to keep black families intact, they by no means delimited their goods and services to black nuclear-type families. The exclusion of single-parent families, extended families, or other variations of black family structures did not occur. Single-parent and two-parent families as members of mutual-aid networks were both providers and recipients of goods and services. Because resources were limited, members of the black mutual-aid network developed a complex system for exchanging goods and services. When members of the network had exhausted their available resources, they sought other sources to ensure that the basic needs of black families were met. Individuals were accorded status based on their willingness to assist others. Further, the possession of resources that one refused to give to others was negatively sanctioned. As Staples so aptly stated, in his paradigm on African and European value orientations, one of the benefits black family members once associated with money and material possessions was the ability to share them with each other.[26] For this gesture, black families and other members of the black community bestowed status and esteem. Conversely, negative sanctions were imposed on individuals who refused to share resources that were needed or in demand. These values were so deeply inculcated during the socialization process that, no matter how limited one's resources were, each member of the network felt compelled to share. Stack's contribution in this regard is invaluable, as she revealed examples of mutual sharing even in light of meager resources of both recipients and providers.[27]

Three factors contributed to the ongoing functioning of black mutual-aid networks. They are the recognition of a commonality of interests, a uniqueness of history, and the lack of available alternatives.

THE GOVERNMENT: AN INSTITUTIONAL ALTERNATIVE

In response to the demands of the 1960s social revolution, the federal government intervened and became involved in developing, expanding, monitoring, and funding social services. Blacks and other economically disadvantaged groups demanded that the government supplement existing resources partly because of the dwindling resources available to informal social-support systems and to the families themselves. In addition, the Civil Rights Movement, which served as the conduit for these demands, received mass support from advantaged groups, who linked their dissatisfaction with America's military involvement in Vietnam with the ongoing demands for social and economic equity espoused by black men and women. Moreover, the growing sophistication of the mass media informed large numbers of black families of their relative impoverishment. In fact, the concept's "cultural deprivation," "underprivileged," and "disadvantaged" permeated all layers of society and were believed to accurately described black families and their members.

Thus, the government was constrained to make reparations, which were felt to be immediate, intense, and overdue. All costs were to be borne by the government. Representative agencies were to be established and expanded to provide myriad goods and services to black and poor families. With the formulation of this plan, there was little reason to believe the outcome would not be positive. Further, the initial investment by the government appeared to be sufficient and infinite enough to permanently reduce the burden that families, friends, the church, and other members of the black mutual-aid network had assumed.

Services provided by formal social agencies included financial assistance, child care, educational and job training programs, housing subsidies, and nutrition programs. Description of these programs, including patterns of utilization and monetary expenditures over the twenty-year period from 1960 to 1980, are presented in Chapter 4.

In retrospect, there are many indications that the government's expanded role in social-service delivery was politically motivated, void of deliberate planning, and in dire need of time-specific, attainable goals. Evidence to support this position is found in the manner in which programs were developed, expanded, and amended. For approximately twenty years, social services and legislation were created, amended, and later rescinded, with a great degree of frequency. A prime example of the government's uncertainty in the area of social policy, is apparent by examining the "unemployed parent program." In 1961 the "unemployed parent program" was enacted. This act extended the Aid to Families with Dependent Children (AFDC) program to a child with an unemployed parent. Earlier legislation had defined "dependent child" as a child under age 16 deprived of parental support by reason of a parent's death, continued absence from the home, or physical or mental incapacity. In 1967 the "unemployed parent program" was amended and became the "unemployed father program"; families in need as a result of the unemployment of the father of at least one of the children became eligible for AFDC. In 1979 the "unemployed father program" was amended and once again became the "unemployed parent program." This change was mandated when the Supreme Court ruled it was unconstitutional to make AFDC payments available to unemployed families with an unemployed father, but not to families with an unemployed mother. The development and administration of social programs was characterized by trial and error.

Efforts to gauge the effectiveness of social-welfare programs were unmethodical and fragmentary. Although evaluation and research were highly integrated into nearly all social programs, there was little consensus among policy makers, practitioners, or researchers regarding how to operationally define "success," "effectiveness," and "cost efficient' '— concepts that, in theory, were to determine the fate of social programs and their recipients. Equally problematic was the construction of research designs that could control the effects of a multiplicity of programs on individuals with diverse backgrounds. Because of the inconclusiveness of the findings of numerous social-service studies and for the sake of political expendiency, the government continued this hit or miss approach to the delivery of social service to black and poor families.

It should be noted that not all black families used social-service programs directly; yet it is fair to say that most black men, women, and children were affected by their existence. However, the government's systematic neglect of black families, its subtle and sometimes overt refusal to provide essential social services, and its previous failure to ensure the physical safety of blacks had created a collective sense of distrust of government agents and agencies. For many blacks, their only contact with government representatives had been a police officer or agent of the Internal Revenue Service. Both were perceived as unsympathetic, hostile, and formidable. Before black families could fully use diverse social services sponsored by a government viewed as uncaring and oppressive, blacks had to analyze the costs, rewards, and projected outcomes. In effect, the costs and rewards of using informal social-support systems versus formal social-support systems had to be carefully assessed.

According to Emerson and other social exchange theorists, certain factors influence people to maintain or dissolve relationships.[28] Based on this model, rewards minus costs equal outcome. Accordingly, people tend to remain in relationships if their rewards are satisfactory and there are no available alternatives. Conversely, relationships are likely to be terminated when a person perceives the rewards to be meager and an alternative relationship is available. Of equal importance are the costs that individuals incur in a relationship. During the 1960s and 1970s, the rewards from mutual-aid networks were decreasing. As cited earlier, black families, as members of mutual-aid networks, incurred both monetary and latent costs. The strain of urban living, with high rates of unemployment and underemployment, made it difficult for members of the mutual-aid network to continue to aid others without depleting the resources of their own families. In order to be a member of the mutual-aid network, black families were expected to participate in church activities and to come to the aid of other members of the network. Although these conditions had become antithetical to urban living and the American way of life, both the black church and the mutual-aid network were important to black families. On the other hand, the govenment, with its amorphous and enigmatic nature, appeared to be a service provider without any discernible costs but with definite rewards. Besides, civil rights leaders and other social activists established that the United States, which included the government, had long been a beneficiary of black labor and taxes. So it was the government, with its indebtedness to black families, that had an obligation to discharge. This perception of the government as the recipient and black families as the provider was consistent with the belief that reparations were needed for the social injustices blacks had experienced in America. This rationale helped black families make the transition from the almost exclusive use of informal social-support systems to greater reliance on formal social-support systems.

DECLINE OF MUTUAL AID NETWORKS

Over the last two decades, government-sponsored social-service programs have dissipated the mutual-aid network and diminished its stabilizing influence on black two-parent families. In reality, the government was expected to supplement rather than supplant the black mutual-aid network. However, providing many of the fundamental goods and services, formerly obtained through the mutual-aid network was taken over by government social-service agencies. If formal social-service agencies had been successful in enabling black families and their members to become economically independent, the decline of informal social-support systems would not have had such a devastating effect on black families. Despite modest advances blacks made in the 1960s and 1970s, the overall socioeconomic status of black families did not improve. The decline in mutual-aid networks along with the federal government's ultra-conservative posture in the 1980s, has left black families in a precarious position. This reactionary posture has eventuated in the disallocation of federal moneys to social programs. Presently, the cyclical use of institutional and noninstitutional social-support systems, which has occurred in the larger society, now characterizes black cultural patterns. Recently, the black church has begun to regain its authority. Once again, it is commonplace for black churches to provide food pantries, clothing, and open shelters; to distribute surplus commodities; and to serve as advocates for black and poor families. However, what appears to be occurring at a slower pace is the revitalization of mutual-aid networks for black two-parent families.

In light of this devolutionary trend, there is a definite need for more effective approaches to bring about social and economic progress for black families. Moreover, apart from the decline of black mutual-aid networks, came the shocking realization that this form of government involvement, like any other relationship, is not without its share of costs.

NOTES

1. Carrie Allen McCray, "The Black Woman and Family Roles," in La Frances Rodgers-Rose, ed., *The Black Woman* (Beverly Hills, California: Sage Publications), p. 71.

2. David Rothman, *The Discovery of the Asylum* (Boston, Massachusetts: Little, Brown and Company, 1971).

3. Charles Zastrow, *Introduction to Social Welfare Institutions: Social Problems, Services and Current Issues* (Homewood, Illinois: The Dorsey Press, 1982), p. 19.

4. Niara Sudarkasa, "Interpreting the African Heritage in Afro-American Family Organization," in Harriette Pipes McAdoo, ed., *Black Families* (Beverly Hills, California: Sage Publications, 1981), p. 46.

5. John Hope Franklin, *From Slavery to Freedom: A History of American Negroes* (New York: Alford A. Knopf, 1948), pp. 132–156.

6. Mary Francis Berry and John Blassingame, *Long Memory: The Black Experience in America* (New York: Oxford University Press, 1982), p. 74.

7. Andrew Billingsley and Jeanne M. Giovannoni, *Children of the Storm: Black Children and American Child Welfare* (New York: Harcourt, Brace, Jovanovich, 1972), p. 46.

8. Herbert Gutman, *The Black Family in Slavery and Freedom, 1750–1925* (New York: Vintage, 1976), pp. 498–500.

9. Lambert Maguire, *Understanding Social Networks* (Beverly Hills, California: Sage Publications, 1983), p. 51.

10. Ibid.

11. E. Pattison, D. Francisco, P. Wood, H. Frazier, and J. Crowder, "A Psychosocial Kinship Model for Family Therapy," *American Journal of Psychiatry* 132 (1975): 1246–1251; Christopher Tolsdorf, "Social Networks and Coping: An Exploratory Study," *Family Process* 15 (1976): 407–417.

12. Maguire, *Understanding Social Networks*, pp. 52–54.

13. Gerald Gurin, Joseph Veroff, and Sheila Feld, *Americans View Their Mental Health* (New York: Basic Books, 1960), pp. 364–371.

14. United States Bureau of the Census, *America's Black Population, 1970–1982: A Statistical View*. Series p–10/POP 83–1 (Washington, D. C.: U. S. Government Printing Office, 1983), p. 16.

15. Harriette Pipes McAdoo, "Black Mothers and the Extended Family Support Network," in La Frances Rodgers-Rose, ed., *The Black Womann* (Beverly Hills, California: Sage, 1980), pp. 136–141.

16. Billingsley, *Black Families in White America*.

17. W. E. Burghardt DuBois, "The Function of the Negro Church," in Hart M. Nelsen, Raytha L. Yokley, Anne K. Nelsen, eds., *The Black Church in America* (New York: Basic Books), pp. 77–81.

18. Robert Hill, *The Strengths of Black Families* (New York: Emerson Hall, 1972); Robert Hill, "The Black Family: Building on Strengths," in Robert L. Woodson, ed., *On the Road to Economic Freedom: An Agenda for Black Progress* (Washington, D. C.: National Center for Neighborhood Enterprise, 1987), pp. 71–92.

19. John W. Blassingame, *The Slave Community* (New York: Oxford University Press, 1972), p. 74.

20. Theressa Hoover, "Black Women and the Churches: Triple Jeopardy," in Alice Hageman, ed., *Sexist Religion and Women in the Church* (New York: Association Press, 1974), pp. 63–76.

21. Carol Stack, *All Our Kin: Strategies for Survival in a Black Community* (New York: Harper and Row, 1974), p. 28.

22. Maguire, *Understanding Social Networks*, pp. 51–55.

23. Alvin Ward Goulder, "The Norm of Reciprocity: A Preliminary Statement," *American Sociological Review* 25 (1960): 161–178.

24. Melville Herskovits, *The Myth of the Negro Past* (Boston: Beacon, 1970), pp. 182–184; *Introduction to Black Sociology* (New York: McGraw-Hill, 1976), p. 117; Blassingame, *The Slave Community*, p. 41; Sudarkasa, *Interpreting the African Heritage*, p. 45.

25. Staples, *Introduction to Black Sociology*; Sudarkasa, *Interpreting the African Heritage*, p. 44–46.

26. Staples, *Introduction to Black Sociology*, p. 117.

27. Stack, *All Our Kin*, p. 38.

28. Richard M. Emerson, ''Power-Dependence Relations,'' *American Sociological Review* 27 (1962): 31–41.

4 THE ERA OF LIBERAL SOCIAL POLICY

The decades of the 1960s and 1970s bear a striking resemblance to the Depression Era of the 1930s. Some have argued that the radical change in social policy initiated by Franklin D. Roosevelt set the tone and direction of the sweeping social and economic programs introduced by John F. Kennedy and expanded by Lyndon B. Johnson.[1] Certainly blacks' demands for civil rights and the recognition that federal initiatives were essential to securing social equality were as evident in the Johnson and Kennedy administrations as in FDR's. During the 1960s the revolutionary position of the federal government in planning, developing, and monitoring social programs to facilitate self-reliance and economic independence for black and poor families was more pronounced than in the Roosevelt administration. This transition, beginning in the pre-Roosevelt era, from conservative to liberal, to quasi-conservative, and again to liberal social policy, reflects the cyclical form which social policy took. In the latter case, liberal social policy in the 1960s and 1970s, while innovative in approach, closely paralleled the New Deal in fundamental assumptions regarding poverty. In both cases, federal intervention was to be temporary and of such magnitude as to bring about a permanent change in the circumstances of disadvantaged Americans. The major difference was the composition of the poor, for whom federal programs were geared. In the Depression years, social services were designed to meet the needs of the ''new'' poor, composed largely of whites, as opposed to the 1960s when these programs were targeted to the ''old'' poor, in which blacks were overrepresented. Clouded in sociological lexicon, blacks were defined as victims of slavery and racial inequities that had created structures and patterns of functioning, which, if not corrected, would continue to manifest social anomalies.

It was not that black families were unfamiliar with poverty and its concomitants. What was new was the increased visibility of the debilitating conditions which black and poor families were encountering. The social revolution made all Americans aware of the plight of black families. And rioting, looting, and other civil disturbances forced the majority of Americans, irrespective of race or ethnic background, to experience social problems associated with poverty and social inequality. Essentially, the devastating consequences of occupying an economically depressed status, characteristic of an inordinate number of black families, left the confines of the black community and became a societal rather than a black problem. Until this point in history, few white families had been directly affected by the socioeconomic status of black families. But with mass demonstrations and an upsurge of urban violence, a number of Americans began to seek solutions to the lower status of black families.

Philosophical tenets stressing frugality, productivity, and social rewards commensurate with hard work remained an integral part of the formulation of liberal social policy. It was firmly believed that the cycle of poverty could be broken with global federal assistance. Necessarily, policy-makers envisioned social programs that would enable blacks and the nation's poor to rise from poverty and lead constructive and productive lives. By providing services to meet social, educational, and economic needs and enacting legislation to eliminate racial barriers, the Johnson administration believed it was ensuring that black families, as a collective, would be rescued from material deprivation. Never before in the history of the country had an effort of this magnitude been undertaken. But an investment of this nature was projected to bring a return. Although conservatives argued against federal intervention, not everyone opposed to liberal social policy questioned the ability of the government's plan to produce desired results. Some of the most adamant opponents expressed concerns over the size of budgetary allocations to the proposed social programs. Further, they warned of the disastrous effects to the free enterprise system. Adding to this argument, others articulated the history of immigrant groups who had come to this country penniless and had risen to phenomenal economic wealth on their own merits. Despite the overwhelming dissatisfaction of political conservatives, the federal government put in force social programs and civil rights legislation which had long been sought by black families and their members.

One of the most notable changes was the administrative centralization of social programs. In the years preceding Johnson's War on Poverty, assistance to the poor was almost exclusively handled by state governments. Allowing states to administer their own welfare programs, establishing eligibility and benefit amounts without monitoring, often led to overt discrimination against black families needing assistance. Granted the use of unlimited discretion, many states had such ambivalent and, oftentimes, negative attitudes toward the poor, in which black families were overrepresented, that they held dollar amounts on

AFDC payments to extremely low levels. For example, in 1940 Mississippi had only 104 families on the Aid to Dependent Children (ADC) rolls. Surprisingly, this occurred five years after the program was enacted.[2] Little had changed by 1981, when Mississippi had the lowest welfare payments in the country, $96 a month for a typical welfare family of three, while Wisconsin paid $473 a month for a family of the same size.[3] There is a great disparity in the 4 percent per capita income, which the Mississippi legislature allocates to welfare assistance, versus matching amounts paid by Wisconsin, which at the time was 24 percent of the per capita income. This does not take into account other regional disparities in welfare payments or the methods used by states, prior to the centralization of social welfare programs, to disqualify prospective recipients. One of the most important factors that contributed to the civil rights protests and the subsequent reformulation of social and economic policies was the frustration voiced by blacks regarding exclusionary practices of societal institutions and social-welfare programs.

Despite the trend toward centralization of social-welfare programs, renewed efforts to decentralize social-service delivery and to lessen the federal government's involvement in the delivery of social services became evident during the Nixon administration. Numerous decentralized block grants, such as the Comprehensive Employment Training Act (CETA), Community Development Black Grants (CDBG), and Title XX, were enacted under the Nixon administration. The purpose of such programs was to transfer more responsibility for the provision of social-welfare services to the states. Therefore, job training programs were made available through CETA, cities were permitted to establish priorities for social services through CDBGs, and Title XX gave states more responsibility for social services while limiting the federal government's role in the delivery of social-welfare programs. However, while President Nixon was committed to correcting mistakes of the Great Society programs, many of his proposals for reform conformed to liberalism. For example, Nixon proposed, albeit unsuccessfully, a Family Assistance Program, which would have replaced the Aid to Families with Dependent Children program. The Family Assistance Program would have provided a guaranteed minimum cash income to every family with children who needed it. The passage of the Supplementary Security Income (SSI) legislation, establishing a uniform national minimum cash income to the aged, blind, and disabled occurred under this administration. The food stamp program was also expanded under the Nixon administration.[4]

The Nixon administration, with its propensity for conservatism, has been characterized negatively by some.[5] However, because of the compromising nature of the administration in its relationship with Congress and its overwhelming uncertainty in the arena of social policy, the Nixon administration's involvement in domestic social policy was amorphous at best.

A close examination of social-welfare programs developed and expanded by the federal government during the 1960s and 1970s reveals that while efficacy and design are questionable, few areas reflecting the social and economic needs of black and poor families were left untouched. Basically, the development of social and economic programs had a snowball effect. As programs were implemented, new ones were created. And as social programs increased, so did federal expenditures. Of the large number of social welfare programs in which the federal government played a critical role, the major ones were Aid to Families with Dependent Children (AFDC); food stamps; Medicaid; child development centers; nutrition programs; job training, Work Incentive Programs (WIN), Job Corps, and Comprehensive Employment Training Act (CETA); and subsidized housing. Many of these core programs spread further into related services and served as the basis for the continuous evolution of other social-welfare programs.

Before scrutinizing the extent to which black families utilized social programs, we must examine utilization rates from another perspective, which is purely political. From this vantage point, utilization patterns of black families was one basis which was used to justify liberal social policy. The question asked and answered most frequently, particularly by advocates, was, How many? How many blacks were participants in CETA? How many minorities received educational grants? How many blacks were recipients of housing subsidies? Not only did advocates of liberal social policy raise the question How many? they also provided the public with the answers. Unfortunately, the numbers game they played tended to obscure the disadvantages and the emergence of social problems that needed to be addressed.

Success or failure of social policy should be based on retention and permanence, not merely on utilization. The fact that the number of blacks deriving benefits from social programs increased dramatically should not have led policy makers to infer that the status of black families had significantly improved.

Toward the end of the decade of the 1970s, political conservatives became involved in a numbers game of their own. They began to look at service utilization in terms that triggered strong public emotions. The conservatives' answer to How many? differed significantly from that of proponents of social and economic programs. Blaming the failing economy, high rates of unemployment, and huge federal deficits on out-of-control government spending for social programs, they concluded that far too many federal dollars had been allocated to social-welfare programs without achieving the desired results. However, for them, the question, How many? was applied to a different set of variables, such as, How many black families continue to have incomes below the poverty level? How many black families are female-headed? How many black children are born out-of-wedlock? To these questions of How many? the answers were decidedly different. For both political persuasions, the full implication of the last twenty years was submerged by a myopic view of social policy.

In order to discern the overall impact of social and economic programs on black families, it is essential to examine the extent to which black families became the recipients of newly sponsored government social services. It should be noted that patterns of service utilization alone are not sufficient to explain the relationship between social and economic programs and the stability of black nuclear families. But statistical data reflecting rates of service utilization, in conjunction with program design and administration, are all factors that have contributed significantly to the disintegration of black nuclear families. Theories which attribute the decline of black two-parent families to a changing economy and the decreasing black male labor market participation rate, without examining the relationship between social policy and these occurrences, are ignoring the fact that an efficient, well-designed, and well-monitored service delivery system would have recognized these societal changes and implemented social and economic programs to avert the crisis that now confronts black families.

Trendline data for many of these social and economic programs is difficult at best to obtain. In some cases generic data on patterns of service utilization have not consistently been aggregated on the basis of recipient characteristics. When participants' characteristics have been reported, gender frequently has taken precedence over race. Until the late 1960s and into the 1970s, many social programs reported "race" using the term "minorities," which was all too often a catchall for blacks, Hispanics, and other non-white racial and ethnic groups. In other instances, when data are available on the race of social program participants, definitional changes in obtaining data and other modifications in the instruments used to capture the data make reliability and comparability unlikely. However, since the mid 1970s there appears to be more consistency in reporting data. Still, it is too early to determine if statistical data on participant characteristics will be gathered uniformly and maintained at a central repository. Collecting, reporting and compiling data on social and economic programs is politically determined. This becomes fairly obvious with the Reagan administration and its new thrust for decentralization. This posture has not only reduced program administration to a local level, it also deemphasizes the central reporting and maintenance of social-service data.

SOCIAL WELFARE PROGRAMS

Eligibility

Determining criteria for entitlements has more of a bearing on utilization of social welfare services than any other factor, with perhaps the exception of the fair administration of program guidelines. During the era of liberal social policy, eligibility requirements were substantially altered, thereby extending entitlements to a broader range of black and poor families. Providing social-welfare services to larger numbers of persons, and monitoring to ensure that policies were followed, enlarged the pool of social-welfare beneficiaries. Even though the FDR administration developed federal-state funded social-welfare programs, states continued to maintain a tremendous degree of latitude in determining eligibility. The government's renewed involvement in social-welfare programs brought about changes in the role of the states in governing social-service delivery. The decision to institute centralization was based to some degree on blacks' claims of discriminatory policies and practices at regional and local levels of government, marking a distinct departure on the part of the federal government. Prior to the 1930s, between 1940 and 1960, and in the early 1970's, states' rights or federalism was enmeshed in federal-state relations. It would be pure naiveté to believe that the issue of differential access to social-welfare programs had not been voiced by blacks in the past. In the Depression years, when blacks were confronted with social and economic pressures unparalleled by those of other groups, letters were sent to FDR by black men and women and black leaders who relentlessly stressed their inability to obtain relief throughout the country. The influence of race on states' welfare practices, including the administration of relief programs, did not go unheeded by Roosevelt. Yet he conceded that his priority was one of accommodation to political constituents to obtain support for the passage of social programs. Thus, he felt the need to relegate racial issues in favor of what he deemed political exigency. Roosevelt's sentiments clearly indicated the priorities of his administration when he succinctly stated, "First things come first, and I can't alienate certain votes I need for measures that are more important at the moment by pushing any measures that would entail a fight."[6] In so doing, Roosevelt obtained the votes necessary to pass his emergency relief programs and the Social Security Act, leaving blacks with the formidable task of extracting economic and social support as best they could. This pattern continued for black families until the next era of liberal social policy.

Until the 1960s, social welfare programs, particularly ADC and low-income public housing, continued to narrowly define eligibility with the intent of maintaining exclusivity, thus preventing black families from becoming recipients of various social services. Despite practices to curtail beneficiaries, expenditures climbed at a dramatic rate. As the country's elderly benefited from Social Security, company pensions, and federally financed low-rent public housing, a shift occurred in the composition of the poor. Between 1950 and 1960, the number of elderly recipients decreased from 50 to 37 percent of the public assistance population. Conversely, the Aid to Dependent Children program increased to approximately 3 million recipients by 1960.[7]

In the 1960s the extension of entitlements to a vast array of black and poor families was instituted on three levels. First, major policy changes were initiated in ADC eligibility requirements. Second, the development of new social programs like Medicaid, Medicare, and job training programs subsumed under the 1964 Economic Opportunity Act omitted restrictions for entitlements, which characterized earlier social welfare programs. Third, over a twenty-year period successive amendments to social-welfare programs tended to expand instead of constrict eligibility to individuals and families. Moreover, states' discretion over eligibility was curtailed legislatively and informally through political persuasion.

From this point forward, eligibility for social-welfare programs was established, encompassing larger numbers of individuals and families. By extending eligibility to a vast number of economically disadvantaged families, the government unknowingly facilitated demands from other groups voicing the need for government intercession on their behalf. Observers of the evolution of liberal social policy have subsequently argued that these new contenders for social power—women, elderly, handicapped and other minorities—diffused efforts initiated by blacks and minimized gains made available during the earlier stages of social-welfare expansion.[8] With demands from diverse groups for social justice, eligibiity criteria became unusually broad.

After introducing numerous social and economic programs and legislation designed to respond to the needs and interests of black families, the government and public assumed a wait-and-see posture.

ANTIPOVERTY PROGRAMS

Aid to Families with Dependent Children

One of the most controversial of all public assistance programs is Aid to Families with Dependent Children (AFDC). Today, 1 of every 5 blacks receive AFDC. Since its inception in 1935, (originally called ADC, later called AFDC in 1962), this program represents the largest cash outlay by the federal government. In 1980, nearly $11 billion was spent on the AFDC program.[9] Over the last twenty years, AFDC has been subjected to numerous eligibility and administrational changes. More commonly known as "welfare," AFDC has been stereotypically viewed as a parasitic program for black women, their mates, and children. Persistent inaccuracies have resulted in the proliferation of myths about AFDC recipients.[10] Some of the more popular misconceptions include: most AFDC recipients are black, have large families, and consist of able-bodied individuals who are not willing to work. Since efforts to dispel these myths have been restricted to academic circles, the general public continues to hold negative attitudes toward government assistance and recipients. Expanding AFDC to include unemployed parents, particularly fathers (AFDC-UP), fostered the belief that men too lazy to secure employment were benefiting directly from public assistance.

Regarding the AFDC program, public outcry has risen to a level commensurate with the number of recipients. The number of AFDC families rose from 1.3 million in 1967 to 3.2 million in 1979. This increase over a twelve-year period represents a 162 percent and 165 percent increase for white and black families respectively. What is surprising is that these increases exceeded the percentage increase of white and black female-headed families with children, which rose 90 and 108 percent respectively. Despite the drastic increase in the number of families receiving AFDC, the composition of these families in the caseloads remained fairly stable. In 1979 white families comprised 52 percent of the AFDC recipients, down from 53 percent in 1967. Blacks represented the same proportion of the AFDC caseload—44 percent—in 1967 and 1979. Currently, approximately 3.9 million families receive AFDC. In general, the average family receives welfare benefits from 18 to 24 months. Of this number, 900,000 have been on the program for more than five years.[11] Ten percent have received benefits for 10 years or longer.[12] Another indicator of the level of service utilization is the rate at which families return to AFDC and other public assistance caseloads. However, reliable data reflecting a national pattern of repeated social welfare service use is not available.

Work Incentive Programs

An adjunct to public assistance, Work Incentive programs (WIN) were created in 1967. By design these programs mandated that recipients be referred by the states for either gainful employment or vocational training. Some exclusions which exempted individuals are as follows: (1) under age 16, (2) ill or incapacitated or attending school, and (3) those who needed to be continually present in the home because of the illness or incapacity of another member of the household. Thus, female heads of households with dependent children, who are recipients of AFDC are permitted to claim exemption due to the latter stipulation, which excludes women with children under 6 years of age. By 1971, WIN policies became even more stringent, as all AFDC current and prospective recipients were required to register for a manpower training program or seek employment. Failure to comply with this mandate could mean the loss of benefits.[13]

In 1976, the total number of WIN registrants was 1,740,085; 928,519 (53.4 percent) were white, 705,054 (40.5 percent) were black, and the remaining 106,512 (6.1 percent) included American Indians, Hispanic Americans, and other minorities. By 1983, WIN guidelines had once again undergone modification. New federalism resulted in states having the option of providing WIN, or other forms of employment-oriented programs, in an effort to reduce welfare rolls. At this time, in the 34 regular WIN states, a total of 1,325,879 participants were registered. Of this number 581,606 (43.9 percent) were white, 418,915 (31.6 percent) were black, 227,716 (17.2 percent) were Hispanic, and the remaining 97, 642 (7.4 percent) were American Indian, Alaskan Native, Asian and Pacific Islander, and other minorities. Comparing these two categorizations of the racial and ethnic characteristics of program participants for 1976 and 1983 illustrates that observable changes occurred in data collection, reporting, and compiling.

The enactment of the Manpower Development and Training Act (MDTA) in 1962, along with the passage of the 1964 Economic Opportunity Act and the Emergency Employment Act, represents the development of contemporary federal manpower programs. Principally the goal of such programs was to assist the young urban poor, included in which are black youth, in acquiring and refining marketable job skills.[14]

Another employment and job training program established under the Nixon administration to enable black and white underclass families to acquire economic independence was the Comprehensive Employment and Training Act program. Distinguished by various Title numbers, these programs offered manpower training and public jobs to disadvantaged youth and adults. In 1976 and 1981, the cumulative totals remained under 3 million participants, 2.5 and 2.9 million respectively. During this time the percentage of white participants declined from over 50 percent in 1976 to 45 percent in 1981; while the proportion of black CETA participants, over this period, increased from 29 percent in 1976 to 37 percent in 1981.[15]

An interest in creating job opportunities for low-income families was also indicated by the Carter administration, as was the belief that income-support programs should be consolidated into one system. In 1977 President Jimmy Carter presented the Program for Better Jobs and Income. Essentially, this program, while exempting the aged, blind, disabled, and single parents with children under seven, required the principal wage earner in each family seeking public assistance to participate in a five-week program to secure a job. If a job could not be found, then a public sector job would be made available. Ultimately the wage earner was to obtain a private-sector job. In addition this proposal contained a provision that individuals who did not generate sufficient incomes could receive a direct cash benefit or an expanded earned-income tax credit. Accordingly, the principal wage earner would be able to keep $3,800 of earned income, after which federal cash benefits would be reduced 50 cents for each dollar. The earned income tax credit was designed to encourage private sector employment by providing income tax credits on annual earnings in the labor market. This portion of the plan was to be administered by the Internal Revenue Service. However, Carter's welfare proposals, focusing largely on increasing private sector employment for poor families, failed to receive congressional support. In general, the Carter administration's propensity for liberalism was thwarted by a mood of conservatism, which had begun to engulf the country.[16]

Opponents of social welfare programs did not look favorably upon policies that prevented recipients from engaging in employment or activities that would not rapidly lead to a job. This sentiment increased when large numbers of women sought employment in the labor market. At this time the expression of compassion and empathic understanding for women remaining in the home to care for children rapidly diminished. There was even less tolerance for women who remained in the home because they were recipients of social welfare services.

To give women with children an opportunity to acquire and refine marketable job skills, as well as to mediate the concerns of those who saw public assistance as a means of avoiding employment, child-care centers proliferated. The relationship between WIN, CETA, and other employment-oriented programs and government-funded child-care centers became obvious. Each program was designed to enable single-parent heads of households, typically women, to ultimately secure and retain employment. Prior to 1975 when federal and state governments increased funds to day-care centers, under Title XX of the Social Security Act, public financial support for child-care services had dwindled considerably since the Depression and post-World War II period, as the number of women workers in industry began to decline. The timing of the government's influx of funds to day-care centers cannot be taken lightly. Although practitioners argued for mechanisms that would support women willing and eager to acquire job skills and secure employment, the visibility of married and unmarried female workers with children was sufficient evidence that given adequate child care women could become productive outside the home. In 1974, one year before the revitalization of child-care centers, 30 percent of women with children under the age of three were in the labor force, and 33 percent of married women with children between the ages of six to seventeen were working outside the home. Added to this number, 67 percent of female single parents with school-age children were employed, and 54 percent of these women had children under the age of six.[17] Suffice it to say, the federal government's decision to provide day care for recipients of AFDC was lauded on many fronts.

Food Stamps

Like many other antipoverty programs, the food stamp program, established in 1939 and ended in 1943, was reinstituted in 1961 during the Johnson administration. Under the auspices of the U. S. Department of Agriculture, food stamps are purchased by eligible persons for a portion of their face value or received without payment based on family size and income, and are used for the purchase of food products in grocery stores.[18] Currently, one of every four blacks is a recipient of foods stamps. The number of food stamp recipients rose from 400,000 in 1965 to 21.6 million in 1983. Examining households which received food-stamps for one year, we find that in 1982, 7.2 million households received food stamps. A racial breakdown reveals that 4.6 million were white and 2.3 million were black. Generally food stamps are available to recipients of public assistance, to supplement their income and ensure an adequate diet. A concern of critics is the use of food stamps for the purchase of commodities that have been deemed frivolous. As a consequence, government policies specify the nature of expenditures that can be made using food stamps. Despite the stipulation that payment cannot be made using food stamps for non-food items, the myth that recipients of food stamps purchase alcohol and expensive cars has been slow to fade.

Another concern has been the selling of food stamps illegally in exchange for money. For the most part, the use of food stamps continues to be a time-consuming and denigrating endeavor, as they are distributed in many states in the same fashion as surplus commodities. In both instances, recipients are compelled to wait in extremely long lines, in and outside, social service offices to obtain food stamps. Despite the inconvenience, the exigency of this transfer program has resulted in a high rate of utilization. Federal expenditures for food stamps have increased from $600 million in 1970 to an estimated $8.7 billion in 1980.[19]

In conjunction with the food-stamp program, the federal government made financial assistance available to state governments willing to provide matching dollars for other nutrition programs. Supplementary food programs such as school lunches and dairy and other nutritional food products have been made available to eligible women and children in programs such as the Women, Infants, and Children (WIC) program.

A look at the school lunch program for one year reveals that a large number of black and white families have relied on these supplementary programs to augment their diets. For example, in 1982 a total of 5.6 million households received free school lunches, 3.5 million were white, and 1.9 million were black. As with other social welfare programs, tremendous furor has been generated over nutrition programs. Many believe that financial assistance and food stamps are more than ample to meet the needs of welfare families. For some, ancillary food programs support the contention that recipients of public assistance are incapable of money management. Arguing for the continuation of food programs by citing high incidents of infant mortality and deaths related to poor nutrition, common among blacks and the poor, proponents have experienced some success in retaining these programs. Although nutrition programs are not offered by all states, monetary allocations have continued to escalate for these programs.

Medicaid

Both Medicaid and Medicare were enacted in 1965 as Title XIX of the Social Security Act. Medicaid defrays medical and health costs primarily for individuals receiving public assistance, while Medicare is designed specifically for the elderly, paying some portion of their health care costs. Originally, Medicaid legislation encouraged states to provide coverage to all self-supporting individuals whose low incomes made medical expenses unaffordable. However, since this condition was not mandatory and states vary on their definition of "medical indigence," only recipients of public assistance are assured coverage.[20] With the exception of Arizona, all states provide for basic health care services for eligible low-income persons.[21]

Critics have argued that Medicaid is dangerously close to socialized medicine and is in part responsible for escalating health-care costs. Statistical data on racial and ethnic characteristics of Medicaid recipients, like other social-service data, was minimally reliable until fiscal year 1980. Prior to 1980, states reported data on recipient characteristics in a dichotomized form using two categories "white, non-Hispanic" and "unknown," for all non-whites who received Medicaid services. On the basis of this typology, data reflect that in 1975, the first year for which such data are available, there were 8,384,300 (42 percent) whites and 11,936,069 (58 percent) unknowns, or minorities who were recipients of Medicaid. However, by 1983 the proportion of minorities receiving Medicaid had decreased to 44 percent and the number of white recipients had increased to 55.8 percent. Specifically, a breakdown of recipients reveals Medicaid was received by the following in 1983: 11,129,942 whites (not Hispanic origin) or 55.8 percent, 7,215,640 blacks or 36.2 percent and 1,590,400 other minorities or 8 percent. The percentage of Medicaid payments made to minorities also declined between 1975 and 1983. In 1975 whites received $7.5 billion or 61 percent, compared to $4.7 billion for minorities or 39 percent. Corresponding figures for 1983 indicate that $11 billion or 70.4 percent in Medicaid payments went to whites and $9.6 billion or 29.8 percent went to minorities. Total Medicaid payments received by blacks for the year was $8 billion or 25 percent.[22] Health-care services due to Medicaid have had a demonstrable impact on attenuating disease and reducing infant mortality for black and poor families. Today one of every four blacks is enrolled in Medicaid, which accounts somewhat for the fact that black Americans have experienced a dramatic reduction in heart disease and have prevented serious health problems through medical screening, and early diagnosis and treatment over the last twenty years.

In spite of the availability of Medicaid, most black families have benefited little from this government-sponsored program. Since most black men and women comprise the working poor, who do not qualify for government-subsi-dized medical care, they are more likely to forego necessary health-care services or to incur enormous hospital and medical expenses when medical care is an imperative. Johnson says that the working poor can manage adequately until a medical emergency arises. At that point, he states the medically indigent can be confronted with a financial disaster which is difficult to overcome.[23]

Recognizing the importance of health services to families who do not qualify for cash welfare programs, which automatically entitle them to Medicaid, ap-proximately 29 states include families in their definitions of the medically needy. Medicaid benefits are extended to families whose incomes do not meet welfare requirements or whose medical expenses reduce their incomes to medical needy levels.[24]

Subsidized Housing

In 1983, 54.7 percent of all black families were renters compared to 32.7 percent of white families in the United States.[25] Hence, available and affordable rental units are extremely important to black families. During the riots in the 1960s, blacks drew attention to substandard and overcrowded housing, which characterized their communities. The term "ghetto," which defined the physical and psychological limitations imposed on inhabitants of metropolitan areas, gen-erally on the periphery of the inner city, became synonymous with absentee slum landlords, dilapidated housing, and overcrowding.

However, concern for inadequate housing for the poor did not begin in the 1960s. The first federally sponsored housing program had its beginning in the New Deal era. In 1934 and 1937 the federal government passed the National Housing Act and the Housing Act, respectively. Just as social policy in general created public employment, pensions, and financial assistance for many who were economically disadvantaged, the housing program in the 1930s was ben-eficial not only to the poor but was also advantageous to the middle and upper classes. To say that the destitute did not benefit from the government's social policy in housing would not be completely true. Indirectly, blacks and the poor were able to obtain suitable housing through the trickle-down effect. When middle-class families becamed upwardly mobile and migrated to suburban areas, their homes were placed on the market for working-class families to occupy.[26] In addition to insuring loans to stimulate the housing market and to allay the fears of individuals faced with loan defaults, the Wagner-Steagall Housing Act of 1937 created the United States Housing Authority. Through the USHA loans were made available for the construction of low-income dwellings.[27] Equally important, the housing act enabled states to provide low-rent public housing to the needy.[28]

Unsurprisingly, black familes did not benefit much from these new housing measures. Since the FDR administration espoused government decentralization, local government officials mediated social programs in their own geographic areas. In effect, racial discrimination made it difficult for blacks to receive the benefits of social-welfare programs, including adequate low-cost housing. As late as 1944, seven years after the passage of the Housing Act, 83,000 of the 92,476 housing units in which blacks resided were totally segregated or had quotas limiting black occupancy.[29] Moreover, in Buffalo, New York, where 76 percent of the city's 5,343 dwelling units remained unoccupied, government officials refused to permit the temporary use of these units by blacks.[30] In contrast to this period, a resurgence of federal funding of housing along with the enactment of Fair Housing Legislation in the 1960s and 1970s produced gains in housing ownership and improvements in overall living conditions for some black families.

One of the oldest and widely used programs under the aegis of the U. S. Department of Housing and Urban Development (HUD) continues to be low-rent public housing. Because a disproportionate number of black families are renters, as opposed to homeowners, the availability of public housing is essential. However, despite increases in the occupancy rates of public housing, the proportion of these units occupied by black families has decreased. In 1972, black families occupied 49 percent and white familes 43 percent of the occupied public housing units. Comparitively, in 1978, the proportion of low-rent public housing units occupied by black families had declined to 47.1 percent and 38.4 percent for white families. Increases in occupancy, which took place during this six-year span, largely affected the Hispanic population. For this cultural group, public housing occupancy rose from 7 to 12.2 percent.[31]

Aside from the government's increased participation in the aforementioned social-welfare services, other government-funded social and economic programs were provided to bring about parity in employment, education, and private enterprise, not to mention a myriad of social services to address the social and emotional needs of blacks and poor families. The latter services generally took the form of community mental-health centers, drug abuse programs, delinquency prevention projects, and so on. While many of these and related programs attempted to transform poor black and white families into viable social and economic units, black working- and middle-class families sought policies to further enhance their status. Other than grants and loans for education, housing, and business ownership, many of these families were unable to derive immediate benefits from the expansion of social-welfare services, as their incomes precluded entitlement.

Meeting the needs of the growing black middle-class required substantially more than increased monetary expenditures in social welfare programs. What black middle-class families also expected was a change in discriminatory practices in education, employment, and housing. For instance, in 1960 and 1970 the proportion of blacks employed in managerial and professional occupations was 7 and 10 percent respectively.[32] Finding inequities in the labor market, middle-class blacks challenged the federal government to enact legislation and empower government agencies with enforcement capacity to effect social justice. Hence, affirmative action laws, by design, were to bring about parity in institutions that had historically excluded blacks.

AFFIRMATIVE ACTION

Employment

Resistance to affirmative action programs was undoubtedly greater in this area of social policy than in any other. Still, the government, under demands from black leaders, the black student movement, and coalitions of blacks and white liberals took a giant step forward by mandating that blacks be given equal access to employment and educational opportunities. To enforce affirmative action laws, various entities were established to issue legal sanctions for noncompliance. Both the public and private sectors were subjected to this legislative edict. To soften the blow, monetary incentives in various forms such as tax breaks were offered as inducements for adherence to affirmative actions laws. Evidence suggests that corporations implemented diverse policies to comply with federal initiatives. However, more often than not these measures were established reluctantly and resulted in a paucity of token jobs.[33] Some blacks did benefit from affirmative action in employment. In this regard, who? and how many? are pertinent. Hill indicates that blacks were not the only ones to benefit from affirmative action legislation and policies. He states that between 1974 and 1977, 53 percent of all new jobs in the private sector went to white women. White males acquired 26 percent of new jobs, Hispanics 12 percent, and blacks and Asians secured a mere 5 percent. Moreover, only 1 of every 1,000 jobs created between 1970 and 1983 went to black males.[34]

In the corporate sector, executives found a catchall position for blacks, in human resources, which rarely led to promotion into higher-paying positions in other divisions within the company. In the main, trepidation regarding the loss of sizable government contracts was somewhat sufficient to evoke affirmative action policies from the most conservative corporate entities. The federal government, being the initiator of such policies, was one of the largest employers of blacks. However, the government as a role model was nothing new. During the Depression, the percentage of blacks in federal employment outnumbered their proportion in the population. This trend continues today, as blacks and other minorities constitute one of every four federal workers.[35]

ENTREPRENEURSHIP

In addition to the opportunities offered to blacks in the labor force as a consequence of affirmative action, the government made numerous loans available to blacks to establish, maintain and expand businesses. Data on government loans to black-operated small businesses are sparse. However, available data reflect that in 1970 a total of 15,100 loans were approved for small businesses; 6,300 (41 percent) went to minority-operated businesses, compared to 1980 when 31,700 loans were approved and 6,000 (19 percent) were for minority-operated businesses. By 1982 loans to small businesses were down to 15,400. In the same year, loans to minority operated-businesses had fallen substantially, to 5,900 or 13 percent, 28 percent below the level which existed more than two decades earlier.[36] The data indicate that considering the small percentage of minority-operated businesses, a large proportion of minority firms received loans from the federal government during the 1960s and 1970s. For instance, in 1977, of nearly 10 million industries, black firms constituted only 231,000 of 2.3 percent. When the dollar value of these loans is considered, the proportion of actual dollars minority firms received was far less than the percentage of total loans which were made to these businesses. Specifically, in 1970 the value of total loans made to all small businesses was $710 million, of which $160 million (23 percent) went to minority-operated small businesses. By 1982, small businesses received loans in the amount of $2.5 billion dollars, and $238 million (13 percent) was received by minority-owned firms.

Education

Barriers in educational institutions were also addressed. Although equal percentages of blacks and whites were enrolled in school, in 1970 the median level (in years) of education for blacks was 10.2 years, 12.0 for whites. An even greater disparity existed between black college graduates and their white counterparts.

Only 6 percent of blacks had college degrees, compared to 17 percent of whites who had graduated from college in 1970.[37] Adding to this problem was the systematic exclusion of blacks from predominantly white colleges and universities. Moreover, professional-school enrollment for blacks was significantly less, thereby producing a negligible pool of black lawyers and judges (1 percent), physicians and surgeons (2 percent), and teachers (8 percent). At this time actual black enrollment figures for law and medical schools were as low as 3 percent. Almost ten years later, in 1979, the enrollment of blacks had risen to 4.2 and 5.7 percent in law and medical school respectively. Furthermore, the percentage of blacks majoring in business in 1969 and 1979 had increased from 5 to 8 percent.[38] Attributing low enrollments in white colleges and universities to limited financial resources and discriminatory practices, the federal government sought to alleviate both factors by appropriating moneys to make grants and loans available to blacks and poor students. Furthermore, the federal government threatened to withdraw federal dollars from colleges and universities that failed to admit a reasonable number of black students. This approach began to narrow the educational gap between blacks and whites. Thus, the entrance of larger numbers of blacks into predominantly white institutions of higher education was successfully accomplished. In 1980, 80 percent of all blacks enrolled in colleges and universities were at these institutions.[39] With affirmative action in place, numerous social-welfare programs and the 1965 Voting Rights Act, policy-makers clearly envisioned that black families would be strengthened through these social, economic, and political initiatives. At last it appeared that reparations were being made for past social inequities, which would permit, and even facilitate, black's joining mainstream America. As such, the prognosis for black families was one of optimism.

Community Mental Health Centers

It was not sufficient for the Johnson administration to seek solutions for curing the social and economic ills of black families. The proclivity for wholism surfaced in the expansion of mental-health services to black and low-income families. In 1963, when President Kennedy pushed for and succeeded in obtaining the passage of the Community Mental Health Centers Act, black and poor families were designated target groups whose emotional status was considered as precarious as their financial one. In effect, this law, like similar laws enacted by states throughout the 1950s, shifted the care of the mentally ill from state hospitals to community facilities.[40] The trend toward deinstitutionalization, transferring responsibility to local community agencies for persons with mental disorders, was assigned to model cities organizations and various components within community action organizations. It came as no surprise that black families were labeled as a high-risk group. The social and psychological indicators that mental health practitioners use to determine groups in need of mental-health services—female-headed families, children living in female-headed families, and families subsisting on incomes below the poverty level—were descriptive of a larger proportion of black than white families.[41] Added to the projected mental-health needs of black families was the high rate of institutionalization for black men, women, and children. The population of mental institutions consisted of 21.7 percent black males and 46.3 percent black females in 1960, when blacks comprised only 10.6 percent of the U. S. population.[42] In addition, differential U. S. mental hospital admission rates based on race for the year 1975, per 100,000 population, were as follows: for males, 214.2 for whites versus 444.5 for blacks and other races, and for females, 111.2 for whites versus 212.0 for blacks and other races.[43] Similarly, blacks were overrepresented in correctional institutions. An estimate of the population of correctional institutions in 1960 reveal that black males and black females represented 55 percent and 11 percent respectively. These and other factors were associated with poverty and defined as indicators of the need for mental-health services.[44]

The expansion of community mental-health services throughout the decade had a two-fold goal of rehabilitation and prevention. By placing service delivery at the community level, the stigma and distrust of service providers was to be lessened. As a consequence, black clients were to establish a greater degree of rapport and confidence in the therapist because facilities were in a familiar milieu. In addition, governing boards were formed with representatives of the community, who came to be known as "grassroots" persons, capable of proffering suggestions for treating black families. Still, there was a larger number of blacks who could not qualify for free mental-health services, because their incomes were slightly higher than the poverty index. The passage of Medicaid and Medicare extended mental-health services to these individuals and families. Furthermore, the incorporation of a sliding fee scale and private insurance coverage of mental-health services gradually made services available to all families with mental-health needs.

In terms of the chronology of social policy, it would appear as if the enactment of Medicaid and Medicare and the earlier passage of the Community Mental Health Centers Act were a part of one great master plan. But there is little evidence to support this contention. Had there been strategic planning, the subsequent receptivity to and usage of community mental-health centers by blacks would have been substantially greater. Instead, black familes resisted such services and continued to view them with suspicion.

Black families' underutilization of community mental-health centers was met with consternation and chagrin by both practitioners and policy-makers. Few could understand blacks' reluctance to voluntarily seek and continue participation in mental-health services. After all, prevalance studies showed higher rates of schizophrenia among black males and females, higher rates of institutionalization, and a preponderance of conditions indicating proneness to mental-health disorders.[45] Given these projections, it is fairly obvious why practitioners expected black families to be overrepresented in the utilization of community-based mental-health services. In no way am I suggesting that blacks did not utilize community mental-health services, but their use of these services did not reach projected levels. Recognizing the goals of mental-health policy, administrators convened meetings, seminars, and public forums to identify methods of increasing blacks' utilization of services. Lefley and Bestman state that the NIMH's 1974 Mental Health Demographic Profile of community mental-health centers revealed that policy recommendations were necessary to address underutilization by nonwhites.[46] Moreover, it was found that blacks who had utilized community

mental-health centers had drop-out rates as high as 74 percent, which led researchers to conclude that drop-out rates are invariably higher for black clients
than for whites.[47]

In general, community mental-health centers represent the major social-service
program that was underutilized by black families. When black families did utilize
these services, their use was frequently mandated by the courts, social-welfare
agencies, or some other entity with legal authorization to impose negative sanctions for failure to comply with their order.

REASSESSMENT: A PRELUDE TO RETRENCHMENT

By the late 1960s, the federal government was firmly entrenched in establishing
and expanding social programs. As gaps in service delivery were discovered,
the government responded by either appropriating more dollars, amending legislation, or creating new programs. From the administration's perspective, unfair
practices in social-service delivery by states and local governments were sure to
be minimized by federal monitoring and enforcement agencies. During the late
1960s and the 1970s, a growing cadre of social conservatives began reassessing
liberal social policies.

The emphasis on inculcating a strong work orientation, in exchange for social-
welfare services, paralleled vocal opposition to the expanded role of government
in the delivery of social services. One of the gravest errors policy-makers made
was their attempt to mold black families into a unit resembling white middle-
class families, at the expense of jeopardizing vital black formal and informal
structures. The unique experiences of black Americans relative to economic
deprivation and racial discrimination were responsible for the evolution of the
structure and dynamics of family life, based on a complex informal exchange
system. Although the mutual supportive network was unable to meet all the
economic needs of black families, it continued to provide invaluable social
services. Further, it was not the government's responsibility to replace traditional
black formal and informal institutions. Instead, the government was expected to
augment these social and economic systems. In the event that social and economic
programs had succeeded in creating progress for black men and women, dis-
banding these support structures would still have had a detrimental effect on
black families. Sufficient evidence exists in Jewish and Asian cultures to demonstrate that, although racial and ethnic minorities can achieve economic assimilation, socially they must maintain a strong sense of cultural unity. In fact, one
of the ways in which racial and ethnic groups have acquired economic and
political power is to retain traditional cultural institutions, which ensure unity,
support, and a collective sense of responsibility. Using other successful racial
and ethnic groups as a barometer, it is fairly safe to conclude that the structures
necessary for black upward mobility were weakened by liberal social policies.
In effect, social programs that set out to improve the plight of black families
contributed to their instability.

Overall, Johnson's War on Poverty was a failure for the majority of black families. The inability of blacks to ascend into the mainstream and the steady decline of traditional social support systems has exacerbated the problems already confronting black families before the era of liberal social policy. Believing that the government had embarked upon a permanent position of ensuring parity— through affirmative action programs, the voting rights act; civil rights laws; affirmative action legislation; housing, educational and small business grants and loans, and social welfare programs—it was difficult for anyone to expect the rescission of liberal social policy.

Further, there was evidence to confirm the belief that blacks were making significant gains. Government reports and studies showed positive gains for blacks, which pointed to the success of social and economic programs. There was little indication that liberal social policy had brought about anything other than positive outcomes for black familes. Reports of the 1960s were so convincing that the demands from other contenders for social and economic power became stronger. It was no coincidence that policy-makers and program administrators generalized advances made by some blacks to the black population in general. Furthermore, social and economic factors tended to perpetuate these efforts. First, during the 1960s and 1970s, numerous jobs had been created, not simply for blacks but for whites as well. These were subject to elimination if social and economic programs were deemed ineffective. Second, after 200 years of being economically disadvantaged, twenty years of government assistance was too soon to determine success or failure. Third, political reasons precluded objectivity in evaluating social programs and their impact on black families. Most of these reasons were easily translated into numbers in the form of constituents and, in election years, votes. Suffice it to say, policy-makers considered it unwise to acknowledge that social programs, as designed, were incapable of solving the problems of black families. And identifying problems that these social programs had created for black families would have been even more disastrous. It became evident during the era of liberal social policy that this "either-or" aproach to the formulation and implementation of social-policy rendered social and economic programs virtually ineffective. When social policy is more accurately viewed as a continuum, it is not "either-or," rather it is "more-or-less."

While civil rights organizations and federal authorities sought to uncover service gaps and inconsistencies in the provision of social and economic programs, countercurrents became more pronounced. Critics argued that expenditures for social programs were rising at an alarming rate and were too exorbitant for the taxpayer to bear. According to Guzzardi, federal grants-in-aid to states for transfer payments exceeded the growth of inflation. He states, "For over two decades federal grants grew after inflation at an average annual rate of 10 percent; in fiscal 1978 they hit a high of 17.3 percent of federal outlays. Further, he adds that in 1981 federal grants were around $95 billion, or 14.5 percent of federal outlays."[48]

In order for social programs to be effective, they must be subjected to critical evaluation and redesign without the fear that opponents will charge total failure. In the main, social policy should be perceived as a process that leads to a well-designed, well-implemented and well-evaluated plan.

Finally, in 1980 the federal government began to reassess its carte blance approach to social policy. Under pressure from various groups, the government had to justify escalating expenditures for social programs. This took place as governmental agencies identified social and economic gains, which were touted as indicators of benefits that black families were deriving from social programs. However, black families were experiencing other "gains," which surprisingly were overlooked.

NOTES

1. Robert McElvaine, *The Great Depression: America, 1929–1941* (New York: Times Books, 1984), pp. 188, 334–336.

2. Ibid., p. 309.

3. Walter Guzzardi, Jr., "Who Will Care for the Poor?" *Fortune* (February, 1982), 34–42.

4. Beulah Roberts Compton, *Introduction to Social Welfare and Social Work* (Homewood, Illinois: The Dorsey Press, 1980), p. 537.

5. Alphonso Pinkney, *The Myth of Black Progress* (New York: Cambridge University Press, 1984), p. 168.

6. Robert McElvaine, *The Great Depression: America, 1929–1941* (New York: Times Books, 1984), pp. 188–189.

7. June Axinn and Herman Levin, *Social Welfare* (New York: Dodd, Mead and Company, 1975).

8. James E. Blackwell, "Persistence and Change in Intergroup Relations: The Crisis Upon Us," *Social Problems* 29 (1982): 325–346.

9. Charles Zastrow, *Introduction of Social Welfare Institutions: Social Problems, Services and Current Issues* (Homewood, Illinois: Dorsey Press, 1982), p. 105.

10. Wayne Johnson, *The Social Services: An Introduction* (Itasca, Illinois: F. E. Peacock Publishers, 1982), pp. 57–59.

11. Muriel Feshbach, "Dynamics in the AFDC Caseload, 1967-Present" (Washington, D. C.: Department of Health and Human Services, 1982), unpublished report.

12. U. S. Department of Health, Education, and Welfare, *Findings of the 1973 AFDC Study: Part I.* (Washington, D. C.: National Center for Social Statistics, 1974).

13. U. S. Department of Labor, *WIN Handbook.* No. 318 (Washington, D. C.: U. S. Government Printing Office, 1984), I–1.

14. Compton, *Introduction to Social Work*, pp. 543–545.

15. "1982 Employment and Training Report to the President: Selected Tables," *Employment and Training Reporter*, The Bureau of National Affairs 14 (February 9, 1983), pp. 670–671.

16. Compton, *Introduction to Social Work*; Charles Zastrow, *Introduction to Social Welfare Institutions: Social Problems, Services and Current Issues* (Homewood, Illinois: The Dorsey Press, 1982), pp. 520–521.

17. Therese W. Landsburgh, "Child Welfare: Day Care of Children," *Encyclopedia*

of Social Work, 17th issue (Washington, D. C.: National Association of Social Workers, 1977), p. 138.

18. Johnson, *The Social Services*, pp. 62–63.

19. "Still More Billions for Food Stamps," *U. S. News and World Report* (May, 1980): 7.

20. Zastrow, *Introduction to Social Welfare Institutions: Social Problems*, pp. 103–104.

21. Johnson, *The Social Services*, p. 151.

22. U. S. Department of Health and Human Services, "Statistical Report on Medical Care: Recipients, Payments and Services." Health Care Financing Administration, unpublished report, 1984.

23. Johnson, *The Social Services*, p. 60.

24. U. S. Social Security Administration, "Aid to Families With Dependent Children," *Social Security Bulletin, Annual Statistical Supplement* (Washington, D. C., Department of Health and Human Services, 1982).

25. United States Bureau of the Census, *Statistical Abstract of the United States. National Data Book and Guide to Sources* (Washington, D. C.: U. S. Government Printing Office, 1984).

26. Johnson, *The Social Services*, pp. 397–399.

27. McElvaine, *The Great Depression*, p. 303.

28. Chauncey A. Alexander and David N. Weber, "Social Welfare: Historical Dates," *Encyclopedia of Social Work*, 17th issue (Washington, D. C.: National Association of Social Workers), pp. 1497–1503.

29. William L. Evans, *Race, Fear and Housing in a Typical American Community* (New York: National Urban League, 1946).

30. Ibid.

31. 1979 Statistical Yearbook, United States Department of Housing and Urban Development, Superintendent of Documents (Washington, D. C.: U. S. Government Printing Office, 1979), p. 206.

32. United States Bureau of the Census, *The Social and Economic Status of the Black Population*, p. 74.

33. Theodore Cross, *The Black Power Imperative* (New York: Faulkner Books, 1984), pp. 808–809.

34. Robert Hill, "What's Ahead for Blacks?" *Ebony* (January, 1980): 27–36; "America's Underclass, Broken Lives: A Nation Apart," *U. S. News and World Report* (March 17, 1986): 20.

35. Milton Coleman, "Reagan's 'Rising Tide' Sinking Blacks," *The National Leader* (February, 1984), p. 1.

36. United States Bureau of the Census, *Statistical Abstract of the United States* (1984).

37. United States Bureau of the Census, *America's Black Population: 1970–1982, A Statistical View*. Special Publication, P10/POP 83–1 (Washington, D. C.: U. S. Government Printing Office, 1983), p 16.

38. William L. Taylor, "Access to Economic Opportunity: Lessons Since Brown," in Leslie W. Dunbar, ed., *Minority Report: What Has Happened to Blacks, Hispanics, American Indians and Other Minorities in the Eighties?* (New York: Pantheon Books, 1984), p. 31.

39. William L. Taylor, "Access to Economic Opportunity," p. 31.

40. Morton Kramer and Nolan Zane, "Projected Needs for Mental Health Services,"

in Stanley Sue and Thom Moore, eds., *The Pluralistic Society: A Community Mental Health Perspective* (New York: Human Sciences Press, 1984), p. 55.

41. Ibid., p. 57.

42. Ibid., p. 54.

43. Harriett P. Lefley and Evalina W. Bestman, "Community Mental Health and Minorities: A Multi-Ethnic Approach," in Stanley Sue and Thom Moore, eds., *The Pluralistic Society: A Community Mental Health Perspective* (New York: Human Sciences Press, 1984), p. 118.

44. Leo Levy and Louis Rowitz, *The Ecology of Mental Disorders* (New York: Behavioral Publications, 1973).

45. Kramer and Zane, "Projected Needs for Mental Health Services"; Lefley and Bestman, "Community Mental Health and Minorities," p. 118.

46. Lefley and Bestman, "Community Mental Health and Minorities," p. 141.

47. George H. Wolkon, Sharon Moruwaki, David M. Mandel, Jeraldine Archuleta, Pamela Bunje, and Sandra Zimmerman, "Ethnicity and Social Class in the Delivery of Services: Analysis of a Child Guidance Clinic," *American Journal of Public Health* 64 (1974): 709–712.

48. Walter Guzzardi, Jr., "Who Will Care for the Poor?" *Fortune* (February, 1982): 34–42.

5   THE IMPACT OF SOCIAL AND ECONOMIC GAINS ON BLACK FAMILIES

There has been considerable debate over the extent to which gains were made by black families and their members between 1960 and 1980. These adavances apparently correspond with the social programs implemented during this period. What remains as a point of contention is which and how many black families and their members made advances over the twenty-year period. A related area of uncertatinty is assessing the magnitude of social and economic progress for black families. Increasingly, there appears to be some consensus that the social and economic progress that occurred was differentially experienced by black families and their members. Undoubtedly, disparities in upward mobility for black families were related to social class. Furthermore, there were differences in the rate of progress among members of black families as well. In this case, differential progress was based on gender. That is, not all black families nor their members experienced mobility as a consequence of innovative social policies. To the contrary, many black families remained static, while others descended into poverty. Of the latter group, black families whose lifestyles have become deeply entrenched in poverty are said to be among a growing permanent underclass.[1] This alone is evidence that liberal social policies enacted over a twenty-year period did have the same positive effect on all black families.

Considering the gains that were made by blacks during the 1960s and 1970s, it becomes obvious that social class played a critical role. At that time, black Americans with middle-class status were able to solidify their positions and continue their ascent on the social and economic ladder.

There is little consensus among scholars as to which indicators should be used in defining the black middle class.[2] Though some agree that income is an important determinant of stratification among blacks, there is considerable disagreement about what range constitutes various social-class levels. Thus, the income range for black middle-class families is found to vary from $15,000–$30,000 annually. However, Robert Hill, a black sociologist, states that in 1970 when the U.S. Bureau of Labor statistics (BSL) intermediate level was set at $10,664, 24 percent of all black families were "economically middle class." And by 1979, the percentage of black middle-class families (those with incomes over $20,517) had risen to 26 percent.[3] Not only did the majority of black middle-class families remain stable during this period, their numbers also increased.

For the most part, black middle-class families were in a better position to benefit from massive liberal social policies in the 1960s and 1970s. Educational grants and loans, affirmative action, and civil rights legislation served to reduce the rigidity and exclusivity that had characterized traditional institutions. Thus, social policies enabled members of black middle-class families to access educational, political, economic, and legal systems. Prior to the 1960s and 1970s, the same institutions had either prevented the entrance of blacks or had established conditions that resulted in inequitable treatment for blacks once they were granted entree. One reason black middle-class families benefited more than other black families is that they were already successfully participating in the same institutions on a microcultural level. In other words, before the 1960s, many blacks in this stratum attended institutions of higher education, held professional positions, established and owned businesses, and were buying rather than renting their homes. Therefore, they had already acquired pertinent information about how to gain admission and function effectively in salient social systems. The primary difference was that the institutions in which they participated were generally black-controlled. However, their almost total participation in predominantly black institutions was generally not by choice. Instead, the exclusive nature of black institutions was due to racial segregation and was therefore imposed by the larger society. However, liberal social policy of the 1960s and 1970s eliminated the barriers that had kept blacks from participating in institutions previously available only to whites. Blacks already actively involved in black institutions were able to participate with greater facility in social systems within mainstream America. What was required was simply to generalize knowledge acquired in black institutions to those that were predominantly white. Hence, members of black middle-class families experienced a great deal of success in these institutions. In all, they made the transition from black institutions to white ones with greater ease that did blacks who were members of working-class and lower-income families.

This is not to suggest that only black middle-class families benefitted from social policies enacted during this era. On the contrary, empirical evidence shows that gains were experienced by working-class black families as well.[4] However, advances made by lower-income black families were miniscule compared to those in the working and middle classes. Because of a number of adverse social and economic events that occurred during the era of liberal social policy, the overall effects of these gains are somewhat lessened and obscured. For example, lower-income families might have made greater gains as a result of liberal social policy if old-line industries had not begun to decline. In addition, an economy marked by inflation and recession during this period had a negative effect on all Americans, particularly the disproportionate number of black families at the lower end of the social and economic ladder. In fact, three recessions occurred between 1960 and 1980. According to Robert Hill, the recessions of 1969–71, 1974–75, and 1980 proved to be devastating to the black community.[5] Despite these occurrences, had liberal social policy been effective, there was sufficient time to implement programs to assuage the catastrophic effects of the occupational displacement caused by massive industry shutdowns and layoffs. Clearly, lower-income black families were adversely affected as the economy began to change from highly industrialized to service-oriented. One major reason is that black males were overrepresented in the skilled and semi-skilled occupations. In essence, an inordinate number of black males were employed in industrial jobs as factory workers.

Most of the occupational advances experienced by black males took place between 1940 and 1960. It was during this period that

the proportion of black men working in operative (skilled and semi-skilled) occupations rose from 13 percent in 1940 to 23 percent in 1960, with an additional increase to 26 percent in 1970. By 1970, a higher proportion of black men (one-fourth) was employed in operative occupations than in any other major occupational classification.[6]

In some cases, black men working in these occupations were members of working-class and middle-class families. As a consequence, the occupational displacement of the 1970s tended to lower their social class, causing many stable black families to experience downward mobility.

Social class is not the only barometer for measuring differential social and economic gains for black families. Other observable distinctions in advances made by black families occurred among their members. As cited earlier, these differences in progress were also gender-related. For example, disparities can be found in occupational gains for black men and women. Between 1960 and 1980, occupational upgrading occurred with greater frequency for black women than for black men. Moreover, black females made substantially greater gains in education than did black males.[7] It is plausible that black women who experienced occupational upgrading did so in large measure because certain white-collar professions were available to them, but there were no parallel positions for black males to occupy. For the most part, black women who moved into white-collar professions were placed in low-paying jobs in clerical and sales positions.[8] A corollary can be found between black middle-class families and black females. As stated earlier, the black middle-class had a historical precedent for successful maneuvering in salient institutions, albeit black. Similarly black females have generally been enrolled in institutions of higher education in greater proportions than black males. Consequently, familiarity with colleges and universities and the availability of a larger number of female role models and mentors, who had matriculated in these institutions, provided a decided advantage for black females. Unquestionably, these factors placed black females, rather than black males, in a favorable position, particularly in light of the new external institutional support provided in the form of government educational grants, loans, and affirmative action legislation. Thus, black females were not only able to sustain educational gains but were also able to expand educational attainment into areas that had been restricted to both blacks and women. Some may even argue that the feminist movement, which focused on the inequitable access and treatment of women in general, may have had some residual effect on occupational and educational advances made by black women. In all, black women made advances between 1960 and 1980 that were unparalleled by black males. These differences have had a direct impact on the structure and dynamics of black families. What follows is a closer examination of the specific gains made by black families and their members in education, occupation, business and home ownership, life expectancy, and so forth. These changes are discussed as they occurred from 1960 to 1980. Then the impact of these gains on black families will be examined.

GAINS: PROGRESS FOR BLACK MALES AND FEMALES, 1960 TO 1980

Educational Attainment

Contrary to popular belief, there has never been a major disparity in the overall educational attainment for black men and women. Admittedly, black women have had slightly higher rates of educational achievement but, across the board, these differences have not been significant. Where substantial differences in educational attainment for black men and women have existed, they have been found at the collegiate level; historically, more black females than males have attended college. Various theories claim to explain black families' decision, in the years preceding 1960, to send their daughters to college in numbers which greatly exceeded that of their sons. One of the most intriguing, and perhaps more valid, notions is that black females in the 1940s and 1950s had but two occupational choices. They could either become teachers or domestics. The former occupation was available to black females upon whom college diplomas were conferred. Those without credentials were relegated to the status of domestic. Given these rather extreme occupational choices, black families opted to educate their daughters to ensure their chances for a professional career.[9] Conversely, black males could enter a variety of occupations. They had opportunities to become skilled or semi-skilled laborers or to work in the agricultural or service industries. Although these positions did not have the relatively high status associated with teaching and other female-dominated professions, the income, considered by most to be satisfactory, was sufficient to enable the black husband to be the primary breadwinner in most black families. Thus, while most black families had two wage earners, black men generally had higher incomes than their wives.[10]

What emerged from the differential rates of matriculation for black females versus black males in institutions of higher education was a black middle-class family which was in some respects the antithesis of the white middle-class model. In these families, black males, like their white counterparts, made the greater economic contribution to the family income. However, the two families diverge from this point. In the black family, frequently the wife, and not her spouse, had a higher-status occupation. Therefore, many black middle-class families evolved in which high income and occupational status were not possessed solely by the male, as in white families, but were shared by the black husband and wife.

Speaking strictly of educational attainment, in most black marriages the wife is more educated than her spouse. It is estimated that in the past, 55 percent of black female college graduates were married to men whose educational achievement was less than theirs.[11]

The phenomenon of disproportionate numbers of black females vis à vis black males enrolled in and graduating from college continued throughout the last two decades. This same pattern exists today. An overview of college educational attainment for black men and women reveals that in 1956 approximately 62.4 percent of all black college graduates were women. This ratio of black college graduates was maintained until the latter part of the 1960s. It was not until the 1970s that black men began to narrow this educational margin.[12]

Looking at statistics, we come to a clearer understanding of the gains made by black men and women in the educational arena. In 1960, the median years of school completed was 7.7 for black males and 8.6 for black females. By 1975, the impact of the Supreme Court's ruling in *Brown vs. the Board of Education* and the government's affirmative action edict began to significantly alter low levels of educational achievement for the entire black population. At this time, the median years of school completed rose to 10.7 and 11.1 for black males and females, respectively. As further evidence of the effect of liberal social policy on educational attainment, black males reached parity with black females by 1980, when the median years of education for both sexes was 12 years.[13]

College enrollment statistics also began to reflect an unprecendented growth. The increase in the number of blacks enrolled in colleges, especially in predominantly white institutions, was heralded as an indicator of the success of affirmative action. However, when closely examined, those increases reveal that while the number of blacks enrolled in colleges and universities had risen, the actual percentage of black males in these institutions was gradually declining. Thus, black females, not black males, made major gains in attending institutions of higher learning during the 1960s and 1970s. In 1960, of the 134,000 blacks enrolled in college, 48 percent were black males and 51 percent were black females. Over the next twenty years, there was a steady decline in black male enrollment. Simultaneously, black females' college enrollment increased dramatically. By 1980, 688,000 blacks were enrolled in college. Of this number only 278,000 or 40 percent were black males and 410,000 or 60 percent were black females.[14]

Black males not only decreased in numbers on college campuses, they also had a higher rate of attrition, which meant a lower rate of graduation, than black females. Basically, there are three degree levels—baccalaureate, doctorate, and professional—in which black women made gains. Between 1976 and 1981, black women experienced the following percentage increases in these degrees: baccalaureate, 8 percent increase; doctorate, 29 percent increase; and professional, 71 percent. The only area in which a decrease occurred for black women was in the master's degree, which declined by 12 percent. Still, this decline is less than half that of black males, who experienced a decrease of 21 percent at the master's degree level. In essence, black males did not fare as well as black females at any degree level. Degrees for black males declined in all four degree areas, the bachelor's, master's, doctor's and professional levels.[15]

However, as a group, blacks made unprecedented gains at the collegiate level. There were observable increases in black enrollment in professional schools, especially in medical and law schools. Black enrollment in law schools rose from 3 percent in 1969 to 4.2 percent in 1979. Likewise, black enrollment in medical schools escalated from 2.7 percent in 1968 to 5.7 percent in 1980. The significance of this change is evident, as there were 3,000 blacks enrolled in medical school in 1974, during a time when there were only 6,000 black physicians in the entire country.[16]

In spite of disparities in educational achievement for black men and women, blacks as a cultural group made major strides in education during this era. Comparative statistics reflect that whites had a median of 10.9 years of schooling compared to 8 years for blacks in 1960. Two decades later, in 1980, the educational gap had been significantly bridged, as blacks were almost approaching parity with whites. At this time, blacks had a median of 12 years of education compared to 12.5 years for whites.[17] However, the increase in the number of black female college graduates along with the constant decline in black male college graduates during this twenty-year period continues to impact on the structure of black middle-class families.

Occupational Mobility

There is a direct correlation between education and occupation in contemporary American society. Although there is a definite relationship between education and income for whites, inconsistencies in earnings based on race and gender result in the association being tenuous for blacks.[18] Affirmative action is often cited as having granted blacks access to occupational areas that had been closed or severely restricted to black men and women before the 1960s.

Major occupational changes did occur between 1960 and 1980. During this period, blacks made significant advances, moving from service and semi-skilled occupational groupings to white-collar jobs. Only 16 percent of all employed blacks were working in white-collar jobs in 1960, compared to 47 percent of employed whites. By 1980 the percentage of blacks in white-collar occupations had risen 36.6 percent. The comparable proportion of whites in white-collar occupations had increased to 53.9 percent.[19] Nevertheless, two factors should be taken into consideration in interpreting these data. First, the mere fact that blacks are categorized, for census purposes, in white-collar positions does not mean that they have white-collar incomes.[20] As such, positions which are most likely to be considered white-collar tend to be low-paying or entry-level. For example, the percentage of black women working in clerical and sales jobs increased from 1 percent in 1940 to 9 percent in 1960. Additional increases occurred as this proportion climbed to 21 percent by 1970, and later reached 34 percent in 1980. Decreases in the proportion of black women domestics also took place from 1940, when 60 percent were employed in household service work, compared to 1970, when the proportion had dropped to 15 percent.[21] Moreover, the greatest percentage decrease in black female domestics occurred over the ten-year period from 1960 to 1970. Still, when all service occupations are included, such as nursing aides, attendants, cooks, and so on, the proportion of black women in service-related occupations in 1980 was more than one-fourth (29 percent or 1.5 million).

Second, occupational segregation remained egregious, as the homogenization of workers in high-status and high-income positions was maintained. Gains by blacks moving into professional occupations did not take on the magnitude of other occupational shifts for blacks over the twenty-year period, and the progress was still modest.[22] Again, black women were more successful in moving into the ranks of professional occupations than were black men. Black women showed a percentage gain, moving from 10 percent in 1970 to 11 percent in 1980. Black males advancement into professional occupations was even less as their numbers increased from 5 percent in 1970 to 5.5 percent in 1980. Occupational gains made by many black men and women were in occupations traditionally held by women, such as teaching, nursing, and social work. To a degree, both black men and women, particularly the latter, made some inroads into professional occupations in which they had been highly inconspicuous two decades earlier.

ECONOMIC GAINS

Income

In looking at an overall picture of black progress in the area of income, it is inaccurate to categorically describe what occurred as gains or losses. Primarily, what took place was that one segment of the black population registered gains in earnings, while other sements of the black population continued to lag behind whites. Positive increases in income were experienced by black two-parent families. In addition, black females increased their earnings at a rate that exceeded that of black males. During this period, black females began to significantly reduce the income differenetial that had existed between themselves and black males.

Income for black two-parent families climbed 6.9 percent from 1971 to 1981, which reflected an increase from $18,370 to $19,620 in constant dollars. The figures for white families were $25,130 in 1971 to $25,470 in 1981. Even in the most optimal situation, when intact black families are compared with white husband-wife families, black families have an income of only 77 percent of the income of white families. Nonetheless, some black families did move into the middle class. Those who did accomplish this significant feat are highly visible, which leads to the regrettable misconception that the majority of black families fared as well. Spratlen states that the rather conspicuous signs of affluence among black families belies this overwhelming evidence that racial inequality has continued to significantly affect the economic status of black families. To illustrate, he points to figures that indicate that the number of black families earning $25,000 or more per year, having increased between 1970 and 1978, from 49,280 to 79,404, remains small relative to white families with similar income. Spratlen further argues that 29.5 percent of all white families versus 13.4 percent of all black families make up this income group, which earns $25,000 or more annually. Thus he concludes there is an ''inequality gap of nearly one white family in three versus one black family in seven.''[23]

Income figures for black families in general are even more alarming when they are considered in total. Black families actually suffered a decline in income, relative to that of white families. In 1971 black families had a median income of $14,460, which was 60 percent of the median, $23,970, of white families. By 1981, the ratio of black family to white family income was 56 percent. One explanation for the decrease in income is the decline in the number of black married-couple families. These families dropped from 74 percent in 1960, to 68 percent in 1970 down to 55 percent in 1982.[24]

One other income-related phenomenon that took place during the 1960s and 1970s was the differential increase in the income of black family members based on gender. Certainly, the differential rate of advancement for black females versus black males in education and occupational areas helped black women to close the income gap that had existed between black males and females. In 1962 black women's median income was 61.1 percent of the median income of black men. At that time, black women's median income was $6,975, compared to $11,414 for black men. By 1982 black women's median income had risen to $12,577, or 75.3 percent of the black male's median income, which had reached $16,710. By contrast, white females in general continue to earn considerably less that white males. While white females did make advances in terms of income, they did so minimally. In 1962 white females earned a mere 59.8 percent of the median income of white males. Specifically, the median income for white women was $11,430 and $19,127 for white males. Twenty years later in 1982, there had been little change, with white women earning $13,847, 62.3 percent of the white males' median income of $22,232.[25]

Black Entrepreneurship

Black business ownership has a definite impact on black families. In many instances, black-owned and operated establishments have been and continue to be sole proprietorships operated by black family members. Moreover, black businesses, like the majority of all small businesses in this country, provide jobs and serve as an economic resource in the community where they operate. Accordingly, there is a direct correlation between the economic solvency and status of black families and black business ownership.

Figuratively, black-owned businesses, particularly those firms operated as sole proprietorships, grew between 1969 and 1980. Data reveal that black entrepreneurship rose from 163,073 black-owned firms in 1969 to 231,000 in 1980.[26] Gross receipts increased during this same period from $4.5 billion to $9.5 billion. This growth represents a 42 percent increase in black-owned firms and a 111 percent increase in gross receipts. Despite this unprecedented growth, black-owned businesses accounted for only 2.3 percent of all firms in 1980. Interestingly, this represents an overall decrease in the percentage of all businesses which were black-owned in the United States. Earlier figures reveal that in 1969 black-owned businesses accounted for 2.6 percent. Thus, it is fairly evident that blacks were not alone in taking advantage of goverment loans and other economic development programs, which aided in the establishment and successful operation of small businesses during this era.

Home Ownership

Home ownership is an area in which black families demonstrated enormous growth over the last twenty years. It was during the late 1960s and throughout the 1970s that black families made significant gains in their transition from renter to homeowner status. In 1980, approximately 49 percent of all black families owned their homes, compared to 38 percent in 1969. However, the rate of homeownership for black families has consistently lagged behind that of whites, with the latter owning 67 percent of the houses they occupied in 1980. Much of the disparity between the rate of homeownership for black and white families can be attributed to higher income levels and the reluctance on the part of financial institutions to lend money to black families for the purchase of property. The growth in homeownership for black families that occurred during this period is a function of increased salaries and governmental programs, both legal and economic, which promoted homeownership among black families and other racial and ethnic groups.[27] It is important to note that while these gains were made, blacks have yet to reach the rate of homeownership that characterized white families nearly 100 years ago. The earliest available data on housing patterns show that in 1890 white families owned 51 percent of the housing units they occupied.

Life Expectancy

Black family members also made notable gains in life expectancy over the last twenty years. Like whites, blacks can attribute these increases to several factors. First, there has been a dramatic improvement in the affordability and availability of health care. Next, a marked decline in infant mortality, although twice the rate of whites, has affected life expectancy. Finally, a decrease in maternal mortality rates has had a positive effect on life expectancy.[28] Statistics bear out the fact that gains made by blacks in life expectancy were greater than those for whites. Still, whites have a life expectancy at birth that exceeds that of both black males and females. In 1981, life expectancy averaged 66 years for black males and 75 years for black females, doubling the life expectancy averages of the earlier decades of the century. Comparatively, life expectancy for whites in 1981 averaged 71 years for males and 79 years for females.[29]

Furthermore, there remains a disparity in life expectancy for black males and females at all ages. These differences in life expectancy for black men and women have had a significant influence on the structure of black families. The fact that black females live an average of nine years longer than black males has numerous implications for black family structure. For example, black women are likely to become single heads of families at some point in the family cycle. While this also holds true for white women, black women are more likely to assume headship due to widowhood at a younger age.

Other factors which contribute to disparities in life expectancy for black men and women are homicide and suicide rates, which are higher for black men than black women.

OTHER "GAINS"

Aside from advances made by black families in the areas of education, occupation, income, business development, home ownership, and life expectancy, increases in other social and economic spheres affected black families immensely. Many of these changes were more subtle in nature. Some of the more conspicuous problems were frequently ignored, and for obvious reasons. One principal reason these ''gains'' were not emphasized, or even acknowledged, was the belief that opponents, having maligned social and economic programs, would point to liberal social policy as the culprit. Using this rationale, it was reasoned that critics would demand the total elimination of social and economic programs. Had there been a precedent for evaluating and correcting ineffective public policies without placing all social and economic programs in jeopardy, in all likelihood social-welfare advocates would have been less reluctant to identify problems and programs that were adversely affecting black families. This dilemma led to the growth of problems that, left uncorrected, began to have a devastating impact on the stability of various black family structures.

It was not until the 1980s that attention began to focus on these other "gains." When policy-makers did turn their attention to these social and economic problems, it was exactly for the reasons proponents of social welfare programs had projected—to eliminate liberal social policy. What follows is an examination of "gains," which have been equated with the retrogression of black families in America.

Civilian Labor Force Participation

Given that one of the chief purposes of liberal social policy was to enable black families and their members to become economically independent by increasing blacks' participation in the economic sector, it is imperative that we examine the extent to which black family members became active in the civilian labor force. This in conjunction with income, is an important indicator of the overall impact of social and economic programs on the status of black families.

An historical overview reveals that following the Depression the black labor force continued to increase, albeit more slowly than the white labor force. From the mid 1950s until 1965, a new pattern began to emerge, as the black labor force began to grow at a rate that exceeded that of whites. Over the next ten-year period, both the black and white labor forces grew at essentially the same rate. In 1982, approximately 11 million blacks were in the civilian labor force, accounting for nearly 10 percent of the total civilian labor force; this figure represents an increase of 2.7 million persons over 1972, or a 31 percent increase.[30]

Historically, blacks have had a higher civilian labor force participation rate than whites. One explanation for the greater proportion of blacks in the labor force is that more black women were gainfully employed. However, with larger numbers of white women entering the labor force in the 1970s, this disparity began to gradually disappear. The numbers of black and white workers began to coincide around 1970, when both groups had a 57 percent labor-force participation rate.[31]

Two factors apposite to any assessment of the civilian labor force participation rate of black family members are age and gender. While black women made positive adavances by increasing their numbers in the civilian labor market, the opposite was true for black men. Instead of increasing their participation in the labor force, the percentage of black males outside the civilian labor force climbed steadily over the last two decades.

In looking at black women's labor-force participation rate, it becomes clear that the percent of black women in the labor force under 65 has continued to increase. In effect, the proportion of black women in the labor force rose from

48 percent in 1960 to 54 percent in 1982. Conversely, the proportion of black men in the labor force declined from 83 percent in 1960 to 70 percent in 1982.[32] Here the "gain" is recorded as an increase in the percentage of black men outside the labor force, many of whom have permanently given up looking for employment. Some researchers argue that this precipitous decline in the black male civilian labor force participation rate is highly correlated with the growth in the number of maritally disrupted black families.[33] Consistent with this notion is the argument that black males who are no longer actively participating in the civilian labor force lack one of the most essential prerequisites for marriage—a job.

The importance of age when examining black labor force participation rates becomes clear when a total picture of employment and unemployment trends are examined.

Employment

The ever-changing economy and industry shifts created high rates of unemployment for black family members at various times over the twenty-year period. Variability in the rate of black male and female unemployment has, unquestionably, influenced the stability of black families. Beginning with a double-digit unemployment rate for black persons of 10.2 percent in 1960, the rate of unemployment for black men and women reached its highest since World War II when it peaked at 18.9 percent in 1982. Throughout the 1960s and 1970s, the unemployment rate for blacks continued to be double that for whites, which was 4.9 percent in 1960 and 8.6 percent in 1982.

Youthful members of black families also felt the effects of a depressed economy, as the rate of unemployment for black teenagers climbed to 48 percent in 1982, exceeding that of white teens (20.4 percent) by more than 100 percent. Differential rates of black teenage unemployment were also discernable by gender. In the same year, black male teens' unemployment rate was 48.9 percent compared to 47.1 percent for their female counterparts.[34] The fact that unusually high rates of black unemployment prevailed for the better part of two decades points to the fact that various social and economic programs had not adequately provided black men, women, and youth with the necessary job skills or financial solvency to thwart the effects of an economic downturn. Thus, for black families, downward economic spirals continued to be cataclysmic, as their ranks among the unemployed swelled. These increases led to still other "gains."

Poverty Rate

The proportion of black families with incomes below the poverty level fluctuated throughout the twenty-year period from 1960 to 1980. In 1960 approximately 1.9 million, 48.1 percent, of all black families had incomes below the poverty level. Declines in this figure became evident as the percentage of black families in poverty dropped to a low of 27.1 percent in 1975. However, in spite of government intervention in social-service delivery up to this point, the proportion of black poor families began a gradual surge upward. By 1980, the percentage of black families in poverty had increased to 27.6 percent.[35] An equally striking occurrence was the increase in the number of these families consisting solely of women and children.

Female-Maintained Families and Their Children

In recent years the dramatic growth in the number of black families maintained by women has generated much debate. In general, female-headed families are the fastest growing segment of the poor population. One reason black female-maintained families, like their white counterparts, have attracted considerable attention is due to concomitant problems associated with female headship. A major concern of these families is financial. In 1982, the growing proportion of black families headed by women accounted for 70 percent of all black poor families in this country. In 1960, only 22 percent of black families were headed by women; this figure had risen to 46 percent by 1982.[36] Further, it has been projected that if these trends continue, the number of families headed by black women is expected to reach 59 percent by the year 1990.[37]

The strain encountered by black families maintained by women is not solely financial in nature. Studies reveal that female heads of families are more likely to be victims of physical and mental illness than their married counterparts.[38] Clearly, black women who maintain families are not the only family members experiencing the ill effects of a family structure in which no male is present. Black children in families headed by women also are faced with poverty and related social anomalies. The fact that the poverty rate among black children is rapidly growing is an understatement. Presently, the poverty rate for all black children under the age of 18 is higher than at any time since 1967.[39]

More specifically, the percentage of black children living with one parent increased sharply, from 25 percent in 1960 to 49 percent in 1982. Although the proportion of white children living with one parent more than doubled, from 7 percent in 1970 to 17 percent in 1982, only 42 percent of all black children were living in two-parent families in 1982, compared to 81 percent of all white children.[40]

Growth in the number of black women maintaining families is largely a function of still other increases. A rise in the divorce rate, a low remarriage rate for black women, and an increase in the number of births occurring to black unwed mothers are correlated with the disproportionate number of black female single-parent families.

Marital Disruptions: Separations and Divorces

One of the most dramatic influences on the structure of black families has been the increase in the number of marriages disrupted by separation and divorce.

Until 1980 separations outnumbered divorces for black men and women. In 1960, of all black males and females between 25 and 54 years of age who had ever married, 8.2 percent and 12.4 percent respectively were separated; in 1980, 10.4 percent of black males and 18.7 percent of black females of the same group were separated. A significant increase in the divorce ratio for black men and women took place between 1960 and 1982. Defined as the number of divorced persons per married persons, the ratio of divorced black males reached 151 per 1,000 in 1980, compared to 45 per 1,000 in 1960. The divorce ratio for black females rose from 78 per 1,000 in 1960 to 257 per every 1,000 married persons in 1980. While the divorce ratio for white males and females also showed an unprecedented growth during this same period, the divorce ratio for black men and women more than doubled the rates for their white counterparts. More specifically, the divorce ratio for white men was 27 per 1,000 in 1960 and 74 per 1,000 in 1980. White women had a considerably higher divorce ratio of 38 per 1,000 in 1960, compared to 110 for every 1,000 in 1980. In short, over two decades the number of divorces grew at a rate of 300 percent for white couples and 400 percent for black men and women.[41]

Out-of-Wedlock Births

There has been a steady rise in the percentage of births born to unwed mothers among black and white females since 1960. Figures reflecting the number of out-of-wedlock births should be interpreted with the knowledge that they are computed based on the number of births to married women. Thus, as the percentage of births to black married women has declined, the proportion of births to black unmarried women has risen. In 1960, the percent of births to black (21.6) and white (2.3) unmarried women was appreciably less than in 1982, when 55 percent of all births to black women occurred out of wedlock, compared to white women whose out-of-wedlock birth rate had risen to 11 percent.[42] As cited earlier, a related causal factor in the growth of black families with female heads can be attributed to the growing number of black women with children who never marry. One major factor that accounts for the disproportionate number of out of wedlock births among black women is that, over the last twenty years, the rates of adolescent marriages dropped 45 percent for black teens. By contrast, marriages for white teens declined only 4 percent during the same period.[43]

Suicides

At the end of two decades, blacks experienced a relatively new phenomenon. During the twenty-year period, the rise in suicides for black women was negligible. But for black men and black male youth the suicide rate had shown a definite increase. The suicide rates for black males, up from 8 per 100,000 in 1960 to 10.8 per 100,000 persons in 1980, continued to be less than one-half the rate of suicides for white males (18 per 100,000 in 1970 to 20.2 per 100,000 persons in 1980).[44]

It is interesting to note that age is a salient factor in differential suicide rates for black and white men. Suicides for white males tend to take place in greater numbers in the 65 and over age range. On the other hand, the highest rate of suicides among black males occur between the ages of 25 through 34.[45] While suicides have a profound impact upon family structure and dynamics, irrespective of the age, race, or ethnic background of the suicide victim, the fact that black males tend to commit suicide at younger ages is likely to have a profound impact on the structure of black families. For example, individuals in this age group fall within the pool of males eligible for marriage as well as those who are married and in the early stages of the family life cycle. Thus, in addition to creating female-headed families, black males who commit suicide are more likely to leave dependent children.

Given that suicide is likely to be an indication of an individual's perception of self-worth, and that our society measures self-worth, particularly for males, on the basis of one's socioeconomic status and the acquisition of material objects and status symbls, it seems reasonable to assume that white males nearing the end of their professional careers might question their usefulness and ability to make valuable contributions. Resultant frustration may lead to suicide. Likewise, a growing number of young black men, unable to attain societal goals and conform to the traditional definition of men as providers and protectors, are also committing suicide. In both cases, the actual age is not as much an issue as is being socially consigned to a position of helplessness and forced unemployment. The obvious question is, what effect did liberal social policy have on the increased ratio of suicides among black males? It appears paradoxical that the percentage of black male suicides would increase during a period when innovative social programs were created to enhance social and economic opportunities for black family members. However, high rates of unemployment, a low civilian partic-ipation rate, and the acceptance of a value orientation that equates individual self-worth with one's ability to produce and consume create a better understand-ing of why increasing numbers of young black males experience the same lack of purpose as do white males approaching the age of retirement. There is little doubt that visible gains made by some black family members have overshadowed the overall lack of progress by others.

Crime

Over recent years the rise in the proportion of crime affecting black families has become an issue of great concern. An increase in the number of black males as victims of homicides took place over the last twenty years. Becoming a homicide victim is highly correlated with race, gender, and age. Data reveal that black men are the most likely victims of homicide. Between 1960 and 1980 the rate of homicides for white males more (3.6 per 100,000) more than doubled.

Furthermore, in 1960, the homicide rate for black males was 36.7 per 100,000. In 1980 black men had the highest homicide rate (60 per 100,000), followed by black women (13 per 100,000), white men (10 per 100,000) and white women (3 per 100,000). As can be seen, the homicide rate for black males exceeded the rates for white males, black females, and white females combined. Again, the implications for black families are serious. For example, black males are most likely to be victims of homicide between the ages of 15 to 24. This not only creates a female-maintained household due to death, but another one resulting from incarceration.[46] Typically, this occurs because the majority of black male homicides are perpetrated by other black males. Thus, dual female-maintained families are generally the end result of black male homicides. According to some, this gives further credence to the idea that black males began to experience mounting frustration and anger, which increasingly became manifested as displaced aggression, when goals and expectations set at the beginning of the turbulent 1960s failed to come to fruition.

UNDERSTANDING THE GAINS AND "GAINS"

Liberal Social Policy: Mission and Assumptions

It is fairly evident that not all segments of the black population experienced social and economic gains similarly. Moreover, race, age, gender, and social class were important determinants of the level of advances made by black families and their members. How social policy of the 1960s and 1970s contributed to the success of some and the failure of others is of paramount importance. To understand this phenomenon, we must examine the tenets and underlying assumptions associated with liberal social policy.

First was the assumption that, in order for black families to become viable economic units, they must become an integral part of mainstream America. A second and related condition for remedying the social and economic ills of black families was embodied in the notion that black families should strive for and be transformed into the idealized nuclear family. Underlying each of these expectations was the belief that extant black families were in need of change in terms of their structure and dynamics. Because of this conceptualization of black families, academicians and policy-makers set forth theories characterizing black families using the culture of poverty and matriarchal and criminal subculture paradigms.[47] To this end, black families were categorized similarly and without delineation based on regionalism, education, occupation, or income. In the main, there was little recognition that a form of stratification existed among black families. Nor was there an understanding that there were structurally functional systems operating in the black community, which, if tampered with, could have negative consequences for black families.

A significant amount of emphasis was placed on the need for integration of black Americans in social institutions. Support for the internalization of mainstream values and norms abounded from both the academic and nonacademic communities.[48] Furthermore, it was held that if blacks and whites were placed in the same social and economic milieus, whites would become more tolerant and sensitive to the needs of blacks. Blacks too were expected to acquire norms, values, and other benefits from this association. Hence, liberal social policy was based on a thesis that defined black families as culturally deprived and socially inadequate. And given that Moynihan, in his work *Family and Nation*, finds the growth in black underclass families as vindication for his earlier analysis and projections, it becomes questionable whether the real issue of blaming black families for their economically depressed status and other concomitants of poverty will ever be properly addressed by policy-makers.[49] From its onset, liberal social policy was fraught with problems, which emanated from the failure to adequately assess and integrate the strengths of black families into social and economic programs.[50] The end result has been an illusion of assimilation and a decline in systems (e.g., mutual-aid networks and black institutions), which had previously ensured the survival of salient black family strucutres.

In trying to understand the impact of liberal social policy, which resulted in some black families experiencing greater social and economic gains than others, it is useful to distinguish the underclass from more advantaged black families. The latter group, composed largely of working- and middle-class families, were among those for whom social and economic gains occurred with greater frequency.[51] Black underclass families were not as successful.

According to Miller, the underclass consists of those persons and families who experience continuous unemployment and whose incomes tend to fall below the poverty level as established by the U.S. government. Miller categorizes families with incomes exceeding the poverty line as working-class or middle-class.[52] The ensuing emphasis on submerging black family values, which were diametrically opposed to those of the general society, began to occur as blacks were permitted access to various social, economic, and legal systems.[53] Before the formulation of liberal social policy, there was convergence on the part of black and white families regarding some societal values.[54] However, since black families' means of attaining these goals were restricted, their goals were also more narrowly defined. Inasmuch, the goals which black family members sought to attain, being within the realm of realism, were not as broad as those of their white counterparts. In other words, a black male child, unlike his white counterpart, may have aspired to become a president of a black-owned business rather than a chief executive officer of a major corporation.

Differential access to opportunity structures caused by economic and racial discrimination has affected the level of goal setting by black middle-class family members and is responsible for the greater divergence in the goals of black underclass families and other families in society. To be sure, working- and middle-class black families are more likely to predispose successive generations

to becoming successful.[55] Because of massive governmental intervention, resources that black working- and middle-class families possessed were enhanced
by liberal social policies.

Though differential gains can be isolated by social class, emergent conditions
arose in which the social position of black families became irrelevant to the
overall debilitating effects of liberal social policy on their structure.

Black families in assuming values inherent in the dominant culture, began
establishing goals and expectations consistent with this orientation.[56] Seeking
and gaining admission into predominantly white institutions, black families began
to anticipate outcomes commensurate with their own social, psychological, and
economic investments. In other words, black men and women assumed that new
social programs and legislation would effectively deemphasize race as a criterion
for success. The increase in the scope and magnitude of social and economic
programs seemed ample proof that "race" was losing its significance in determining an individual's life chances in our society. Mass media reports corrob-
orated this perception that affirmative action programs and the Voting Rights
Act were augmenting economic development programs and assuring black families equitable opportunity for upward mobility. Had liberal social policy been
effectual, the extent to which an ethnic group became integrated in a majority
culture would be purely academic. That this did not occur makes this an issue
that warrants consideration. An assessment of black progress over the last twenty
years suggests that black families and their members became only partially
assimilated and experienced modest positive gains. Subscribing to the values of
the society at large is useful, to the extent that individuals can reasonably establish
and attain goals that represent those of the larger society. For blacks, other ethnic
minorities, and women, this has not held true. Although black family members
can now establish goals broader than those they were limited to before liberal
social policy, in no way are these goals parallel to those that can be reasonably
established, pursued, and attained by members of white families, particularly
white males. Some social scientists cite examples of racial and ethnic minorities
who were able to achieve economic wealth and political power by maintaining
interdependent family units that engage in mutual cooperation, thereby consol-
idating their resources.[57] However, autonomy on an individual and familial level
is a norm stressed as both important and essential for adequate functioning in
western culture.[58]

In sum, economic independence and growth did not become a reality for many
black families. For the most part, the growth that occurred did little to promote
ongoing economic independence for black families and their members. As the
government began to withdraw fiscal responsibility for various social and economic programs, it became clear that advances made by black families were
tenuous and temporary. Much of the growth that black families had experienced
in twenty years was predicated on government involvement and restrictive participation. This has been true in virtually all social and economic areas. Positive
gains made by black families were difficult to sustain without continued gov-

ernmental support. Anderson's discussion of the proprietary versus participatory nature of black enterprise is a poignant illustration of the continued marginal and dependent status of blacks in general and black families in particular. In assessing black entrepreneurship, he posits that,

Participatory Black entrepreneurship means that Blacks simply share or participate in the execution of a firm's policy. Where Black proprietary entrepreneurship exists, Blacks decide or make the policies. In the past 25 years, most of the civil rights legislation and affirmative action policies aimed toward giving Blacks the opportunity to function within the business mainstream of the society have been only participatory in effect.[59]

Although Anderson focuses on black enterprise, his analysis is equally applicable to the relationship of black families to American institutions in general. Needless to say, although greater numbers of black families are participating more fully in a larger number of social institutions, neither their participation nor the economic benefits are equal to that of white families. A chief reason for the peripheral relationship between black family members and social and economic systems can be found in the consignment of blacks to positions, job sectors, and organizational units that are of low to moderate esteem and status. The increasing proportion of blacks participating in institutions creates the myth that great gains were made by black families. However, aside from the inordinate number of entry-level positions that they have assumed, blacks who make up professional and managerial ranks are generally located in enclaves. This form of neosegregation operates in a fashion quite similar to de facto housing segregation. In the latter case, there is generally evidence that black families reside in virtually all geographical areas within a given city; yet, closer observation shows that while this may be true, blacks tend to be concentrated in certain blocks or subareas within any designated region. Therefore, black families tend to be isolated from and have limited contact with white families who, while living in the same community, are separated by physical and social distance. As this relates to institutional gains of black family members, a number of examples of this phenomenon can be found. In the corporate sector, blacks tend to be isolated in human resources; in government, blacks became concentrated in community development and human services departments; and within academia, the largest percentage of blacks were employed in Black Studies departments. The end result was that blacks secured positions within traditional institutions, yet remained outside of the mainstream. Thus, as C. Eric Lincoln posits, black Americans need to not only be in the place but in the process.[60] The skills acquired and personal and professional contacts obtained through these positions seldom have intra- or interinstitutional generalizability. That is, these positions are likely to lead to lateral rather than vertical mobility for blacks.

What appeared to be conformity to liberal social polciy was in many instances institutional resistance. Employing blacks in positions of limited utilitarian value did more to promote dependence than economic independence. Rather than fostering economic independence, liberal social policy created a level of dependence that has been relatively unknown to black families. Clearly, the hopes and aspirations for many black men, women, and children were dashed. For others, they were realized only in part.

The adverse consequences of liberal social policy for black families has been inestimable. It cannot be denied that liberal social policy has had sociopsychological implications. The replacement of a value system that emphasized personal qualities and collective responsibility with one that was more object-oriented, focused on the acquisition of goods, social isolation, and independence, combined with unfulfilled expectations, has left many black families with feelings of frustration, consternation, and confusion.

Idealized Nuclear Family

The ultimate goal of liberal social policy was the transformation of black families into self-sufficient economic units akin to the ideal nuclear-family model. Along with the nuclear-family model came traditional male and female role expectations. These role expectations defined men as the sole breadwinners and assigned women to an affective role, whose primary responsibilities were domestic. During the development and expansion of social and economic programs, it appeared as though black families who wished to embrace this model would be able to do so. Aside from the fact that economic progress for black families did not become a reality as projected, the resurgence of the women's movement in the 1970s brought about the evolution of new gender role definitions. As larger numbers of white women became financially independent because of their increased labor-force participation, they challenged traditional definitions that relegated wives to positions subordinate to their husbands. Simultaneously, white middle-class families, based on the ideal nuclear family model, began to dissolve as marital disruptions throughout the general population increased. This role confusion had an equally devastating effect on black families who had yet to attain the white middle-class nuclear model. Faced with high rates of black male unemployment and underemployment, failure of black businesses to thrive, a differential rate of progress for black families, disparate social and economic gains for black males and females, and continued institutional isolation, black families began to undergo strain brought on by these and other inexorable social and economic pressures.

A Challenge to Black Family Stability

There is little doubt that the distintegration of the black nuclear and extended families is related to liberal social policy. Attendant problems facing black families, such as poverty, low civilian workforce participation rates for black males, and the like, are also indicators that becoming a viable member of our society is far from a reality for many black men, women, and children.

It was assumed that black families interested in upward mobility had only to follow social prescriptions, which encompassed taking advantage of various social and economic programs and accepting a value system considered more amenable to success in an urban post-industrial society. However, liberal social policy was not equipped to efficiently and effectively address the needs of displaced workers, to challenge institutional recalcitrance, and to cure an economy plagued by inflation and recession, thus creating feelings of inadequacy and hopelessness among black families and their members. In addition, racial inequities became more covert but continued to have a counteractive effect on liberal social and economic programs. Clearly, institutions that obeyed the letter rather than the spirit of civil rights legislation gave rise to what became popularly known as institutional racial discrimination. While there is a dearth of research on the effects of this surreptitious form of discrimination on blacks and other ethnic minorities, its uncertain and elusive nature is undoubtedly detrimental to the psychological well-being of black families.

Thus we conclude that structural factors as well as liberal social policy with its mission and underlying assumptions requiring a social and economic metamorphosis, failed to bring black families to a position of financial well-being. This failure has contributed significantly to the high rate at which black nuclear and extended families dissolved over the twenty-year period.

Liberal social policy notwithstanding, black families in general were not prepared to take full advantage of the social and economic programs for which they were the designated beneficiaries. Having been systematically excluded from societal institutions, black families lacked critical information necessary for accessing social institutions and making optimum use of the myriad social programs available. Therefore, many blacks were without critical information necessary to make adequate decisions that affected the academic and professional careers of adult and child family members. According to Naisbitt,

In an industrial society the strategic resource is capital. But in our new society, as Daniel Bell first pointed out, the strategic resource is information. Not the only resource, but the most important. With information as the strategic rescource, access to the economic system is much easier.[61]

Considering the limited knowledge black families possessed of the complex social, political, and economic systems, the gains made by black families are commendable. Undoubtedly, much of this can be attributed to the high achievement and work orientations of black families.[62] In general, there were far too many factors that militated against positive gains for an inordinate number of black families.

In the main, black families' assimilation was social-psychological rather than economic. Thus, they adopted the norms and values of mainstrean American society but continued to be permitted limited access to economic opportunities. The illusion of blacks having made monumental gains and the myth that social institutions have become sufficiently malleable to ensure equity for blacks are responsible, in part, for the trend to rescind liberal social policy that emerged in the 1980s.

NOTES

1. Doubles G. Glasgow, *The Black Underclass* (San Francisco: Jossey-Bass, 1980), p. 3.

2. Alphonso Pinkney, *The Myth of Black Progress* (New York: Cambridge University Press, 1984), pp. 99–103.

3. Robert Hill, *Economic Policies and Black Progress: Myths and Realities* (Washington, D.C.: National Urban League, 1981), pp 39–43.

4. Robert Hill, *The Strength of Black Families* (New York: Emerson Hall, 1971), pp. 28–32.

5. Robert Hill, *Economic Policies and Black Progress*, pp. 15–17.

6. U.S. Bureau of the Census, *The Social and Economic Status of the Black Population in the United States: An Historical View 1790–1978*. Current Population Reports, Special Studies, Series P–23, No. 80. (Washington, D.C.: United States Printing Office), 1979), p. 62.

7. Robert E. Staples, "The Black Professional Woman: Career Success and Interpersonal Failure," in *Black Working Women: Directions Toward a Context for Social Science Research* (Berkeley, California: Center for the Study, Education and Advancement of Women, 1981), pp. 197–210.

8. United States Bureau of the Census, *The Social and Economic Status of the Black Population of the United States*, (1979), p. 62.

9. Staples, "The Black Professional Woman," pp. 197–210

10. Hill, *The Strengths of Black Families*, pp. 11–15; K. Sue Jewell, "The Changing Character of Black Families: The Effects of Differential Social and Economic Gains," *Journal of Social and Behavioral Sciences* 33 (1988), pp. 143–54.

11. Graham Spanier and Paul Glick, "Mate Selection Differentials Between Blacks and Whites in the   nited States," *Social Forces* 58 (March, 1980): 707–725; Staples, "The Black Professional Woman," pp. 197–210.

12. Staples, "The Black Professional Woman," pp. 197–210.

13. U.S. Bureau of the Census, *Statistical Abstract of the United States, National Data Book and Guide to Sources*. (Washington, D.C.: U.S. Government Printing Office, 1981).

14. Ibid.

15. Staples, "The Black Professional Woman," p. 197–210.

16. William Taylor, "Access to Economic Opportunity: Lessons Since Brown," in L. W. Dunbar, ed., *Minority Report: What Has Happened to Blacks, Hispanics, American Indians and Other Minorities in the Eighties* (New York: Pantheon Books, 1984), pp. 31–32.

17. U.S. Bureau of the Census, *America's Black Population: 1970 to 1982, A Statistical View*. Special Publication, P10/POP–83–1 (Washington, D.C.: U.S. Government Printing Office, 1983), p. 16.

18. Cayton S. Drake, "The Social and Economic Status of the Negro in the United

States,'' in Talcott Parsons and Kenneth B. Clark, eds., *The Negro American* (Boston: Beacon, 1965), pp. 16–20.

19. Gai Berlage and William Egelman, *Experience with Sociology* (Reading, Massachusetts: Addison Wesley, 1983).

20. Hill, *The Strengths of Black Families*, pp. 11–12; Hill, *Economic Policies and Black Progress*, p. 41.

21. United States Bureau of the Census, *The Social and Economic Status of the Black Population*, (1979), p. 62.

22. Alphonso Pinkney, *The Myth of Black Progress*, pp. 86–87.

23. Thaddeus H. Spratlen, "The Continuing Factor of Black Economic Inequity in the United States," *The Western Journal of Black Studies* (Summer, 1982): 73–88.

24. United States Bureau of the Census, *The Social and Economic Status of the Black Population, 1979*, p. 103; United States Bureau of the Census, *America's Black Population, 1983*, pp. 18–19.

25. K. Sue Jewell, "The Changing Character of Black Families," 1988.

26. United States Bureau of the Census, "Current Population Reports," United States Department of Labor (unpublished report), 1984.

27. United States Bureau of the Census, *The Social and Economic Status of the Black Population* (1979), p. 126.

28. Ibid., p. 117.

29. United States Bureau of the Census, *America's Black Population, 1983*, p. 18.

30. United States Bureau of the Census, *America's Black Population, 1983*, p. 9.

31. United States Bureau of the Census, *The Social and Economic Status of the Black Population* (1979), p. 60.

32. United States Bureau of the Census, *America's Black Population, 1983.*

33. T. Joe and P. Yu, *The "Flip" Side of Black Families Headed by Women: The Economic Status of Black Men* (Washington, D.C.: The Center for the Study of Social Policy, 1984).

34. United States Bureau of the Census, *America's Black Population, 1983*, p. 9.

35. United States Bureau of the Census. Department of Labor, 1984.

36. Joe and Yu, *The "Flip" Side of Black Families Headed by Women*, 1984.

37. Joe and Yu, *The "Flip" Side of Black Families Headed by Women*, 1984; Alphonso Pinkney, *The Myth of Black Progress.*

38. Lois M. Verbrugge, "Marital Status and Health," *Journal of Marriage and the Family* (May, 1979): 267–285; Robert E. Staples, "Family Life in the 21st Century: An Analysis of Old Forms, Current Trends and Future Scenarios," in Ida Makinson et al. (eds.), *Family Nursing* (Englewood Cliffs, New Jersey: Prentice Hall, 1988), in press.

39. Marian Wright Edelman, "The Sea Is So Wide and My Boat Is So Small: Problems Facing Black Children Today," in H. McAdoo and J. McAdoo, eds., *Black Children* (Beverly Hills, California: Sage, 1985), pp. 72–82.

40. United States Bureau of the Census, *The Social and Economic Status of the Black Population*, 1979, p. 101; United States Bureau of the Census, *America's Black Population*, 1983, p. 18.

41. United States Bureau of the Census, *Statistical Abstract of the United States, 1981.*

42. Ibid.

43. Louise Meriwether, "Teenage Pregnancy," *Essence* (April, 1984): 96.

44. United States Bureau of the Census, *Statistical Abstract of the United States, 1981.*

45. Walter Leavy, "Is the Black Male an Endangered Species?" *Ebony* (June, 1983): 41–46.

46. Ibid.

47. E. Franklin Frazier, *The Negro Family in the United States* (Chicago: University of Chicago Press, 1939); Daniel P. Moynihan, *The Negro Family: The Case for National Action* (Washington, D.C.: Office of Policy Planning and Research, U.S. Department of Labor, 1965); Lee Rainwater, *Family Design* (Chicago: AVC, 1965, pp. 308–309; Hyman Rodman, "Family and Social Pathology in the Ghetto" *Science* 161 (1968): 756–762; Marvin E. Wolfgang, *The Culture of Youth* (U.S. Department of Health, Education and Welfare, Washington, D.C.: Government Printing Office, 1967).

48. Elliot Leibow, *Tally's Corner* (Boston: Little, Brown, 1966); Moynihan, *The Negro Family*, pp. 3–8.

49. Daniel Patrick Moynihan, *Family and Nation* (New York: Harcourt Brace Jovanovich, 1987), pp. 134–135.

50. Robert Hill, "The Black Family: Building on Strengths," in Robert L. Woodson, ed., *The Road to Economic Freedom: An Agenda for Black Progress* (Washington, D.C.: The National Center for Neighborhood Enterprise, 1987), pp. 71–88.

51. Pinkney, *The Myth of Black Progress*, pp. 99–114.

52. Seymour Michael Miller, "The American Lower Classes: A Typological Approach," in Arthur B. Shostak and William Gomberg, eds., *Blue Collar World* (Englewood Cliffs, New Jersey: Prentice-Hall, 1964).

53. Robert E. Staples, *Introduction to Black Sociology* (New York: McGraw-Hill, 1976), pp. 76–78; Wade A. Boykin, "The Academic Performance of Afro-American Children," in Janet T. Spence, ed., *Achievement and Achievement Motives* (San Francisco: W. H. Freeman and Co., 1983), p. 328.

54. Wade A. Boykin and Forrest D. Toms, "Black Child Socialization: A Conceptual Framework," in H. McAdoo and J. McAdoo, eds., *Black Children* (Beverly Hills, California: Sage, 1985); John H. Scanzoni, *The Black Family in Modern Society: Patterns of Stability and Security* (Chicago: University of Chicago Press, 1977); John H. Scanzoni, "Black Parental Values and Expectations of Children's Occupational and Educational Success," in H. McAdoo and J. McAdoo, eds., *Black Children* (Beverly Hills, California: Sage, 1985), pp. 113–122.

55. Scanzoni, *The Black Family in Modern Society*, p. 153.

56. Boykin and Toms, "Black Child Socialization," pp. 33–51.

57. Thomas Sowell, *The Economics and Politics of Race* (New York: William Morrow and Co., 1983).

58. Talcott Parsons and Robert F. Bales, *Family, Socialization and Interaction Process* (Glencoe, Illinois: Free Press, 1955), pp. 10–11.

59. Talmadge Anderson, "Black Entrepreneurship and Concepts Toward Economic Coexistence," *Western Journal of Black Studies* 6 (Summer, 1982): 80–88.

60. C. Eric Lincoln, "Black Studies and Cultural Continuity," *Black Scholar* (October, 1978): 12–18.

61. John Naisbitt, *Megatrends* (New York: Warner Books, 1982), p. 15.

62. Hill, *The Strengths of Black Families*, pp. 1–4.

6 *EXPECTATIONS VERSUS REALIZATION*

SOCIAL WELFARE: A MARRIAGE DISINCENTIVE?

Disagreement over the effects of liberal social policy on black families can be seen in its most dramatic form in the area of social-welfare recipiency. Controversy, which centers on the causal relationship between social and economic programs and black family stability, invariably finds its locus in the analysis of tranfer payments provided by government-sponsored social welfare programs. Although considerable attention has focussed on the advantages and disadvantages of social welfare programs on the structure of black families, a tremendous amount of inconclusiveness and uncertainty remains. Because the urban black welfare recipient is highly visible, and because the percentage of blacks who receive welfare, 34 percent, exceeds the 12 percent of the U.S popuplation comprised of black Americans, inordinate attention is drawn to this segment of the population. The inability to establish a correlation between the receipt of welfare benefits and black familial instability is generally ignored by those outside academic circles. Thus, policy-makers take unswerving positions on whether welfare causes black family instability. In so doing, they use studies that substantiate their arguments as evidence in support of social-policy decisions. Unlike studies that rely on census data, welfare benefits, and other secondary data sources, primary research, in which data has been gathered from questionnaires administered to welfare recipients, has yielded findings that indicate that there is no correlation between black women's receipt of welfare and marital breakups.[1] Using this method, the only correlation between welfare recipiency and black women's marital status is that black women who receive welfare have lower remarriage rates. However, the extent to which this factor alone contributes to lower remarriage rates for black women who receive welfare is questionable. Other factors, such as imbalanced male-female sex ratios and black male unemployment and underemployment, are also likely to play a significant role in the relatively low rate of remarriage for black women. After all, lower-income black females who receive welfare benefits are not alone in having low rates of remarriage. Rather, black women across all socioeconomic levels tend to remarry at a rate lower than their white counterparts.[2]

THE ECONOMIC MOTIVATION ARGUMENT

One reason for conflicting findings of studies that sought to measure the relationship between welfare recipiency among black females and marital disruption is that the primary unit of analysis is economically based. Using the normative paradigm, where economics is thought to be a primary determinant of marital stability, economic feasibility in determining marital disruption is likely to result in findings that reveal either no relationship or a spurious one when black families are studied. Not that there is no economic basis for marital disruption, but that other factors aside from economic ones are likely to be a greater determinant of marital breakups among black men and women.[3] Even in the general population, Mott and Moore challenge the importance of economic factors in determining marital disruption. They assert that marriages are not economically determined, and, as a consequence, neither are dissolutions. Again, this is not to imply that economic solvency does not play a role in marital stability, only that marriages are not likely to be dissolved simply because they are economically weak. However, evidence suggests that welfare recipiency is a significant factor in marital disruptions among lower-income white women.[4] In such cases, it is plausible that economic factors, while not being the sole determinant of marital stability among white couples, may be more important to white females than to black females. Thus, it is not surprising that studies reveal white females generally experience status elevation through marriage.[5] Further, it has been empirically verified that black women, while earning less than black men, do not have as great a salary differential as do white men and women. Moreover, in many marriages black women may have education equal to or greater than their spouses. And in occupational areas black women may have a higher-status position, either in a service or high-tech industry. Thus, although economic factors are likely to be more important in determining marital stability among whites, their value is greatly diminished for black married couples. Those who expect to find logical explanations for marital disruptions among black welfare recipients by using an economic incentive model are likely to continue to meet with disappointment.

Does this mean that welfare recipiency positively affects marriages for lower-income black families? To the contrary, social-welfare programs by design and administration have had a debilitating effect on black families. The fact that welfare places black men, women, and children in a position of ignominy is difficult to disprove. Moreover, following marital disruption, black female heads of households and their charges all too frequently become immersed in a vicious cycle of poverty and welfare recipiency, the latter of which can only be escaped temporarily. One of the most unfortunate consequences of the current social-welfare system is its inability to enable recipients to become socially and economically independent. Some social scientists rely on statistics on the relatively short duration of welfare recipiency of black families to refute arguments that the U.S. welfare system produces chronicity for families with incomes below the poverty level, but they overlook the fact that far too many black families subsist in a state that narrowly exceeds the poverty line, which qualifies one for welfare. Furthermore, the welfare recipient's anxiety and relentless struggle associated with the cyclical pattern of rising and falling in and out of the social-welfare system is clearly a position not to be coveted. Coupled with being black and female, occupying the status of a welfare recipient does little to enhance the already double negative status held by black women. In addition to economic barriers, black women who receive welfare must overcome their psychological and sociological inferior statuses that may prevent upward mobility, because of both intra and interpersonal factors. In many cases, the obstacles, including welfare recipiency, that black female heads of households are forced to overcome are insurmountable in the absence of considerable support from external sources.

Because welfare programs have been basically ineffective in improving the standard of living of lower-income black families, there are few options available to elevate the status of black poor families.

A SOCIAL-PSYCHOLOGICAL EXPLANATION

In the past, support from mutual-aid networks had a stabilizing effect on black two-parent families. Because of an increase in demand for assistance from informal social-support systems, a decrease in resources (due largely to high rates of black unemployment), and an economically depressed economy, the support that informal self-help groups now make available to black families maintained by women is not likely to be sufficient to permanently alter the family's economic status. Thus, the tenuous nature of the member's resources, those of the mutual aid network or kinship network, and societal proscriptions severely limit the extent to which informal helping systems can assist families, whether intact or maritally disrupted.

Still other problems produced by the social welfare system negatively affect black families that are recipients. A welfare system that provides services to two-parent families, yet has as its primary recipients the mother and children, is divisive in nature. The extent to which social welfare programs are detrimental to intact families is related to their policies and practices, which exclude males in black two-parent families. Hopkins, in his study of the treatment of black males by social service agencies, cites the manner in which administrators and practitioners relegate fathers to a position of unimportance.[6] As Hopkins asserts, black fathers whose families are recipients of welfare are seldom asked for input into decisions that will affect their family. The fact that needed goods and services are provided by government-supported agencies is not justification for a paternalistic approach to social-service delivery. Given that the black father's perception of his self-worth and competency in relation to his family is a determinant of marital stability, social-service agencies can influence family stability by the way they relate to the father. Thus, social-psychological attributes are greater predictors of marital outcome among black families than are economic ones. Specifically, Hampton found that the husband's "self-satisfaction, efficacy, and sense of trust-hostility . . . or the degree to which he feels that he is competent in handling his own destiny" are factors that determine whether the marriage will be sustained or disrupted.[7]

Because separation is a common form of marital dissolution among lower-income black families, social-welfare programs should be designed to relate to absent as well as resident fathers, particularly when reconciliation is possible. Accordingly, social-welfare programs should incorporate marriage, family, and employment counseling into their services for adult family members. The tendency to overlook and dismiss black fathers is one of the obvious ways that social-welfare services disrupt black families. The most common image social-welfare agencies maintain of black fathers and husbands is directly related to the black male's inability to provide financially for his family. Despite the reason for the family's need for welfare—whether due to layoff, disability, or unemployment—the perception of the irresponsible, lazy, nonproductive black male influences the service-delivery process. The fact that underclass black families occupy a position of economic dependency generally means that powerlessness is experienced by both mothers and fathers. When social-welfare agencies become the chief provider of services, they tend to assume an authoritarian posture relative to recipient families. The provision of social-welfare services by service providers who perceive themselves as the ultimate authority on matters pertaining to the family's well-being contradicts the societal definition of masculinity, and the black male's role is usurped. Thus, social welfare programs, not wives, push the black father and husband out of the family. Furthermore, the black father, forced out because of his inability to provide financially, is then defined as a liability rather than an asset by social agencies. In view of these circumstances, it is understandable how social agencies can foster discordant relationships in families who receive welfare.

The fact that black fathers love their children and are sensitive to their needs is an attitude which, as Hopkins indicates, is rarely given serious consideration by service providers in social-welfare agencies. He adds that the seed of the self-fulfilling prophecy is sown as black fathers are perceived as being of marginal utility and are ignored. The end result is the emasculation of black fathers by a social-welfare system that is impervious to the holistic needs of black underclass families. Hence, the exclusion of black fathers serves to facilitate their departure.

This gives rise to the image, and stereotypic view, of the female-headed black underclass family, whose absent father is synonymous with black male irresponsibility.

To the extent that social-welfare programs are correlated with female headship, this phenomenon is more likely to be related to the familial disruptiveness caused by the policies and practices of receiving social welfare. Thus, marital disruption caused by social-welfare programs is largely related to the extent to which the black father's role is undermined by social-service agencies. Moreover, social-welfare policy affects the economic stability of intact black families when occupationally displaced fathers are not successfully retrained and equipped with skills that will enable them to regain or exceed their earlier occupational and economic status. This being the case, efforts to correct social-welfare programs should focus on programmatic and policy changes that will provide planning and programming for all family members.

STATUS OF THE POSTDIVORCE BLACK FEMALE-HEADED FAMILY

It is highly unlikely that black lower-income females are unaware of statistics that reveal that postdivorce women and their children are more likely to experience such disruptions as a drastic decline in their standard of living, adolescent pregnancies, high school drop-outs, drug abuse, delinquency, crime, and mental and physical illness than are members of two-parent families.[8] Yet, marital disruption continues to escalate among black couples.

Unlike black women, white women generally remain in a postdivorce status for a period of five years. After remarrying, a white female's second spouse is more likely to not only increase her divorced standard of living but to provide an income which exceeds that of her previous marriage.[9]

While it is easy to focus attention on the effects of marital dissolution on underclass black female-headed families because of the multiplicity of problems they face, marital disruption has consequences damaging to black families at all socioeconomic levels. Furthermore, marital disruptions occur at a faster rate among college-educated black females than among black females in the general population. Corroborating this statistic, Robert Hill found that in 1980 female-headed households were increasing ten times faster among college-educated black women than for black females who had not completed high school.[10] While there is reason to concede that women in the middle and upper classes have greater resources available for accessing social institutions, abundant evidence supports the contention that female-headed families, irrespective of socioeconomic level, have a plethora of problems to overcome. In addition to problems in the labor market, which are related to discriminatory practices and limited opportunities in educational institutions for black children, still other problems arise because of society's differential treatment of individuals based on race, gender, and class. What this means is that female-headed families cannot function at the same level as male-headed or two-parent families, irrespective of income. However, the basis for the lower-level functioning of female-headed families, in general and black-maintained families in particular, is not inherent in the structure. Rather, two-parent families are able to optimize their capacity to function because of the presence of the male. For instance, males are guaranteed higher earnings and greater opportunities for promotion and are better able to devote a larger percentage of their careers to work than are mothers with children. The expectation that husbands perform instrumental roles and become the family's chief breadwinners contributes significantly to the preferential treatment of men in the labor market. Since men are treated more favorably, two-parent families derive economic rewards from the male's presence. In effect, these benefits enable two-parent families to function at levels higher than families whose structural arrangements differ from the nuclear type.

Because race and gender also differentially affect income and societal treatment, it is understandable that black female-headed families, even under optimum conditions where the black female's income is moderate to high, are likely to have a reduced level of functioning compared to two-parent families. Moreover, because it is highly improbable that a male will be present in the household, because of relatively low remarriage rates, problems faced by the black female-headed family are likely to persist. Thus, for black women who experience marital disruption, the real conflict between expectations and realization centers on the fact that the expectation of marital stability is all too often incongruent with the reality of marital dissolution. And in many instances where intact black families receive welfare, marital disruption, the inability of couples to reconcile, and low remarriage rates could be favorably affected by an effective social-service delivery system. Hence, marital disruption is not likely, as economic motivation theorists suggest, to be a function of the black female's expectations that her postdivorce standard of living will be improved.

Remarriage: Private Versus Public Transfer Payments

Postdivorce black females are unlikely to receive compassion or understanding as an institutional response for their economic destitution. The position of the Los Angeles Court of Domestic Relations, which to a large extent is reflective of courts throughout the country, is that following divorce, women who wish to increase their resources have but two choices. In substance, they can either receive public assistance or remarry. Additional support for remarriage as a solution to poverty among female heads of households is provided by the men and women who make up the New Right.[11] The difference between the proponents of this conservative persuasion and the American judicial system is that the former, while supporting marriage as a viable strategy for economically depressed females who maintain families, also seek the total elimination of welfare. This lack of sensitivity to the economic problems of divorced women is inexorable when one considers that race, age, and number of children affect a woman's ability to remarry.

While there is evidence to support the notion that second marriages, for many women, appear to be more economically motivated than first marriages, compelling women to rely on remarriage as a primary method of elevating their economic status is hardly a viable alternative. And when race is a variable, the chances of remarriage improving the black female's standard of living is diminished due to an imbalanced sex ratio and unemployment and underemployment among black males. Duncan and Hoffman, in their study of the economic consequences of marital dissolution, discovered that in their sample after a five-year period of divorce, new husbands of remarried black women earned $8,813 a year, compared to $15,125 for whites. Moreover, when they calculated an average husband's projected earnings for a woman who was currently divorced, hypothetically a new husband for a white woman would earn $8,000. By contrast, hypothetically a new spouse for a black woman would earn $4,000 annually. They concluded that women who remain divorced were less likely to attract men with high incomes.[12] Thus, the belief that remarriage is a viable alternative to the economic insolvency that typifies the divorced female who heads a family is untenable. Further, Staples found the existence of a hierarchy of attractability among black singles.[13] This "pecking order" assigns single black females with children to the position of least desirable for purposes of courtship and marriage. Thus, remarriage for black women with children is negatively affected by their ability to secure eligible mates as well as by other factors over which they have no control.

Limiting the alternatives for greater economic independence for female single parents to choosing between public assistance or remarriage is tantamount to accepting and reinforcing female dependence. That is, females are expected to be unable to adequately provide for their families without depending on external sources of support. This concept supports the differential treatment of women in the labor market, which is translated (among other things) into pay inequities and the underrepresentation of women in mid- and high-level positions where greater economic rewards can be secured. Clearly, the assumption here is that since women are not perceived as the primary source of financial support for their families, there is no justification for paying them wages comparable to those of males with equal qualifications and job responsibilities. Along this line of reasoning, it is the male, not the female, irrespective of her marital status, who is primarily responsible for meeting the financial needs of the family. Therefore, following divorce, females are expected to remain dependent and to transfer their dependency from their former spouses to either the public welfare system or a new spouse. The real irony is that during the era of liberal social policy, social and economic programs were developed to reduce female dependency by fostering the acquisition of skills, particularly for women who were heads of households, yet the judicial and public welfare systems offered little support.

The paradox is that American society expects female single parents to be financially independent, yet the American judicial system, one of the most important of American institutions, does little to assuage institutional or individual dependency. For black underclass women, the extent to which the courts and other societal institutions were truly interested in promoting economic independence for female heads of households is even more questionable. Statistics reveal that, on the average, black women have only a 34 percent chance of being awarded any child support by the courts, compared to a 67 percent chance of receiving child support awards for white women.[14] Moreover, figures show that in 1978 one-third of all separated women received child support payments compared to one-half of all divorced women.[15] Never married women are at an even greater disadvantage when it comes to receiving child support, as a mere 6 percent of the women in this group received any financial support from their children's father during that year. It is little wonder that single mothers, including black women who head families, experience dire economic conditions. Furthermore, the inordinate number of lower-income black families that terminate marriages by separation rather than divorce, along with an increase in the percentage of black families headed by never-married women, means that many black women are in the two categories where absent fathers are least likely to fulfill their financial obligations for child support.[16] Equally alarming is the finding that the 50 percent of divorced fathers who do contribute to child support pay less than $2,000 per year.[17] Based on the modest child support the courts award to women in general and black women in particular, in conjunction with the laxity with which nonresident fathers comply with child support awards, the institutional response that perceives welfare or remarriage as a feasible alternative to the plight of female single parents is damaging to female-maintained families.

This idea that female heads of families should receive either public or private transfer payments rather than contribute significantly to their own families conflicted with the societal value of individual autonomy. While efforts were being undertaken to enable black men and women to develop skills that would promote more independence, counterefforts were encouraging female economic dependence. These double messages served to confound and thwart economic stability for black families.

THE NEVER-MARRIED BLACK WOMAN

The black woman whose marriage is dissolved is not alone in experiencing conflict between expectations and realizations caused by marital status. There is a growing number of black women who are joining the pool of never-marrieds. Included in this segment of the black population are increased numbers of female-maintained families with children. In addition, there is a definite growth in the number of black women with college degrees who do not marry. Though these women are at opposite ends of the spectrum, theories that have been set forth to explain black singlehood, with or without children, are similar in nature. The notion has been advanced, in the case of the underclass black female with children born out of wedlock, as well as the better educated, more financially independent black woman, that the paucity of eligible black males accounts for their inability to enter into a marital union. As such, the chances of their remaining single tend to increase rather than diminish with age. Here the conflict over expectations versus realization is related to the propensity for individuals to marry at some point in their lives, since blacks, like their white counterparts, continue to value marriage as an institution.

The never-married black woman with children is not a new phenomenon, yet the proportion of single black women with children who do not marry has increased over the past twenty-five years. Many attribute the growing number of black single women to a shortage of black males, but at the beginning of the era of liberal social policy black males and females envisioned a society in which blacks would assume traditional gender role positions as husbands and wives. However, liberal social policy was unable to create significant occupational advances for black males, which would have enabled them to earn substantially larger incomes and to have a greater degree of security in the market place. Replacing discriminatory practices with those that lead to greater job retention and promotions would have reduced the proportion of single black females.

One consequence of the industrial displacement of black males, many of whom have become chronically unemployed, is manifested in retreatist behavior. Having given up hope of becoming gainfully employed, and frustrated with their inability to find permanent employment, many of these once-eligible marriage partners have withdrawn from the labor market entirely. Having done so, they are represented among others within society who, like themselves, have given up the American Dream. They have adopted a life style that by most standards is its antithesis. Thus, for some underclass black males whose labor is only temporarily in demand, drug abuse, alcoholism, and mental illness are the collective responses of alienation caused by the overwhelming lack of opportunities for participation in mainstream institutions. Other self-destructive behaviors, such as homicides, are more spontaneous in nature, but also reflect cultural disaffection and the lack of control over one's destiny. These forms of apathy and aggression, while undoubtedly a reaction to thwarted goals and aspirations, tend to seriously attenuate the number of black males eligible for marriage.

BLACK TWO-PARENT FAMILIES

Not all black families are maritally disrupted. Approximately 55 percent of black families are intact and remain so against extraordinary odds. These families, like other families, irrespective of structural arrangement, share the same expectations for familial stability and social and economic progress. When one considers that some black families remained intact, recorded gains throughout the 1960s and 1970s, and continue to demonstrate upward mobility in the 1980s, there is little doubt that these families have accomplished an extraordinary feat.

Certainly, these families can provide invaluable insight into establishing strategies that ensure the sustenance and viability of the black family as a unit. Specifically, they are likely to possess critical information on the use of social-support systems, the ability to establish and reformulate goals, and the capacity to synthesize important cultural values inherent in the larger society with those within the black community. All too frequently, structures, particularly those within the black community, that manage to survive and progress seldom receive the attention essential for providing clues to their survival. To this end, a number of questions can be raised for which answers are definitely needed.

NOTES

1. Stephen Bahr, "The Effects of Welfare on Marital Stability and Remarriage," *Journal of Marriage and the Family* 41 (August, 1979): 557; William A. Darity, Jr., and Samuel L. Myers, Jr., "Does Welfare Dependency Cause Female Headship? The Case of the Black Family," *Journal of Marriage and the Family* 46 (November, 1984): 766–767.

2. Robert Staples, *The World of Black Singles: Changing Patterns of Male–Female Relations* (Westport, Connecticut: Greenwood Press, 1981), p. 71.

3. Frank L. Mott and Sylvia F. Moore, "The Causes of Marital Disruption Among Young American Women: An Interdisciplinary Perspective," *Journal of Marriage and the Family* 41 (May, 1979): 363–364.

4. Bahr, *The Effects of Welfare*, p. 557.

5. Staples, *The World of Black Singles*, p. 186.

6. Thomas J. Hopkins, "The Role of Community Agencies as Viewed by Black Fathers," *Journal of Orthopsychiatry* 42 (1972): 508–516.

7. Robert L. Hampton, "Institutional Decimation, Marital Exchange, and Disruption in Black Families," *Western Journal of Black Studies* 4 (Summer, 1980): 134–135.

8. Lenore Weitzman, "The Economics of Divorce: Social and Economic Consequences of Property, Alimony and Child Support Awards," *UCLA Law Review* 28 (1981): 1228; Lois M. Verbrugge, "Marital Status and Health," *Journal of Marriage and the Family* 41 (May, 1979): 267–283.

9. Christopher Jencks, "Divorced Mothers, Unite!" *Psychology Today* 16 (November, 1982): 73.

10. Barbara Ehrenreich and Karin Stallard, "The Nouveau Poor," *Ms.* 11 (August, 1982): 222.

11. Lenore Weitzman, "The Economics of Divorce: Social and Economic Consequences of Property, Alimony, and Child Support Awards," *UCLA Law Review* 28 (1981): 1228; Barbara Ehrenreich and Karin Stallard, "The Nouveau Poor," *Ms.* 11 (August, 1982): 223.

12. Greg J. Duncan and Saul D. Hoffman, "A Reconsideration of the Economic Consequences of Marital Dissolution," *Demography* 22 (1985): 493–495.

13. Staples, *The World of Black Singles*, p. 167.

14. United States Bureau of the Census, *Statistical Abstract of the United States: National Data Book and Guide to Sources*, 106th Edition (Washington, D.C.: U.S. Government Printing Office, 1986): 286.

15. Ehrenreich and Stallard, "The Nouveau Poor," p. 219.

16. Jencks, "Divorced Mothers Unite!" p. 74.

17. Jencks, "Divorced Mothers Unite!" p. 74; Ehrenreich and Stallard, "The Nouveau Poor," p. 219.

7 THE 1980s: A PERIOD OF SOCIAL CONSERVATISM AND SOCIAL REAWAKENING

A CASE OF SOCIAL TRAUMA: SHOULD WE PULL THE PLUG?

The "patient's" vital signs were rapidly deteriorating, blood pressure was rising, temperature climbing, and pulse throbbing. Eventually, the overall system was in a state of disequilibrium.

Code Blue was called.* Attendants and other experts rushed in and confirmed the "patient's" declining status. Initially prognosis was uncertain, yet there was room for hope. Later, it was thought that with emergency treatment and artificial life-support systems, the patient's condition would improve markedly. Although the "patient" would be in a total state of dependency, experts believed that the use of life-support systems would allow time for monitoring, stabilization, and experimentation with new treatments, designed to bring about an improved level of functioning. Barring complications, recovery seemed likely.

A sigh of relief could be heard from those concerned. Now that chances for survival appeared good, a series of questions were posed to the experts. Will the "patient" survive? How long will it take for full recovery? Will the level of functioning remain at the pretrauma level, improve, or decrease? What will be the monetary costs for treatment? The answers to these and similar questions remained ambiguous and inconclusive. A wait-and-see attitude prevailed.

With the passage of time and the application of numerous modalities of treatment, the "patient" continued to remain in a state of dependency. The prolonged use of artificial

---

*Code Blue means human life is at risk, and immediate intervention is necessary.

life-support systems became a point of contention, as dependency resulted in rising costs. Earlier considerations, once liberal, became conservative as the experts' prognosis for improved functioning was grim. Since continued dependency on artificial means failed to result in independent functioning, hope began to fade. At this time, concern for the emotional and monetary costs to others began to take precedence over earlier considerations for the "patient." The question now posed to the experts was, "Should we pull the plug?"

This scenario, more commonly applied to patients undergoing medical crises, is equally applicable to individuals experiencing social trauma. Taking place on a grand scale in the 1960s, the "patient" represents the inordinate number of poor and black families; the "experts," the policy-makers; and the "concerned," the more economically advantaged and socially informed American men, women, and students.

Underlying the massive change in social policy in the 1960s and 1970s was the belief, held by civil rights activists and others concerned with the plight of the poor, that economically disadvantaged groups were faced with social and economic exigencies requiring emergency measures. This trauma was manifested in its most dramatic and volatile forms by social movements, urban violence, and student protests. The new social and economic programs were considered temporary measures to allow for stabilization and ultimately to enable poor and black families to function better by increasing their participation in the mainstream United States. Moreover, these efforts were considered social and economic remedies to make up for the past injustices to blacks. Accordingly, the "recovery" hoped for was a level of functioning for black families that, according to black scholars, had been destroyed by slavery. Thus, subsidized housing, liberalized public assistance, child-care development centers, Medicaid, foodstamps, job training programs, affirmative action, and so on, were intended to promote economic independence for poor and black families.

Unfortunately, complications set in as inflation grew, established industries declined, and a multiplicity of social and economic programs failed to curb social isolation for poor and black families throughout society. After monitoring the progress of poor and black families for more than a decade and assessing the mounting costs for government-supported programs, the country entered into a period of reassessment. Many American taxpayers were disenchanted with the depressed economy and believed that social policies were benefiting poor and black families at the expense of the majority. Policy-makers who represented the taxpayers began to raise questions regarding the costs and utility of such efforts. It was then concluded that dependence in this state appeared permanent, probability for improvement was slim, and that social and economic life supports should be removed. Because they were dependent and powerless, the approximately 5.3 million poor families in America in 1980, 1.7 million of whom were black, had little input into this decision. Irrefutably, the artificial measures had not enabled social policy experts to identify viable methods for effecting financial independence for poor and black families. In the case of medical emergencies, when life-support systems are withdrawn, some patients survive, while others do not. How well poor and black families in America would survive in the absence of formal social-support systems became an issue of much heated debate. On one side were advocates who indicated that formal social-support systems had not been maintained long enough. Critics argued that poor and black families had had sufficient opportunities to benefit from these measures, which their constituents were no longer willing to pay for. What began to surface from this conservative persuasion was the prevailing attitude that poor and black families had not demonstrated the will to live. Hence, the onus for survival was transferred from the government to its dependents: poor and black families.

Reassessment and Retrenchment

The social and economic climate of the late 1970s and the 1980s indicated that poor and black families were unlikely to progress beyond a level of social and economic dependency.

Emphasis on needs began to shift from the economically disadvantaged to problems encountered by other members of society. Increasingly, attention was focussed on majority families, especially those with middle-class status. The change in government policy in the 1980s was due to many of the same social and economic factors that had adversely affected black families. High rates of unemployment, escalating crime rates, growing out-of-wedlock births, and an increase in marital disruptions were among the many problems that made policy-makers reexamine governmental expenditures. However, these problems, while critical, were not exclusively responsible for the mood of conservatism that engulfed the country in the 1980s. Of paramount importance was the public's declining confidence in the government's ability to stabilize the economy, maintain a lower debt ceiling, and assure employment for numbers of displaced workers.

Understandably, the focus of attention was placed on government spending. When the country's economic woes were blamed on runaway government spending, domestic programs came under vicious attack. This not only set the stage for a careful reexamination of social and economic programs but for a reassessment of the status of the recipients of such programs. The outcome of such analyses was to restore the economy and American families' confidence in it.

Ushered in on a platform of social reform, the Reagan administration began to reformulate social policy. In so doing, conservatives highlighted negative conditions facing poor families in general and black families in particular. By attributing these problems to liberal social policy, rather than to regulations, administrative policies, and pre-existing conditions that mitigated the effectiveness of liberal social policy, social conservatives proposed the rescision of social and economic programs.

While the Reagan administration claimed to be following a public mandate to make major changes in social policy, liberals maintained that support for these undertakings was not as prevalent as suggested.[1] Naisbitt, asserts that while 43 million people voted for Ronald Reagan, 42 million voted against him.[2] For this reason, some have questioned the level of public support for these major changes in social policy. Nevertheless, the Reagan administration was not influenced by admonitions from individuals opposed to this reactionary form of social policy. What followed were proposals for and the eventual implementation of budgetary cuts to existing social and economic programs. Aside from advocating that civil rights legislation, such as affirmative action and the 1965 Voting Rights Act be rescinded, the Reagan administration invoked the furor of its political adversaries by espousing the complete decentralization of government, known as ''New Federalism.'' The establishment of new governmental priorities, designed to end what was labeled as reverse discrimination and economic injustices to majority families, resulted in the reformulation of a plethora of social policies. What began as a period of reassessment made the 1980s a decade of retrenchment.

Reformulation of Social Policy

The Reagan administration's agenda encompassed massive, and what some refer to as radical, reform. Efforts to bring government spending under control for the purpose of balancing the federal budget was expressed as the fundamental basis for making drastic cuts in domestic programs. Supported by welfare revisionists, a return to true conservatism was imminent as the withdrawal of government involvement in social-welfare programs was proposed and quickly implemented in 1981. The new set of government policies placed defense as a top priority and relegated social-welfare programs.[3] Just as liberal policy-makers had found an abundance of academic support for their inventive programs, conservatives from the academy came to the aid of welfare revisionists by advancing theories and postulates that discounted the effectiveness of liberal social policy. Traditionalists were among the growing list of scholars claiming that the number of families in poverty was substantially lower than reports would indicate. By relying on a new set of criteria for measuring poverty, which entailed counting all welfare benefits, cash and noncash, as income, one such report indicated that the number of persons in poverty had been overestimated by 4 million in 1976.[4] Lending even more support for abandoning social-welfare programs, other scholars, such as Roger Freeman, were convinced that changes proposed by the Reagan administration would cause distress only to those who, as Freeman states, were getting too much in the first place anyway.[5] Among the various programs affected by these new conservative social policies were Aid to Families with Dependent Children, Medicaid, educational grants, federal subsidized housing, food stamps, and affirmative action. Left virtually unaltered were Social Security, Medicare, and veterans' benefits.[6]

Other changes became apparent as the decade progressed. The Reagan administration, after a second electoral victory, resumed their program of government decentralization of and disengagement from social services. Legislation intended to buttress a return to community and private responsibility was proposed and in some cases enacted. For example, the Reagan administration supported bills that enforced paternal responsibility for child support. Such measures proposed the withholding of overdue payments through seizure of federal and state tax refunds and reducing welfare benefits for women who remarry by expecting stepfathers to provide financial support for stepchildren. The ultimate aim of these laws was to relieve the government of its financial responsibility in this area.

The abrupt rescission of various programs on which black families had become dependent revealed the extent to which progress had truly taken place. As conservative social policies began to unfold, it became apparent that many black families who appeared to have escaped to the middle class had done so only peripherally. For them, ascent was merely temporary.

SOCIAL POLICY REFORMULATED

New Federalism

New Federalism was designed to return to the states the power and authority to make critical decisions regarding the establishment of priorities and the administration of social-welfare services. Delegating additional responsibility to state government for the delivery of social services was proposed to give states more latitude in policy formulation and the dispensation of funds. Specifically, New Federalism entailed the federal government taking over Medicaid costs, while the states assumed responsibility for food stamps, Aid to Families with Dependent Children, and other welfare programs. Considerable disagreement took place over the capacity of state governments to run social programs efficiently and fairly. At this point, glaring differences were apparent in the percentage of government funds that states allocate for social-welfare services to the poor. Because states do not uniformly treat social services as a priority, the effects of New Federalism can result in minuscule benefits to black and poor families solely on the basis of geographic residence.

From Collective to Private Responsibility

The conservative policy initiated by the Reagan administration, intended to absolve the federal government of its responsibility for social-welfare programs, involved more than the transference of authority for welfare programs to the states. Included in this attempt to reduce the federal government's commitment to social-welfare programs was an effort to ensure that the private sector assumed a greater share of the responsibility. The argument conservatives advanced to substantiate this move was that the expanded role of government had served to reduce charitable contributions to private organizations.[7] It was suggested that the private sector's enormous resources had remained untapped over the two preceding decades and that the sheer magnitude of resources needed to care and provide for the poor had to be provided in part by others, particularly the private sector. To effect this transition, proposals entailed tax breaks and various incentives, such as collapsing the Comprehensive Employment and Training Program (CETA) and transforming this job training effort to Private Industry Councils throughout the country. Support for this program, which reassigned the government's function of social-service delivery to the private sector, came from the trickle-down theory. The government held that by easing regulations and providing corporations with incentives and financial opportunities for expansion, the private sector would respond by creating jobs, thereby reducing unemployment and poverty. In this same vein, the federal government encouraged and supported the introduction of what proved to be unsuccessful legislation to lower the minimum wage. Arguing that a lower minimum wage would result in numerous jobs for youth (rather than their exploitation, as opponents of this bill argued), the Reagan administration remained undaunted and determined to effect this controversial change in social policy.

The shift from collective to private responsibility included more than a greater role for the private sector. Volunteerism was promoted as a moral obligation and an avenue that had been underutilized over the twenty-year period during which the government was predominant in the provision of social-welfare services.[8] Government reports indicated the extent to which volunteers were already an integral part of social-service delivery systems, especially those geared to children in child-development centers and the aged in area agencies for the aging. According to these same government sources, evidence indicated that innumerable volunteers were available representing untapped resources, which, if utilized, would reduce government expenditures. This approach to social-service delivery, in which communities were expected to shoulder more responsibility for their own members, was further evidence that the country had gone full circle, from neighbors helping neighbors to institutional responsibility and back to self-help.

Workfare Mandated

Based on the philosophical tenets that welfare recipients are inherently lazy and lack any real incentives to work, workfare programs took on greater importance. The 1981 Omnibus Budget Reconciliation Act, which shifted welfare responsibility to the states, offered three optional programs from which the states could select: Community Work Experience (workfare), Work Supplementation, and the Work Incentive Demonstration Project. A year later the government transferred even greater responsibility for social-service delivery by having states assume the administration of employment programs.[9]

The purpose of such programs was to reduce welfare caseloads. Moreover, workfare was the government's attempt to inculcate welfare recipients with acceptable work habits and to convince the general public that an economic exchange system was still in place. The government's stance was designed to allay the concerns of those who shared the welfare revisionist's conviction that welfare recipients should work in exchange for benefits, irrespective of the nature of the work in which they were engaged.

To further heighten the already punitive stance of neoconservatives regarding social welfare reform, the U.S. Senate on June 17, 1988, overwhelmingly voted to approve a bill that its supporters labeled the first federally mandated work program for able-bodied welfare recipients. The bill, which must be resolved in a Senate-House conference, requires states to provide education, training, and jobs for able-bodied adults on welfare, except those with children under three. Further, this legislation seeks to increase child support payments by requiring states to withhold wages of absent fathers and requires that fathers in two-parent families work a minimum of sixteen hours each week in community service in exchange for welfare benefits.[10]

Other Policy Changes and Their Outcomes

Following the Reagan administration's first year of leadership, considerable changes in social policy had already begun to take place. In addition to cutting millions of dollars from the federal budget for social-welfare programs, eligibility requirements had reduced the number of welfare recipients. Efforts were being made to lower expenditures for still other social programs, but the political resistance and opposition voiced by liberals prevented them. For example, controversy turned into outrage as the federal government was accused of total insensitivity when efforts to reduce the federal budget resulted in government nutritionists classifying pickle relish and catsup as vegetables. Although the Department of Agriculture did make cutbacks in school breakfasts and lunch programs, this latter proposal was discarded, as the federal government was unable to withstand the barrage of criticism it elicited.[11]

The fact that not all domestic programs underwent budgetary cuts raised questions regarding the federal governments partiality for various segments of the population. The most vocal and ardent foes of welfare revisionists were quick to point to the government's protectionist attitude toward middle-class Americans, who were the beneficiaries of social programs that remained virtually untouched. These groups of individuals whose benefit levels were not reduced were beneficiaries of Social Security, veteran's benefits, and Medicare. When objections were made to budgetary cuts that affected the poor but not the middle-class, the government's retort was that the truly needy among the poor would also be provided for. Thus, safeguards were provided, which theoretically guaranteed that families who could demonstrate, using revamped means tests, that they were destitute would be eligible for and receive federal assistance. Those exempted from benefit reductions were protected by what Reagan termed a "safety net."

Policy changes were not limited to social-welfare programs alone. As cited earlier, civil rights legislation was subjected to a complete reappraisal. Both affirmative action plans and the Voting Rights Acts of 1965 and 1968 underwent reassessment. The number of litigations for affirmative action and voting rights violations greatly diminished in number during the first six months after Reagan took office.[12] Moreover, companies with federal contracts who were mandated to report their affirmative action contracts were no longer compelled to adhere to this stipulation unless their contract met the new fiscal criterion: The minimum was raised from $50,000 to $1 million. Thus, companies receiving federal contracts under the $1 million amount were exempt from submitting affirmative action plans. Other firms were notified that their affirmative action plans would be reviewed only every five years.[13]

This radical shift in social policy from liberal to conservative did far more than reduce moneys to social and economic programs. It established a new social climate with a growing intolerance for conditions facing black and poor families in the United States. In making monumental changes in social policy, the federal government insisted that middle-class families had been ignored and had become the caretakers of black and poor families for twenty years. Using this rationale, the government decided that greater benefits would be realized by all if the following occurred: the federal government placed greater emphasis on and appropriated more dollars for defense, budgetary cuts in social-welfare programs were made, and the government deregulated industry and implemented tax incentives for big business to boost the economy.

The federal government moved rapidly toward attaining its goals. By cutting the food stamp and Aid to Families with Dependent Children programs, welfare recipients with earnings were among the poor to feel the impact of these initiatives, which were supposed to balance the budget and restore economic and moral stability to the country. Levitan and Johnson assert that these budgetary cuts raised marginal taxes substantially, which meant that many black families who constitute the working poor were no longer eligible for any form of welfare assistance. These policy changes caused the disposable income of the average AFDC family with earnings, to fall in every state in 1982. In addition, this created the very work disincentives that conservatives had attributed to liberal social policy. Thus, in twelve states a nonworking AFDC parent with two children was better off financially than a working non-AFDC parent in comparable circumstances.[14] In 1981 budgetary cuts in social programs had removed 400,000 families from federal and state welfare.[15] Moreover, Joe and Rogers assert that the Reagan administration failed to replace work incentives to the working poor, in spite of the fact that this group displayed the "self-supporting" behavior that the administration was interested in promoting.[16] While these were some of the more immediate effects of the implementation of conservative social policy, continued efforts in this direction resulted in even more changes.

Advocates of liberal social policy expressed considerable dissatisfaction over policy goals and objectives that they considered grossly insensitive to the needs of black and poor families. Nevertheless, the federal government did not halt its effort. Rather, the administration continued working to bring reactionary policy to fruition. After four years of conservative policy, the federal government claimed that the economy had made a phenomenal recovery. The social and economic policies to which the Reagan administration referred, also known as "Reaganomics," generally impressed conservatives and repulsed liberals. Reaganomics could be defined as a strategy to return the country to economic stability and to return government to the people; the latter goal was to be achieved by giving responsibility for social programs to the states, the private sector, and the community. However, for many black families, Reaganomics symbolized a return to the pre-1960s era, when civil liberties could not be taken for granted. The "good old days" the welfare revisionists so frequently lamented were ones that civil rights activists and advocates of liberal social policy had directed tremendous effort to change.

Blacks, instrumental in the social revolution that precipitated liberal social policy, perceived these revisionists policies as more than mere attempts to shore up the economy. In general, the Reagan administration was considered an ally to the rich and an adversary to poor and black families. Although other groups demanded that power and wealth be redistributed, black families, with the exception of those few who belonged to politically conservative interest groups, were appalled by the measures taken by welfare revisionists. In the main, black intellectuals believed that the welfare revisionists' attempts to extend policy recommendations—from cutting the federal budget for social programs, to attacking affirmative action, the Voting Rights Act, and educational grants and loans—would have a definite impact on black families across all socioeconomic classes. Even the more conservative element among blacks, generally represented by black businessmen, expressed dissatisfaction over the government's proposal to reduce support for federal guaranteed loans to small businesses.

Black families' disillusionment was largely rooted in the negative assumptions that underscored conservative social policy. The social inadequacy theory of black family life, once used by liberals as the basis for the social and economic programs of the 1960s, was now used by conservatives to explain the necessity for eradicating social and economic programs. Black families, they believed, had been receiving undeserved benefits from social and economic programs. They also believed that the disproportionate number of black families receiving welfare had other alternatives for producing and consuming than relying on the federal government for support. The prevailing image was one of welfare recipients as able-bodied individuals whose abuse and fraudulent behavior at the taxpayer's expense would no longer be tolerated. To be fair, the image of of welfare being synonymous with black families was not peculiar to any one political persuasion. However, the notion that somehow there was a parasitic relationship between black families, in all strata, and the government was novel.

This stereotype of black families, created by the development of social programs and civil rights legislation, made some people feel that the government was solicitous and unduly generous toward all black families in America. People also believed that black families were benefiting at the expense of white families, and that the rewards black families received were more than commensurate with their efforts.

In many respects, this non-discriminative perception of black families set in motion a slow but gradual rekindling of racial unity and activism among middle-class black and intellectuals, the significance of which cannot be understated, as blacks who were active participants in the civil rights movement, once again, began to recognize their commonality of interests with black families in the underclass. Heretofore, social activism among blacks had reached the predictable lull that characterizes social revolutions, as they peak and recede in a cyclical fashion.[17] The contention was that black families were prospering at a rate that surpassed that of the average American family, because it was believed that opportunities were being made available to black families in inequitable proportions; this attitude led the Reagan administration to emphasize the need to restore institutions to their pre-1960s state. In so doing, they argued, blacks would no longer receive preferential treatment at the expense of other cultural groups. The implication was that blacks were receiving benefits to which they were not entitled. Because of the contention that many undeserving black families were receiving government goods and services, while other families were going wanting, the administration became preoccupied with ensuring that the work ethic become the focal point of all social programs, particularly social-welfare services. The assumption of policy revisionists was that liberal social policy had given rise to social and economic programs with built-in work disincentives.[18]

The trend toward lowering the federal budget by reducing the federal government's involvement in social-welfare programs continued throughout Reagan's first term and was reemphasized when he resumed office for a second term. Between 1980 and 1985, the Reagan administration took credit for economic growth and a reduction in the overall rate of unemployment. The economic upturn, frequently mentioned by administration officials, was labeled by Reagan as a sign that the country was experiencing an economic recovery. The withdrawal of government support for social-welfare programs and the laxity of monitoring and enforcing civil rights legislation were considered—along with other policy modifications, including tax inducements to big business—as having contributed to the improved economic conditions during Reagan's first term in office. Given their high degree of success, the welfare revisionists continued to move forward with similar policy goals in the second term of the Reagan administration. Depending on one's political persuasion, the Reagan administration's social-policy initiatives can be categorized as conservative or radically conservative.

It became increasingly clear following Reagan's election to a second term of office that the country had become polarized. Disavowing the administration's claim of an economic recovery, blacks offered little support for Reagan in the 1984 national election.

Although many argued that the general public remained reticent and ambivalent regarding conservative social policy, the tenor of feelings and attitudes regarding black and poor families in 1984 had changed little from those of 1980. In fact, the undercurrent of dissatisfaction with government's expanded role in providing social programs was more firmly rooted in 1984. It was no longer considered socially unacceptable to voice disapproval for the continued inability of black and poor families to rise out of poverty. The continued economically depressed status of black and poor families and attendant problems were considered further evidence of moral turpitude. Moreover, the public's increased awareness of intergenerational poverty, interpreted by culture-of-poverty theorists as inspired by a deviant value system and life style, provided ample justification for eliminating welfare programs, which were perceived as exacerbating the cyclical nature of poverty and dependency. The media was unrelenting in its portrayal of poor black families as morally corrupt, which lent further credence to welfare revisionists' position that black underclass families were contributing to the annihilation of traditional American cultural values. Embraced by a growing cadre of supporters who had combined religious beliefs and political action and calling themselves the Moral Majority, the Reagan administration vigorously pursued the mission of improving the economy by offering economic incentives to industry to boost the free enterprise system. At the same time, efforts were made to safeguard against what was believed to be the further moral decline of society by removing social-welfare programs that were considered work disincentives for poor families. In this context, equity and social justice were felt by conservatives to be lacking. Where violations of civil rights were said to occur, conservatives argued that the nonpoor were the victims rather than the poor. Old arguments that stressed the frugality of poor immigrant families who had successfully ascended from poverty resurfaced. Along this line of reasoning, George Gilder, in analyzing social-welfare programs and the lack of parity between black families and their white counterparts, suggested that the triumvirate that was the basis for economic mobility for other ethnic groups was lacking among black families. According to Gilder, those elements "family, work and faith," were all but decimated by liberal social and economic programs.[19] Adding more support for conservative ideologues was Lawrence Mead's analysis of liberal social policy, in which he concluded that the permissive nature of social-welfare programs, whereby the government failed to set up conditions for reciprocal exchange, had resulted in irresponsibility among the poor and an overall deterioration in their moral character.[20] These and similar expositions by Charles Murray and others were myopic and failed to capture the crucial elements that contributed to the failure of liberal social and economic programs to radically alter the despicable conditions facing black and poor families in America.[21] In general, they have chosen to ignore the fact that liberal social policy was ill-equipped to alter societal institutions, making them permanently amenable to affording black families opportunities for social and economic progress. Clearly, intellectuals of this genre have had a profound impact on the proliferation of conservative social-welfare policy during the 1980s. Despite Reagan's campaign promise to balance the budget within two years by making drastic cuts in social and economic programs, the country's debt grew uncontrollably. The federal budget deficit soared from $74 billion in 1980 to an unprecedented $221 billion in 1986.[22]

A major occurrence that raised serious questions regarding the government's future role in social-service delivery was the passage of the Gramm-Rudman-Hollings plan in December 1985. This law, more popularly known as Gramm-Rudman, was designed to gradually eliminate the federal deficit, which in 1985 exceeded $200 billion by imposing mandatory spending cuts in domestic programs. Considerable disagreement existed over the constitutionality of this law, which invoked an automatic formula for mandatory cuts in domestic programs in the event that the administration failed to enact voluntary reductions in federal spending. There was also genuine concern over the effects of this legislation on social-welfare programs. On the one hand, social-welfare advocates wondered how these programs would fare under this edict. Alternatively, ardent supporters of conservative welfare policy voiced reservations and trepidation over the potential of Gramm-Rudman to make deep cuts in the defense budget. One pivotal issue centered on whether the government's reluctance to raise taxes would lead to drastic cuts in budgetary allocations to social-welfare programs. The fact that these programs had already been subjected to earlier budgetary cuts and policies that had reduced the level of benefits and beneficiaries, generated suspicion that Gramm-Rudman's effect on social-welfare programs would be ominous and far-reaching. Under the terms of Gramm-Rudman, the federal government was compelled to make budget cuts to reach a zero deficit by 1991. To eliminate the $200 billion federal deficit, a reduction of $144 billion was projected by 1987. Further, an additional $36 billion budget cut a year was deemed necesesary to achieve a zero deficit by 1991. Given the Reagan administration's conservative policy and disaffection for social-welfare programs, liberals believed that the programs that would be voluntarily cut to prevent the invoking of automatic reductions would be social-welfare programs. The provision that liberals found objectionable—and which the U.S. Supreme Court ruled unconstitutional, citing that it violated the constitutional requirement that the executive and legislative powers of government be kept separate—stipulated that if Congress and the President could not reach a consensus on how to trim the budget, automatic cuts would occur that would either reduce or eliminate many federal programs. Still, the court's ruling does not allay doubts over policy-makers' sensitivity towards the poor during an era of conservativism.[23] Further evidence of the Reagan administration's social policy failures (and of the failure of their assurances of an economic recovery) was the 1987 stock market crash. On Monday, October 19, 1987, stock values plummeted, causing a worldwide economic panic. Furthermore, many economists believe that the 1987 Wall Street crash had negative economic consequences exceeding those of the 1929 crash.[24]

In sum, social policy throughout the first half of the decade of the 1980s continued to reflect social conservatism. What is striking about social neo-conservatism is the redefining of the victims of social injustice. In this sense, neo-conservatism replaces black and poor families as victims of social inequities with majority families. Moreover, the perpetrators also change places. Accordingly, blacks and not society are blamed for the lack of parity between black and white families in America. Hence, social policy formulated with a conservative undergirding operates on a zero-sum basis; whereby, equity for black families is thought to result in social inequities for majority families.

Social Conservatism and the Black Community

It is not always easy to separate the effects of one phenomenon from another. In many respects, a number of years that yield repeated observations are necessary to isolate the impact of social, political, and economic events on major institutions. Another salient factor in determining the effects of social phenomena on various societal systems is the fact that the effects of pre-existing phenomena cannot always be successfully controlled. In this case, where do the effects of liberal social policy end and the impact of conservative public policy begin? The answers to this and related questions are not clear-cut, particularly in the case of conservative social policy, since it is still in the process of being formulated. As conservative social policy takes on new dimensions, brought on by policy-makers, current and future events, and political opposition, it is impossible to predict with a high degree of reliability the overall impact of the new wave of conservatism. It is difficult to accurately gauge the total array of factors that may militate against a continuation or escalation of conservative social policy. However, it is clear that the formulation of conservative social policy is responsible for some discernible changes that have begun to occur in black families. Moreover, changes in the structure and dynamics of other institutions and patterns of interaction are becoming increasingly apparent within the black community.

Revitalization of Mutual-Aid Networks

The welfare revisionists' insistence that communities assume more responsibility for social-service delivery when authority is transferred from the federal government to state and local governments, the private sector, and volunteers, is coming to fruition. The increased participation of these segments of the population is not solely due to the demands of social conservatives. Greater involvement of these entities has occurred out of necessity, rather than being directly related to a strong sense of moral responsibility. After all, the values in our society place heavy emphasis on social isolation and familial autonomy, and they continue to govern the lives of economically advantaged families in this country.

In general, there is sufficient evidence that community self-help is on the rise. The interesting issue, however, is who is helping whom. As one looks closely at the growing rate of networking throughout society, it is increasingly the case that most of these efforts take place in the inner city. Local church groups and other organizations that are centrally located and easily accessible to the poor (who lack the money to afford transportation) are in the vanguard of self-help efforts, Moreover, civic and neighborhood associations have been the prime sponsors of numerous social services to the poor. That is not to say that individuals residing on the periphery of and outside major metropolitan areas do not contribute to less advantaged families. In fact, there has been a conscious effort to donate foodstuffs and other essentials not only to poor families in the United States but to those living abroad as well. The growing concern about and consciousness for alleviating U.S. and world hunger arose from famine relief efforts for Ethiopia, largely promoted by well-known entertainers.

The stimulus for black families to revitalize mutual-aid networks has not been limited to radical changes in social-welfare policy alone. While the increase in black unemployment has necessitated a resurgence of community self-help, the increasing percentage of black families headed by women due to separation, divorce, and out-of-wedlock births has also been an impetus for the resurgence of mutual-aid networks. As stated earlier, black women have historically been in the vanguard of self-help groups. Moreover, the vital functions of child care and the exchange of goods and services that mutual-aid networks perform are particularly critical to black female single parents, of which there are a growing number. Thus, mutual-aid networks must provide basic goods and services to individuals who, because of new policy guidelines, no longer qualify for public assistance, as well as those whose earnings have been diminished by loss of employment and marital break-ups. The fact that many black families have become downwardly mobile because of inordinate rates of marital disruption, the lack of marketable job skills, and unemployment places an added burden on mutual-aid networks. For example, the fact that black female heads of households experience a greater need for financial support from informal support systems than their married counterparts underscores specific needs brought about because of the male's absence.[25]

Structural arrangement is the basis for the middle-class status of many black families; hence, familial structure is to a great extent a determinant of economic status in the black community.[26] Still, it should be noted that the higher economic status of black married-couple families is socially determined and is not inherent in the structure itself. Given that the high rate of unemployment and underemployment for black males requires both the husband and wife to be employed outside the home, combined with the fact that males have a higher earning potential than females, it is understandable that these families had a median income of $20,586 in 1983 compared to the median income of $14,506 for all black families in the same year. The importance of male presence in reducing the need for financial support from informal support systems cannot be overstated. According to James McGhee, even in black married-couple families where the wife was not in the paid labor force the median income in 1983 was $16,348, approximately twice that of female-headed households whose median income was $7,999. In the case of the latter group, the median income was less than one-third that of married-couple families with both the husband and wife in the paid labor force.[27] This is not to suggest that black middle-income families do not receive financial support from mutual aid networks, only that the nature of support tends to be emotional rather than monetary.

Though they continue to provide essential services to black families, mutual-aid networks in the black community are faced with a problem of supply and demand, which makes the adequate provision of goods and services difficult at best. The greater demand for black families to give to each other, following what appeared to be substantial growth in the number of black middle-classs families, makes even more vivid the fragility and transitory nature of the nouveau black middle-class family.

The Black Church

Because of the traditional role of the church in providing and coordinating goods and services to black families, the black church has assumed its primary function as overseer and mediator of the increasing number of self-help activities. There is a certain degree of irony associated with the increased visibility of the black church. For example, during the 1960s and 1970s, the enhancement of black churches and other black institutions vital to the functioning of black families and the total black community could have had a profound impact on black family stability.[28] Instead, the government's method of formulating and implementing social and economic programs ignored black institutions, including the black church. However, the reactionary posture of welfare revisionists— which extols traditional institutions, values, and norms and attempts to restore to societal institutions a high level of authority for reestablishing social order and moral responsibility—has enhanced the position of the black church. Consequently, the black church began to reaffirm its mission to economic development of the black community through myriad entrepreneurial initiatives.[29] The government's social conservatism is not the sole reason that the black church as well as other religious organizations are resuming an honored position. As social anomalies related to the family continue to escalate, without any apparent methods for prevention or control, the black church with its moral obligation is expected to provide answers.

Moreover, cutbacks in federal spending that reduce monetary support for social services, such as community mental-health services, result in the church assuming greater responsibility for pastoral counseling. Because black families are faced with the debilitating effects of high rates of unemployment, economic hardships, marital break-ups, and a demoralizing social-welfare system, the black church has an extremely important role to play. In many respects, black churches must not only address these problems using their own resources but must identify other sources to address the myriad needs of black families. Black churches function as the dispenser and coordinator of resources, a difficult role to play, not only because of limited resources but also due to the still impersonal nature of an urban environment. It is obvious that mutual-aid networks consisting of consanguine as well as fictive kin are antithetical to the value orientation, which became pervasive over the last twenty years, that prescribes personal and familial autonomy as an ideal characteristic for American families. One conclusion that can be drawn from the move from liberal to conservative social policy is that the black family, among other black institutions, must assume the formidable task of addressing problems caused by the social and economic programs that created unattainable expectations and aspirations. Conservative social policy of the 1980s has compounded the already egregious conditions facing black families by indiscriminately reducing federal expenditures for social programs, further dashing the hopes and dreams of black families who have yet to gain entrance or permanence in mainstream America. In addition, conservative policy has created disillusionment for those black families whose middle-class status is not only predicated on a married-couple family with both husband and wife in the paid labor force, but for whom economic status is based on civilian labor force participation of one or both spouses in government service.

Status of Black Families

The black family, like the white family, had already begun to undergo significant change when social conservatives began exploring ways to implement deep domestic budget cuts, which would move the federal government away from social-service delivery. Interestingly, welfare revisionists maintained that policies which were being enacted were for the express purpose of reversing the debilitating effects of liberal social policy. Since the implementation of conservative social policy, a number of changes have taken place. For example, in 1980, 8 million or 34 percent of American blacks were in poverty. By 1985 the proportion of blacks with incomes below the poverty level was still at 34 percent. Moreover, the jobless rate among black males was was still double that of white males—13.1 percent in 1985.[30] So while the Reagan administration assumed credit for bringing about an economic recovery and lowering the rate of unemployment, these improvements did not affect black families similarly.

By all indications, black families, particularly those who constitute the underclass, felt the greatest impact of the illusion of acculturation and mainstream society participation brought on by liberal social policy. Furthermore, the rescission of these policies has worsened the status of many black families. However, renewed efforts are underway to identify strategies from within the black community, which will enable black families to effectively solve social and economic problems caused by liberal social policy and further exacerbated by a new breed of policy-makers with a predilection for conservatism. The continual plunging of black families into poverty as a result of radical changes in social policy substantiates the extent to which upward mobility and enhanced economic status were ephemeral for an overwhelming number of black families. What occurred when liberal social policy was succeeded by social conservatism is akin to big business lending its support to a small but struggling business, exploring methods to remain viable. In such cases, when a larger enterprise contractually agrees to provide the failing business with the basic necessities and adds to these fundamentals an abundance of other resources, such as equipment, facilities, supplies, and contacts, eventually the small business begins to thrive. In addition, the small business establishes long-term goals and reaches a level of economic solvency. However, while the small enterprise is progressing, it has not acquired sufficient resources to sustain its growth independent of the larger corporate concern. Let's assume that big business decides that maintaining the contract is no longer in its own interest. Therefore, at the end of the contract, big business decides not to renew the agreement and withdraws the abundance of support. In such a case, it is highly probable that the small business is worse off because of the relationship. In fact, the small business is likely to have become dependent on the larger company, operating at a level far exceeding that at which it functioned before entering into the contractual relationship. Thus, when the contract is abruptly terminated the small business suffers immensely becasue it does not possess the resources nor the capacity to sustain operations at this higher level. And in many cases, the smaller business folds. This raises the question, would the smaller business have failed without the added support? The answer is, not necessarily so. First, the larger enterprise could have shared its expertise which would have assisted the smaller business in developing its own capabilities, which would enable the small business to operate independently. Secondly, the smaller business could have elected to consolidate with similar companies. The range of options which a fledgling business could pursue are too numerous to explore. However, when a struggling business enters into a contractual agreement with a big business, it should do so recognizing that while such an arrangement appears palatable, the risks of such a relationship are in direct proportion to the rewards.

In many respects, this is what happened to black families and their members due to the radical shift from liberal to conservative social policy. To suggest that liberal social policy during the 1960s and 1970s created real opportunities for blacks to gain access to, and compete in, an open market ignores the fact that blacks' participation in traditional institutions was based on legislative edict, in the form of affirmative action, grants and loans for financing education and black-owned businesses, and the like. At the beginning of the 1980s, when the federal government began to "pull the rug" from under black families by withdrawing social and economic programs upon which they had become dependent, the overall effects were pernicious.

Previous experience indicates that economic instability is accompanied by increased levels of nuclear family stability.[31] In times of economic crisis, families generally become more unified and consolidate their resources. Clearly, the current economic recession and inflation, unlike before, did not reduce the number of marital breakups for black families. Given the systematic high rates of unemployment for black men and women and the growing number of black families who are becoming members of the impoverished class, the standard of living for black families has not improved substantially. In addition, the dire economic exigency that black families face has not been a unifying force in keeping families together. The same appears to hold true for white families as well.

Although it may be premature to assess the overall impact of social conservativism on the disintegration of black married-couple families, conservative social policy unequivocally must shoulder responsibility for the growing number of men, women, and children who are without a familial structure. In effect, cuts to federal programs have increased the number of individuals in our society who are categorized as the homeless. According to recent studies conducted on this population, the homeless represent people who for the most part have exhausted both kinship and mutual-aid networks. Afterwards, with limited or no financial resources, the homeless find themselves outside any familial structure. The trend toward deinstitutionalization, which began over twenty years ago, left many individuals, who otherwise would receive institutional support, without an adequate support system. Added to this situation is the welfare revisionists' determination to make even deeper cuts in institutional and community-based programs. Though social conservatives tend to minimize the pervasiveness of this phenomenon, figures for the homeless range from 192,000 to 2.2 million. Many of these individuals were previously members of some type of family arrangement.[32]

More than halfway into the decade of the 1980s, the black family continues to be confronted with severe economic and social problems. For the most part, this return to true conservatism, while failing to halt the decline of black married-couple families, has resulted in an increase of individuals without families and in other social anomalies, all of which are associated with the economic destitution and hopelessness that confront a growing number of black underclass families. However, one aspect of conservative social policy that should not be overlooked is the fact that although not by intent, it has unveiled the myth that the advantages of liberal social policy outweigh the disadvantages. On the other hand, liberal social policy did have definite advantages for some black families. In fact, one can even argue that some black families made advances that are sure to fortify their positions in the middle class. Still, gains made by an inordinate number of black families were temporary. The rescission of liberal social policy indicates that, though the short-term effects of social and economic programs may have had some positive consequences, the long-range effects of liberal social policy must be measured, interpreted, and presented with extreme caution.

Liberal social policy has had devastating consequences for black families and the conservatism of the 1980s has not brought about a dimunition of these problems, but has shifted the government's attention away from the status of black families. The responsibility for identifying strategies to solve the problems confronting black men, women, and children rests almost exclusively on the shoulders of black families, particularly those black families whose middle-class status is more solidly based, either due to intergenerational economic advantage or the nature of their occupational marketability.

NOTES

1. "Reagan's Polarized America," *Newsweek* (April 5, 1982): 17

2. John Naisbitt, *Megatrends: Ten New Directions Transforming our Lives* (New York: Warner Books, 1982), p. 103.

3. Floyd W. Hayes, "The Political Economy, Reaganomics, and Blacks," *Western Journal of Black Studies* 6 (1982): 90.

4. Martin Anderson, *Welfare* (Stanford, California: Hoover Press, 1978), p. 163; "Report of the Department of Health and Human Services before the Subcommittee on Public Assistance and Unemployment Compensation" (June 23, 1982), unpublished report, p. 2.

5. "Life Below the Poverty Line," *Newsweek* (April 5, 1982): 25.

6. "Reagan's Polarized America," *Newsweek* (April 5, 1982): 17–18.

7. Sar A. Levitan and Clifford M. Johnson, *Beyond the Safety Net: Reviving the Promise of Opportunity in America* (Cambridge, Massachusetts: Ballinger Publishing Company, 1984), pp. 74–80.

8. Levitan and Johnson, *Beyond the Safety Net*; "Report of the Department of Health and Human Services," p. 2.

9. *Employment and Training Reporter*, (Washington, D.C.: The Bureau of National Affairs (August 23, 1982), p. 64.

10. "Senate, 93–3, Votes Welfare Revision Mandating Work," *The New York Times* (June 17, 1988): A-1.

11. Manning Marable, "Reaganism, Racism, and Reaction: Black Political Realignment in the 1980's," *Black Scholar* (Fall, 1982): 3.

12. Marable, "Reaganism, Racism, and Reaction," p. 3.

13. Ibid., p. 2.

14. Levitan and Johnson, *Beyond the Safety Net*, p. 43.

15. Marable, "Reaganism, Racism, and Reaction," p. 3.

16. Tom Joe and Cheryl Rogers, *By the Few for the Few: The Reagan Welfare Legacy* (Lexington, Massachusetts: Lexington Books, 1986), p. 116.

17. James W. Vander Zanden, *Sociology: A Systematic Approach* (New York: Ronald Press Company, 1970), pp. 319–320.

18. Levitan and Johnson, *Beyond the Safety Net*, pp. 47–51.

19. George Gilder, *Wealth and Poverty* (New York: Basic Books, 1981), p. 68.

20. Lawrence Mead, *Beyond Entitlement* (New York: Free Press, 1986), p. 1.

21. Charles Murray, *Losing Ground: American Social Policy 1950–1980* (New York: Basic Books, 1984).

22. Bill Barol, "The Eighties Are Over," *Newsweek* (January 4, 1988), p. 44–45.

23. "One Giant Step for Washington," *U.S. News and World Report* (December 23, 1985): 18–19; "Court to Congress: You Cut Budget," *USA Today* (July 8, 1986), p. 1A.

24. Bill Barol, "The Eighties Are Over," p. 44.

25. Harriette Pipes McAdoo, "Black Mothers and the Extended Family Support Network," in La Frances Rodgers-Rose, ed., *The Black Woman* (Beverly Hills, California: Sage Publications, 1980), p. 137–138.

26. James D. McGhee, "The Black Family Today and Tomorrow," *The State of Black America* (New York: National Urban League, 1985), p. 4.

27. McGhee, "The Black Family," p. 4.

28. Bill Alexander, "The Black Church and Community Empowerment," in Robert L. Woodson, ed., *On the Road to Economic Freedom: An Agenda for Black Progress* (Washington, D.C.: The National Center for Neighborhood Enterprise, 1987), pp. 45–69.

29. Alexander, "The Black Church and Community Empowerment," p. 51.

30. David Swinton, "Economic Status of Blacks, 1985," *The State of Black America 1986* (New York: National Urban League, 1986), p. 14.

31. Robert Staples, "Family Life In The 21st Century" (unpublished), pp. 13–14.

32. Dee Roth, Jerry Bean, Nancy Lust, and Traian Saveanu, *Homelessness in Ohio: A Study of People in Need* (Columbus, Ohio: Ohio Department of Mental Health, 1985), p. 1.

8 THE FUTURE OF SOCIAL POLICY AND THE BLACK FAMILY

LEARNING FROM SOCIAL POLICY FAILURES

The formulation of liberal social policy, which led to the development of social and economic programs, is strongly related to the decline of black two-parent families and extended familial structures. Nevertheless, some black families, particularly those among the working and middle classes, were prosperous during the era of liberal social policy. In addition, some black underclass families experienced upward mobility. For the most part, black families already enjoying middle-class status before the 1960s continued to make gains in education and occupational areas. As a consequence, their socioeconomic status became more firmly entrenched and less susceptible to adverse changes in the economy. However, black underclass families felt the brunt of industrial displacement, a downward economic spiral, and ineffective social and economic programs. Although modest gains were made, black families across all social and economic levels have been adversely affected by liberal social policies and the overall impenetrability of societal institutions. What liberal social policy did was raise the hopes and aspirations of black families to a level consistent with that of white middle-class families. What it did not do was improve social and economic conditions throughout society or among black families so that the goals and objectives black families shared with their white counterparts could be realized. In considering the positive and negative effects of liberal social policy, analysts ask the inevitable question (which has been systematically used as a rhetorical pawn by the major political parties): "To what extent did social and economic programs sponsored and funded by the federal government lead to widespread economic dependency?''

The most direct response for which empirical verification exists is that government dependency was created by the social and economic programs and legislation of the 1960s and 1970s. The paradox is that the very efforts designed to promote economic independence for black families were, in many ways, responsible for government dependency for an inordinate number of black families. Typically, when one speaks of government dependency as a function of social and economic programs in the 1960s and 1970s, poor families that were recipients of various forms of public assistance come to mind. But government dependency occurred for other black families, transcending socioeconomic levels. However, this is in no way intended to suggest that liberal social policy was totally ineffective; nor does it imply that all social and economic programs had negative outcomes. Even more important is the realization that the federal government does have and should continue to play a strategic role in developing, mediating, and enforcing social and economic programs.

Although some social and economic programs were detrimental to black families, others could be deemed successful. It is difficult to evaluate the relative effectiveness of various social and economic programs, which were developed and expanded during the 1960s and 1970s, without examining other factors that affected their impact on black families. If we remember that the civil rights movement was responsible for spurring the resurgence of the feminist movement and social activism by other members of society, who, like blacks, urged the redistribution of wealth and power, we can understand how social and economic programs initially designed to elevate the status of black families became somewhat diluted. Though other groups, equally disenfranchised, were certainly warranted in seeking redress for past inequities, the concessions made through liberal social policy initiatives did little more than amass a modicum of resources, which were then divided among these contenders. The result was divisiveness, rather than unity, as blacks, Hispanics, women, and others were made to compete for limited ''set aside'' resources.

The way that contenders for economic and political power were forced to bcome social competitors is evident in the history of one significant piece of legislation enacted during the 1960s. Affirmative action, which has received plaudits from supporters of liberal social policy, only superficially created benefits for black families, while generating relatively more opportunities for others in society.

Employment segmentation, the guise by which institutions responded to affirmative action by making job opportunities available to black men and women, yet positioning them in organizational sectors offering limited opportunities for advancement, has already been examined. In addition, the federal government assumed a significant role in hiring large numbers of blacks; thereby serving as a role model to be emulated by others, especially those within the private domain. Another misconception regarding affirmative action is that it has been construed as having created substantial employment opportunities for blacks within the private sector. As previously cited, Robert Hill's findings refute this contention.[1] Despite the financial incentives offered to employers in the private sector, the government was not able to effectively persuade private industry to hire more blacks. For example, a study conducted by the National Urban League revealed that "a majority of employers refused to hire black youth even if their wages were subsidized."[2] Given the small percentage of blacks working in private enterprise, particularly during the 1960s and 1970s, when the government made such ventures financially attractive through tax credits and the like, there is little doubt that barriers still prevent economic independence for black families. Government dependence caused by limited access to employment in private enterprise is not restricted to blacks whose educational attainment is at the high-school level or below. Blacks with college degrees have also derived relatively few employment benefits from affirmative action programs. They too have had to rely quite heavily on the public sector for job opportunities. Martin Canory noted in 1970 that 79 percent of all black female college graduates and 57 percent of all black male college graduates were employed in the public sector.[3]

Many are quick to argue that the inability of black men and women to gain access to private sector employment is a function of academic preparation in nonmarketable areas, rather than the unwillingness of employers to given previously excluded groups an opportunity to compete. However, though this agument has some validity, it loses its strength when income figures for black male college graduates are compared with those of white male high-school graduates. Herein lies a discrepancy for which educational deficiency or the failure to acquire saleable skills is not a tenable explanation. In 1980, the median income of black male college graduates who worked full-time was $17,861, almost $2,000 less than that of white males who had completed only high school, whose median income was $19,857. Comparatively, the median income for black male college graduates was only 68 percent that of white male college graduates, whose median income was $26,139. Further, black male high-school graduates had an annual median income of $15,658, which was 12 percent less than the median income of black male college graduates. Conversely, the annual median income for white male high-school graduates, was 24 percent lower than that of white male college graduates.[4] Thus, despite educational attainment, which increased for blacks during the era of liberal social policy, black men were unable to achieve economic parity with white men with comparable academic preparation or those whose educational levels were decidedly lower.

Other social and economic programs, intended to enhance the status of black families, also proved to be to their detriment. In terms of family structure, black two-parent and extended families were seriously weakened during this period. Social welfare programs, such as Aid to Families with Dependent Children, resulted in welfare benefits that were higher than earned income at the minimum wage throughout the country. Moreover, gearing programs toward mothers, who typically represent the primary recipient, does little more than create divisiveness

between mothers and fathers in families receiving aid. Social-welfare programs
ignored adult males in the family by developing job training and other benefits
primarily for women and their charges; by failing to consider the occupational
needs of adult male family members, the programs were destined to fail—and
to injure the family in the process. Such programs are antithetical to maintaining
two-parent families because they conflict with societal values, which require
males to be the primary providers of their families. The failure of social and
economic programs to include males was particularly detrimental to black families because black males already experienced high unemployment, caused by
the decline of factory jobs when industries were permanently closed. Though
some argue that a disproportionate percentage of black families receiving welfare
benefits are already maritally disrupted, they overlook the fact that a disproportionate percentage of black families receiving welfare benefits are already maritally disrupted, they overlook the fact that a disproportionate percentage of
lower-income black women heading families are separated rather than divorced.
When marriages have not been legally dissolved, appropriate measures con-
ceivably may reunite the family. This is particularly likely when social-welfare
programs are purposely designed to enable families to attain this objective. Since
a large number of lower-income black families choose separation as the preferred
means of marital dissolution, the importance of social programs that are capable
of strengthening the family unit cannot be overemphasized. In order for these
families to reach a level of economic self-sufficiency, husbands and wives must
acquire and enhance marketable job skills, after which, employment opportunities
must not be disproportionately located within the public sector. Anything short
of a wide range of jobs available in both the public and private sectors only
leads to the perpetuity of government dependency for black families.

Still other programmatic, administrative, and social-psychological factors were
associated with the negative impact of social-welfare programs on black two-
parent families. Despite attempts to project positive images that social-welfare
services were acceptable and that black families who were recipients of such
services had an inalienable right to these entitlements, to make up for past social
injustices, these programs continued to be cast in a negative light. While some
of the stigma may have been assuaged due to the liberal nature of the era, social-
welfare services such as food stamps, AFDC, and other programs not provided
to members of society at large, were never free of public contempt. Perhaps this
is one reason the receipt of social-welfare services continues to be perceived as
a temporary emergency measure. It is in this light that, in the past, welfare was
more commonly referred to as "relief."

The dismantling of black extended families had both a philosophical and social
basis. In the latter case, housing subsidies, social security, pension benefits and,
equally important, an emphasis on independent living in our society all contributed to the decline of black extended families over the last twenty-five years.
This decrease is significant when one considers the importance of families con-
solidating limited assets, whether in the form of financial, social, or psychological

resources. Other ethnic minorities entering the United States have commonly pooled their meager resources and engaged in other forms of cooperative behavior until they have established a pattern of intergenerational affluence.

Later, these same groups have altered the family structure to form more independent family units, while maintaining strong kinship networks. However, social and economic factors, in the 1960s and 1970s, resulted in the premature disruption of black extended families. The support offered by extended families cannot be underestimated, particularly when such families contained an older adult relative. Given that in the majority of black two-parent families both the husband and wife are employed outside the home, the extended family has offered relief in the form of child care, cooking and other domestic tasks, and emotional nurturance. The absence of this support frequently results in role strain and later in marital conflict. Although the black extended family, exemplary of the most rudimentary form of strong kinship bonds, was altered, the viability of other kinds of kinship and informal support systems, which have also been the foundation for progress among black families, were also challenged. Both extended families and kinship networks have been viewed by the larger society as impediments to upward mobility for black families. However, as McAdoo states, these support systems are important to black families.[5] Furthermore, she asserts that for black families to experience intergenerational progress, they must continue to support others within their families. Extended family structures and other black kinship support systems enable this type of intrafamilial sharing and mutual cooperation. Further, the absence of communal responsibility is likely to result in each new generation of blacks starting anew, without the benefit of resources that tend to guarantee social advancement. Thus, liberal social policy contributed significantly to the alteration of a process that has contributed favorably to the success of other racial and ethnic minorities.

Conservative social policy, which has been largely responsible for the gradual resurfacing of extended families and other forms of kinship and mutual-aid networks, should not be viewed any more favorably than liberal social policy, which led to their decline. While the reemergence of these structures is fundamental to the progress of black families, the dire economic conditions that engender the proliferation of these family arrangements militate against their effectiveness.[6] Social forces still make their functioning less than optimal. Inexorable problems confront black families. As in the past, black kinship networks, including extended families, must provide basic goods and services, while meeting the growing needs of members. Since these structures have become inextricably infused into the broader society, black families and self-help groups are now confronted with adapting to cultural values—which stress autonomy, competitiveness, individualism, and social isolation—once found primarily in the larger society, that are now a part of the black cultural ethos. This has placed added strain on the black extended family, kinship, and mutual-aid networks. In the future, how well or poorly extent black extended families and informal social-support systems function will depend on their ability to reestablish and strengthen relations with more economically advantaged black families, other racial and ethnic minorities, and whites who are willing to provide opportunities that will lead to increased participation in the private sector. Helping networks in the black community should also look to the federal government for support to resolve social and economic crises facing black families. But the nature of support, short- and long-term objectives, and the parameters of the federal government's involvement must be carefully defined. Simultaneously, the extent to which various family and community structures are beneficial to black families, irrespective of their usefulness in the community at large, is an issue that must be resolved among black intellectuals and black families in general. While autonomy, individualism, competition, and traditional nuclear families may be perceived as essential for majority families, these factors are adversely related to economic mobility of black families.

The overall effect of liberal social policy was to undermine black two-parent and extended family structures as well as to foster a plethora of other problems. However, not all aspects of liberal social policy were destructive. To the contrary, several programs helped black families. Had this not been the case, black families and their members would not have achieved the social and economic gains presented earlier. The progress made by black families is evidence that there are salvageable components of liberal social and economic programs, which, if adapted, can be utilized today to enable black families to secure economic independence. The success of social and economic initiatives in the 1960s and 1970s tended to be limited to younger members of black families. Of the advances made by black families over the last twenty years, the areas where significant progress was made, and for which retrogression in the 1980s has been minimal, are education, infant and maternal mortality, and nutrition. The latter two are related to improved medical and health care, which suggests that Medicaid has also had positive implications for the survival of black families and their members. However, Medicaid, due to its optional nature, was not uniformly incorporated in social-welfare service delivery in all states. Other programs that played a critical role in black family progress were Headstart, educational grants and loans, nutrition programs such as Women, Infants, and Children (WIC), and the Job Corps. This is not to say that other programs and legislation have not resulted in success for some black families in America.

Much of the progress which black families made during the era of liberal social policy was conditional and nongeneric, and it was not sustained in the 1980s. Numerous reasons have been offered to explain the shortcomings of liberal social policy. Many believe that social and economic programs were too narrow in focus. Others maintain that they ended too soon. Still others attribute their lack of effectiveness to the small percentage of money allocated, relative to the total federal budget. Some place the blame on inefficient and insensitive state and local government administrations. While the list of problems which contributed to the failure of liberal social policy is long, there is growing concensus in many circles, and not simply among political conservatives, that social and economic programs created more problems in the long term than they resolved.

This judgment, however, is not an indictment against liberal social policy as we have defined it, in which the government accepts its obligation to ensure that all citizens are guaranteed an equal opportunity to participate in societal institutions. What I am suggesting is that in order for social and economic programs to be truly effective and to meet desired goals and objectives, certain fundamental assumptions and policy directives must be integral to these goals and objectives. Ideally, social policy should be removed from the realm of partisan politics. To do otherwise confounds any attempt to address the needs of poor and black families. Clearly, the political nature of social policy lends itself to a cyclical process. Accordingly we move from individual to community responsibility and back. Further, when social policy relates to black families, a greater degree of complexity surrounds its formulation and implementation. Much of this is due to the necessity for resolving both contemporary problems and historical ones. Because slavery and subsequent events had disenfranchised black men, women, and children, liberal social policy was expected to provide remedies for past injustices as well as to ameliorate ongoing social and economic conditions. The fact that liberal social policy, as defined and formulated in the United States, has been ineffectual in no way vindicates political conservatives who claim that social policy must not interfere with free-market forces. While a disproportionate percentage of black two-parent families before the advent of liberal social policy remained intact, these families, although together in what approximated a nuclear family, did not enjoy the same material privileges as did their white counterparts. Neither liberal nor conservative social policy has successfully elevated large numbers of black families to a solid position of financial comfort. In the case of the former, many problems evolved primarily because the nature, magnitude, and projected success of the federal government's involvement raised expectations among black families that proved to be unattainable, given the realistic parameters of liberal social policy and ingrained systems designed to maintain the status quo. Moreover, liberalism created illusions of progress and gains that were only spuriously related to those achieved through open-market competition. Furthermore, liberal social policy dictated that certain cultural value systems be discarded so that black families could be totally integrated in all spheres of society. A related requirement was that macrocultural systems and ideals replace microcultural ones, such as extended families, the black church, and mutual-aid networks. Finally, if liberal social policy had not operated from the social inadequacy thesis, existing black structures and their inherent dynamics would have been preserved, because they would have been perceived as having utility.

Liberal social policy did not have to take this course. Other avenues for the development and administration of social and economic programs would have worked better. More than any other factor, intransigence in the formulation of social policy is responsible for the extreme forms that social policy has taken.

If social policy were not so highly politicized, a dialectic would not exist in which social policy becomes an either-or proposition. Moreover, if social policy is to be effective it must be supported by objective scientific investigation and should be developed on the basis of the strengths and not weaknesses of earlier efforts. Given the abundance of evidence regarding the outcome of various programs and government interventions, the impact of social policy is no longer capricious. While I do not pretend to know all of the interrelationships between various programs, recipients, cultural backgrounds, and the like, a substantial quantity of data has been amassed and analyzed that can direct the formulation of an effective social policy. For example, few would disagree that various grants-in-aid to college-bound youth would enlarge the pool of college graduates, or that an ancillary service, such as child care, would facilitate skill acquisition or refinement for a mother who is a recipient of AFDC. It would also be difficult to take issue with the beneficence of dual career planning for intact black families, whose adult members are likely to experience unemployment and underemployment by virtue of their race, gender, and membership in the underclass. While the most ardent proponent of conservative social policy would probably concede that these measures are in the interest of economically disadvantaged families, other areas are not as clear-cut. For example, controversy and inconclusiveness continue to abound when attention focuses on the efficaciousness of guaranteed minimum incomes.[7] Relying on scientific inquiry does little to provide answers, as the findings of research conducted in this area have yielded conflicting data. Nonetheless, there remain social problems, which have systematically confronted black families, for which specific policy and programmatic direction is available. What is lacking is agreement over one fundamental social-policy issue. This concern is related to who is responsible for offering correctives for the plight of black American families. Social policy has differed significantly depending on the political climate. The answer to this question has in the past rarely been agreed on.

Whether liberals or conservatives are in a decision-making position, there has usually been either implicit or explicit agreement that the onus for the economically depressed status of black families lies with the families and not the larger society. Although both liberals and conservatives tend to deny that structural factors play a significant role in prolonging economic dependence for black families, advocates of liberal social policy have been willing to permit the federal government to assume an integral role in ameliorating these conditions. While conservatives, like their liberal counterparts, blame black families, conservative policy-makers believe that, since the government is not to blame, it has no obligation to discharge. Therefore, conservatives expect black families to find solutions to their own problems, rather than looking to the federal government for assistance. Ultimately, black families get tossed from one side to the other. On the one hand, they are expected to look to a federal government that assumes a paternalistic posture. Later, when welfare revisionists enact a new set of policies, the approach becomes more punitive. In effect, what occurs relative to the push-pull cycle of social policy is a situation akin to the period following the Civil War. Essentially, in the Compromise of 1877, Rutherford B. Hayes promised to withdraw the federal troops, which had been sent to the South to ensure civil liberties for newly freed blacks, in exchange for Southern Democratic support. At that time, the removal of federal troops resulted in losses for black families both in terms of civil liberties and life. The partisan nature of social policy has resulted in history repeating itself as the "troops," which are tantamount to the federal government's monitoring and enforcing civil rights for blacks and other disenfranchised groups, are cyclically dispatched by liberals and withdrawn by conservatives. Hence, an unspoken compromise continues to affect the status of black families with regard to social policy.

TOWARD A VIABLE SOCIAL POLICY FOR BLACK FAMILIES: SOME CONSIDERATIONS

In order for social policy to be effective the following must be engaged:

1. Specific roles to be assumed by major institutions and segments of the population must be clearly delineated.
2. An understanding and agreement as to what constitutes success and failure for social and economic programs must be developed.
3. Groundrules must be formulated which reflect clear-cut goals and objectives within a reasonably established time frame.
4. Social policy must build on the strengths of extant black families and other institutions and structures within the black community.
5. Strategies for expanding the participation of blacks in institutions in the black community and within the larger society should be identified.
6. A reassessment of traditional and contemporary value orientations within the contexts of the larger society and the black community should create a synthesis that will serve as a moral imperative for black families.
7. New venues must be created for the national dissemination of key information, on legislation, social, economic, and political events occurring on local, regional, and national levels, which are critical to the survival and progress of black families.

Institutional Responsibility

Clearly, while micro systems within the black community must play a major role in efforts to elevate the social and economic status of black men, women, and children, institutions in the larger society that impact upon the lives of black families must also make a commitment to ensure that constructive change occurs.

In the past, the government's involvement in social-service delivery did not move beyond legislating that institutions ensure the civil rights of blacks. Even in this regard, as Derrick Bell so cogently asserts, laws passed during the 1960s and 1970s were inadequate to protect blacks and provide civil rights for them collectively.[8] Handling matters of racial discrimination on an individual rather than a systematic basis represents a less than suitable method of remedying past injustices and curbing invidious social inequities. Moreover, as Bell suggests, the mere fact that in our society the burden of proof lies with the victim, makes eradicating racial discrimination an arduous task. That blacks are faced with proving not only de facto but de jure segregation only confounds the issue of seeking redress for the purpose of ameliorating social and economic conditions for black families. And when one considers the economic constraints of the majority of black families, challenging racial discrimination, whether in housing or employment, is a difficult undertaking at best. Even for those willing to persevere, individual efforts to obtain the equal treatment necessary to enhance their life chances are a highly uncertain endeavor, the outcome of which, even if positive, in no way guarantees that others are any less likely to experience the same treatment.

Given past experience, changing societal institutions requires considerably more than the type of legislation passed during the 1960s and 1970s. Laws must go beyond mandating that rudimentary principles of fairness be met; they must also serve as an edict that the equitable treatment of blacks and other racial and ethnic minorities should occur on a systematic basis. Thus, any evidence of a violation of an individual's civil rights should warrant intense scrutiny to prevent further unfair treatment of minorities. When civil rights violations are proved, penalties should entail substantially more than monetary forms of retribution. The violators should demonstrate through a long-range plan how they will safeguard the rights of minorities.

Laws alone cannot accomplish the eradication of barriers that make upward mobility difficult for black families. Therefore, in conjunction with legislation, members of racial and ethnic minorities must use networks to coordinate their efforts to provide critical information to their members regarding ways to access various institutions. Members of networks internal to various institutions and organizations must gather information regarding institutional needs and goals. This information must be channeled through external networks and disseminated on a local level. Individuals with institutional affiliations must collectively develop methods to encourage greater institutional responsibility and to serve as a conduit for providing valuable information to black families and others outside of the economic mainstream. This form of networking will facilitate greater access to these structures.

Measuring Success

One major flaw in liberal social policy was the amorphous nature of its goals. With the broad goal of eradicating poverty, disagreement over the extent to which social and economic programs were successful is understandable. However, quantitative measures alone are no reliable indicator of the overall effectiveness of these efforts. For example, the number of families in poverty before the government's expanded role in the delivery of social services, compared to the number in poverty at the end of the 1970s, reveals an overall decrease in poverty. However, considerable disagreement continues to exist over whether this decrease should be interpreted as constituting success. In this regard, the issue is whether the goal of alleviating poverty should have been more clearly defined. In other words, is the fact that fewer families had incomes below the poverty level, more than twenty years after poverty programs were implemented, a real measure of the effectiveness of liberal social policy? Or should we take into account the inordinate number of families whose incomes hover just above this arbitrary figure? When we consider the inordinate number of families, particularly black families, who make up the working poor, with incomes slightly above the government-established poverty level, can we say that liberal social policy was effective? Clearly, if social and economic programs in the 1960s and 1970s were intended to bring economically disadvantaged families, in which blacks were overrepresented, to a position where they could enjoy the same material privileges as mainstream families, then liberal social policy was a failure.

Moreover, the absence of short-term goals and objectives made it difficult to determine the effectiveness of certain policies and administrative practices. Thus, programs were permitted to continue relatively unchanged because administrators were left with the task of defining success. In some instances, where decisions of this nature were made internally, one obvious inclination was to maintain programs that were of dubious benefit simply to justify the organization's existence. Therefore, the jobs of service providers were secured at the expense of effecting changes that would have eliminated the program. In addition, establishing short-term, measurable goals is not synonymous with the all too frequent method of measuring program success annually, based on the number of recipients the program or agency serves.

Admittedly, the number of individuals who benefit from diverse services is an important indicator of the capacity of a program to reach those in need. However, quantitative figures that reflect the scope of service delivery should not be interpreted as a measure of success. What is equally important is not merely how many individuals receive a service but the effect which the program has on enhancing the overall status and level of functioning of an individual or group. For example, an increase in the number of blacks receiving educational grants and loans is likely to increase the enrollment of blacks in institutions of higher education but may do little to reduce other barriers that preclude blacks from graduating. In this regard, a number of interrelated goals should be established and measured independently and interdependently to determine the overall impact of educational programs designed to increase the number of blacks who are admitted to and expected to graduate from colleges and universities. All social and economic programs must be developed with agreement relative to what constitutes favorable outcomes. This agreement should take place between policy-makers, administrators, and program participants. In this decision-making process, academicians and others with a history of involvement in and knowledge of social and economic programs should play a key advisory role.

Previous social policies designed to improve the status of black families have been formulated and implemented as though they would last forever. Accordingly, their sponsors have assumed that social and economic programs would be available at optimal levels until the economic status of blacks and poor families in America indicated that the need no longer existed. Such an open-ended approach to effecting social equity is unrealistic and does not allow for the integration of criteria to measure success during various stages of service delivery. Moreover, this method of formulating and administering social and economic programs generates cultural anxiety among program participants, as well as the general public. In addition, the unpredictable duration of social and economic programs makes participants and members of society at large subject to political manipulation. In essence, politicians have been given a free rein to play on the fears and desires of both advocates and opponents of liberal social programs. Establishing concise, time-specific goals is clearly a more tenable and viable way of bringing about needed social change for black families.

Building on the Strengths

Future attempts to develop a social policy capable of elevating the status of black families should embrace the assumption that black families and institutions within the black community are composed of disparate structures which represent adaptations for survival. And like other institutions throughout society, they possess positive as well as negative qualities. If social and economic initiatives are to be effectual, the strengths of institutions in the black community must be recognized, enhanced, and integrated into those efforts. Perhaps the most glaring error in the past was the generalization by policy-makers—with substantiation from select scholars—of social problems affecting subpopulations of blacks to black families in general. Ignoring invaluable strengths and deemphasizing survival strategies employed by black families, the black church, black-owned businesses, and black schools served to attenuate positive advances for black families. Furthermore, this narrow, ethnocentric approach to liberal social policy contributed to the decline of those institutions that before the 1960s, had been responsible for black social and economic progress.

There is sufficient evidence that ethnic and racial minorities that have advanced to a position of economic power have done so in part through group solidarity and cooperation.[9] Moreover, they have become integrated on an economic level but have retained a strong sense of cultural identity and pride.[10] Black leaders involved in the civil rights movement in the 1960s were aware of the importance of black families' acknowledging and maintaining a sense of commonality of interests. Because of this, they placed emphasis on the strengths of black families. Historical images, which depicted blacks as intellectually and culturally inferior, were discarded and replaced with positive imagery of black men, women, and children.[11]

It is difficult to conceive of a social policy that can significantly improve the status of black families that does not utilize existing resources in the black community. Considering that the black church continues to be the most economically wealthy and independent institution in the black community, any social policy designed to help black families that does not give the black church a central role is inconceivable and likely to meet with failure. There are an estimated 65,000 black churches in America with an estimated worth of over $10 billion—strong evidence of the salient role of the black church.[12] Moreover, the familiarity of the black church with social and economic spheres means that the black church can provide guidance and direction in the area of black economic development. Many black leaders have emerged from the ministerial ranks of black churches, such as the Reverends Adam Clayton Powell, Martin Luther King, Jesse Jackson, Andrew Young, U.S. Congressman William Gray III, to name a few, suggesting that black churches are equally equipped to produce those who are adept and participatory in the political process.[13]

Dual Cultural Participation

One major factor, which can lead to either the success or failure of social and economic programs, is the need to develop a working relationship between members of the black community and those within the larger society. That need can be filled by a commission, which would develop, monitor, and recommend changes in social programs. Because this ongoing relationship between these segments of the population is needed on a local, regional, and national level, such an aggregate would take on a tiered configuration. Mutual understanding and respect for both micro and macro systems is vital to the outcome of social and economic programs. An established body of representatives from government, the private sector, academia, the black church, other segments of the black community, and the population at large is not a novel concept. However, such a group now has a wealth of knowledge on which to draw. This information was virtually unavailable in the 1960s and 1970s when similar associations were formed. One factor that would differentiate any future eclectic organization, like the one I have described, is the imperative that they be convened before the formulation of social policy. To do otherwise is likely to result in a lack of the ownership and commitment essential for a body charged with overseeing and providing ongoing input into the policies and practices of social and economic programs.

An important function of an association of individuals from various institutions throughout society is determining strategies that can be employed in conjunction with legislation to increase the involvement of blacks in institutions within the black community as well as in the larger society. And while it may appear to be an easy task to increase the participation of blacks in the black community, there is copious evidence to suggest the contrary is true. For example, a disproportionate amount of the black consumer dollar is spent outside the black community.[14] Specifically, there is evidence which indicates that the transference of black consumer dollars outside the black community increased rather than decreased during the era of liberal social policy. In 1985 black-owned companies received only 7 percent of the total $180 billion spent by blacks, compared to the 13.5 percent of blacks' income that these firms received in 1969. One reason black families spend so little of their income in the black community is economic expediency. For example, in the consumption of foodstuffs, larger supermarket chains are better able to compete successfully for these dollars than are smaller black-owned groceries. In many areas of consumerism, the 1960s and 1970s brought the realization to major white-controlled businesses that black consumers represented a captive, yet untapped, market. At the same time, desegregation and the eradication of Jim Crow laws facilitated black consumerism in areas that had earlier been forbidden. Another example is that of white-owned corporations which began to vigorously pursue black consumer dollars for hair care, cosmetics, and similar products, which had been provided almost exclusively by black-owned companies.

The psychological implications of consumer spending, which have been scientifically determined and reflected in the billions of dollars spent annually in advertising, have a definite effect on how and when consumerism occurs. The inability of black-owned businesses to afford the exorbitant costs of advertising their products and services decreases their visibility and reduces the likelihood that their businesses will prosper. Furthermore, the extent to which larger numbers of blacks become patrons is reduced because of the relative inconspicuousness of black businesses and the absence of legitimation created by the media. The fact that black-owned businesses are not able to successfully compete for black consumer dollars results in an economic drain on the black community. This is particularly true since these businesses, along with underclass black families, tend to coexist in the same residential innercity areas. Because of the complexity of the problem of expanding black involvement in black-controlled institutions, the massive injection of money alone, without a carefully developed plan, will not suffice. Still, in no way is this intended, nor does it begin, to speak to the importance of increasing white consumers' patronage of black-owned businesses.

Increasing the level of black participation in major institutions throughout society must also be adequately resolved if social policy is to be truly effective. Overcoming institutional racial discrimination, which is at the root of the problem, is more difficult to solve. In order to ensure that both the public and private sectors establish and adhere to policies that will increase black participation throughout entire agencies, corporations, and organizations, there must be a nonpartisan commission. Disputes that cannot be settled by this commission would, out of necessity, be referred to the judicial system. However, we must bear in mind that neither the government nor commissions can maintain effective control over privately controlled industry by permitting voluntary compliance with policy directives. The fact that monetary incentives have been unsuccessful is evidence that the private sector, because of its financial independence, is not eager to comply with government edicts or persuasion if they have a choice. Government intervention on a national level can increase opportunities that will enable blacks to acquire marketable skills, but enforcement is essential to assure that blacks are represented in all areas of industry, particularly in mid- and upper-management positions.

When deficits exist within certain occupations, they are eventually filled. To do so, public and private organizations make funds available for individuals to receive academic or vocational preparation in areas where there are shortages. When this occurs, enough individuals become qualified to assume various positions, generally within a projected time frame. The same principle can be applied when there is a paucity of blacks in specific occupational categories. In these cases, it is not sufficient for administrators and managers to argue that qualified blacks are not available without exploring measures to increase their supply. Granted, although this is no short-term solution, it is clearly an option with long-term consequences.

In no way are these recommendations intended to correct all of the deficiencies inherent in social policy. Rather, they are presented as a guide to the careful formulation of social policy. Previous efforts clearly indicate that the formulation of social policy need not be characterized by trial and error. Thus, one facet of social policy, which must be taken into account, is that it cannot be effectively established by any one individual but takes the careful planning of many. Again, actual formulation and planning should remain outside the realm of politics if social policy is to positively affect black families and others seeking economic stability.

It is also imperative that the federal government occupy a position that will promote social justice and at the same time prevent government dependency. Since there is no evidence that the government is able or willing to maintain increased levels of spending, monitoring, and enforcement ad infinitum, it is reasonable to assume that unless the government carefully elucidates the nature, scope, and duration of its involvement, the outcome is likely to be of greater detriment than benefit to black families.

Synthesizing Cultural Values

The current level of ambiguity and confusion, which exists throughout society, relative to redefining norms and values, is also prevalent throughout the black community. Black families, like their white counterparts, are also affected by uncertainty surrounding what constitutes acceptable gender-role definitions. The lack of consensus regarding appropriate role behavior for husbands, wives, and children, is apparent in efforts to determine which cultural values, normative within the larger society, are beneficial to the upward mobility of black families.

Historically, black children were socialized into two cultures, which in some ways were similar. Policy-makers and others whose views were represented by the normative paradigm insisted that black families wishing to achieve had to adopt mainstream values and norms. As a consequence, increased numbers of blacks who gained entrance into societal institutions were expected to discard cultural values and to replace them with those of the majority culture. Moreover, the growing number of schools that underwent desegregation and the increased availability of the electronic media exposed a larger percentage of blacks to competing socializing agents. On one hand black, parents and kin emphasized black cultural values and norms, while schools, employers, and the media transmitted a cultural orientation that often is in direct conflict with that inherent in the black community. During the 1960s values and norms within the larger society were collectively challenged. Before the culmination of this period of liberalism, black values and norms were also expected to change. Policy-makers and controllers of social institutions were usually included among those who believed it was no longer expedient for black families to juxtapose their values and norms with those of the majority culture.

It has become apparent that certain values and norms within both cultural systems will increase the level of participation of black families and their members in the larger society as well as in the black community. Black families should retain the values that increase their overall levels of functioning without impairing or diminishing effectiveness in either sphere. Since it is not plausible to assume that black families, or any families, should or could return to a bygone era, what is needed is a synthesis of values, norms, and behaviors that reflect the essentials of both cultures.

If the stability of black families is to be enhanced and poverty and its concomitants are to be reduced, one of the most important values that must be retained is the black family's propensity for interdependent relationships. The values of cooperative collectivism must take precedence over that of individualism, regardless of the purported benefits attributed to the latter. The importance of collectivism versus individualism exists not only on a short-term basis but has long-range implications for social and economic progress for black families. As Harriette McAdoo has noted, unlike majority families, in black families each successive generation must start anew.[15] Usually black families are unable to leave their offspring with the financial, material, and other critical resources that are necessary to give youth an edge on ascending the socioeconomic ladder. In order to effect a cultural synthesis in which salient norms, values, and behaviors are merged, the black church must serve as the initiator and vehicle for spreading emergent norms and values.

Because the 1960s encouraged the expression of divergent beliefs regarding individual rights versus institutional conformity, individuals can choose between numerous views. Consequently, irrespective of the belief system to which one subscribes or the behaviors that one exhibits, there is usually a segment of the population that will lend its support. This is particularly detrimental to youth, who are in need of specific guidelines for behavior. In addition, the multiplicity of prevailing values and beliefs means there are many role models for youth to emulate. In this regard, the black church and other established black organizations such as the National Urban League and the National Association for the Advancement of Colored People (NAACP), must establish prescribed patterns of behavior, norms, and values, for black families and their members. Activities such as these have already been undertaken by the National Urban League in their efforts to reduce out-of-wedlock births among black adolescents.

The Black Media: Bridging the Information Gap

In order for social policy and other social, political, and economic events within the black community and the larger society to positively affect black families, there must be a medium that will systematically transmit information to blacks throughout the country. Throughout the country, black-owned and black-oriented newspapers contain information primarily regarding local or at best regional activities. In many of these publications, information on national activities tends to appear in the form of editorials and commentaries. Although there are regional and national editions for specific black-oriented newspapers, generally they are not available throughout the country without subscription. For more than forty years, however, blacks have relied on *Jet* and *Ebony*, two major black-oriented magazines, for national news and events.[16] While these publications have bridged the information gap for blacks residing in different regions of the country, the emphasis today is moving in the direction of the electronic media, particularly television. As such, television is a preferred medium for the majority of families in the United States. The same holds true for black families. In fact, studies reflect that a greater percentage of the black population views television than whites.[17] Several nationally syndicated, black-oriented television programs are needed to provide news and commentary on social, political, and economic events. While such programs have been broadcast for years, generally they have been available only through cable networks, which are not as accessible as the major networks.

Many activities necessary to redefine and replace current and previous forms of social-welfare policy are already underway. The major problem with welfare reform in the 1980s is that it is extremely fragmented. The federal government's affinity for decentralization has led to states' wielding greater influence over social programs. Still there is evidence that efforts are being pursued by some states to reduce the welfare rolls, while simultaneously increasing black and poor families' economic independence. But reducing caseloads without enhancing black and poor families' standard of living only reinforces the vicious cycle of poverty. In response to this problem, the state of Massachusetts encourages families who are recipients of welfare to enroll in an employment and training program. In this program the state of Massachusetts assumes responsibility for support services such as child care, transportation, and training costs. These programs, when compared to conservative ones, which mandate that recipients of public assistance participate in workfare, claim to have more success. The extent of their long-term effectiveness remains to be measured.

The success of any one program is inextricably related to the effectiveness of national social and economic programs. Given that regional differences exist in the level of support that states allocate to social-welfare services, the problem of poverty and its prevalence among black families requires national attention. One state may put forth a valiant effort to alleviate poverty among its residents, while another may choose to ignore the problem of underclass families. Although a state such as Massachusetts is to be commended for establishing employment and training programs that offer ancillary services, problems affecting poor and black families have reached a level of complexity that make it necessary that they be addressed through a national social policy. And, in some cases, a reduction in the number of families on welfare may take place. However, although states may lower the number of recipients eligible for public assistance, such figures are likely to be misleading, as individuals have been forced off welfare because of regional and local social policies and practices. Something as simplistic as redefining the means test can eliminate a large number of families from the welfare rolls. Likewise, providing job training for welfare recipients to enter entry-level jobs, which pay minimum wage, may reduce the welfare rolls. But such a reduction is equally deceptive, temporary in nature, and does little to enchance the economic status of underclass families or their members.

Another government-initiated effort involves the private sector in addressing the needs of the urban poor, among whom blacks are overrepresented. Legislation enacted in San Francisco, New York, and Boston requires that residential developers build or rehabilitate housing for the poor or pay into a low-income housing trust fund. Although there is regional variability regarding the actual requirements of the plan, specifically, it requires developers who build or rehabilitate ten housing units outside the inner city to earmark 20 percent of them for low-income housing. In addition, as an alternative to building low-income housing units or paying into the fund, developers have the option of rehabilitating low-income properties to meet the 20 percent criterion.[18]

Clearly, social policy must assume a multifaceted approach to eradicate the social problems poor and black families encounter. However, past methods have been relatively ineffective in reducing poverty or alleviating racial discrimination. Moreover, the failure of black families to become economically independent can be attributed to the absence of a sound social policy void of political interests.

CONCLUSION

A definite relationship exists between social policy and family structure. Given the dynamics and structures of institutions within the black community and the erroneous assumptions that have given rise to both conservative and liberal social policy, it is no surprise that the response of policy-makers in the 1960s was designed to offer a proactive institutional response for replacing systems considered weak and ineffective with systems perceived as more efficacious. Not only has liberal social policy failed to bring about social equity, it has served as the impetus for the decline of salient black structures. Included among black institutions that have shown signs of strain and erosion are black two-parent families, extended families, black-controlled educational institutions, and black-owned businesses. The return to conservative policy in the 1980s has resulted in the resurgence of extended families, an increase in individuals with no familial structures, and the failure to abate the increase in the rate of black family break-ups.

I conclude that neither conservative nor liberal social policy as formulated and enacted in the United States has offered substantial or sustained benefits for black families. However, as in the case of liberal social policy, conservative social policy is not without some benefits. For example, conservative social policy in the 1980s has served to revitalize black institutions, which are essential for black progress. However, to the extent that conservative social policy has merit, it is not because of intent but effect. Analyzing the effects of liberal social policy on black families is important to understanding its mystifying and enigmatic nature. The fact that liberal social policy contributed to many adverse changes which were overshadowed by modest gains is reason for concern. In the case of conservatism, its effects on black families, in terms of institutional exclusivity and rigidity, are overt. However, the unforeseen and subtle consequences of liberal social policy have an effect that is also devastating to the stability of black families.

What we have gained from these experiences is a better understanding of the impact social and economic forces have on black families and their members. Moreover, black intellectuals, politicians, administrators, and leaders are more keenly aware of the measures that must be taken by the black community and those that government and the private sector must take to bring about positive changes for black families. There is little doubt that the wealth of knowledge gained over the past thirty years will have an indelible influence on the relationships between black institutions, government, and the private sector.

Despite the dire social and economic conditions in the 1980s and the failure of liberal social policy (considered a bastion of hope by many), blacks continue to strive to identify and develop means to strengthen the family and other institutions, demonstrating that black families have the will to survive. Indeed, black families, historically, have never occupied a position of passivity, but have been active agents influencing social policy to bring about change. Nevertheless, the extent to which black families are able to reach social and economic parity with white families in America will not be determined by their efforts alone, but will come through a national social policy that reflects a total commitment on the part of the black community, the federal government, and the private sector.

NOTES

1. Robert Hill, "The 80's: What's Ahead for Blacks?" *Ebony* (January, 1980): 27–36.

2. Dennys Vaughn-Cooke, "The Economic Status of Black America—Is There A Recovery?" *The State of Black America* (Washington, D.C.: National Urban League, 1984), p. 10.

3. Ibid, p. 10.

4. Ibid, p. 13.

5. Harriette Pipes McAdoo, "Patterns of Upward Mobility In Black Families," in Harriette Pipes McAdoo, ed., *Black Families* (Beverly Hills, California: Sage, 1982), p. 156.

6. United States Bureau of the Census, *Statistical Abstract of the United States, National Data Book and Guide to Sources*, 106th Edition (Washington, D.C.: U.S. Government Printing Office, 1986), p. 39.

7. Michael T. Hannan and Nancy Brandon Tuma, "Income and Marital Events: Evidence from an Income Maintenance Experiment," *American Journal of Sociology* 82 (May, 1977): 1186–1211.

8. Derrick A. Bell, *Race, Racism and American Law* (Boston: Little, Brown, and Co., 1980), pp. 44–47, 393–395.

9. Thomas Sowell, *The Economics and Politics of Race* (New York: William Morrow and Company, 1983), p. 17.

10. K. Sue Jewell, "Will the Real Black, Afro-American, Mixed, Colored, Negro Please Stand Up? Impact of the Black Social Movement, Twenty Years Later," *Journal of Black Studies* 16 (September 1985): 59–62.

11. Karen Sue Warren Jewell, "An Analysis of the Visual Develoment of a Stereotype: The Media's Portrayal of Mammy and Aunt Jemima as Symbols of Black Womanhood" (Unpublished Ph.D. Diss. Ohio State University, 1976), p. 136; K. Sue Jewell, "Black Male/Female Conflict: Internalization of Negative Definitions Transmitted through Imagery," *The Western Journal of Black Studies* 7 (Spring 1983): 43–48.

12. Bill Alexander, "The Black Church and Community Empowerment," in Robert L. Woodson, ed. *On the Road to Economic Freedom: An Agenda for Black Progress* (Washington, D.C.: National Center for Neighborhood Enterprise, 1987), pp. 45–69.

13. Thad Martin, "The Black Church: Precinct of the Black Soul," *Ebony* (August, 1984): 156.

14. Tony Brown, "The Freedom Philosophy," *Tony Brown's Journal* (October, 1985): 3–8.

15. McAdoo, "Patterns of Upward Mobility," p. 156.

16. "1984 *Black Enterprise's* Top 100 Black Businesses," *Black Enterprise* (June, 1985): 87–105; Robert L. Woodson, "A Legacy of Entrepreneurship," in Robert L. Woodson, ed., *On the Road to Economic Freedom: An Agenda for Black Progress* (Washington, D.C.: National Center for Neighborhood Enterprise, 1987), pp. 1–26.

17. J. Fred MacDonald, *Blacks and White T.V.: Afro-Americans in Television Since 1948* (Chicago: Nelson Hall, 1983).

18. "City May Order Housing for Poor," *Columbus Dispatch* (March 28, 1986), p. 1A.

APPENDIX

Table 1
Households and Families, by Race of Householder: 1960 to 1984

[As of March, Based on Current Population Survey. See Historical Statistics, Colonial Times to 1970, series A-292-295 and A 320-334]

RACE OF HOUSEHOLDER	NUMBER (1,000)					PERCENT				
	1960	1970	1975	1980	1984	1960	1970	1975	1980	1984
Households, total	52,799	[1]63,401	[1]71,120	[1]80,776	[1]85,407	(X)	(X)	(X)	(X)	(X)
White	47,665	56,602	62,945	70,768	74,376	100.0	100.0	100.0	100.0	100.0
Married couple [2]	36,175	41,029	42,951	44,751	45,529	76.2	72.5	68.2	63.2	61.2
Male householder [2]	3,365	4,444	6,295	8,940	9,948	6.8	7.9	10.0	12.6	13.4
Female householder [2]	8,125	11,129	13,700	17,075	18,899	17.0	19.7	21.8	24.1	25.4
Black	5,134	6,223	7,262	8,586	9,236	[3]100.0	100.0	100.0	100.0	100.0
Married couple [2]	3,079	3,317	3,343	3,433	3,446	[3]60.3	53.3	46.0	40.0	37.3
Male householder [2]	579	745	1,002	1,402	1,563	[3]11.0	12.0	13.8	16.3	16.9
Female householder [2]	1,476	2,161	2,917	3,751	4,227	[3]28.7	34.7	40.2	43.7	45.8
Families, total	45,111	51,586	55,712	59,550	61,997	(X)	(X)	(X)	(X)	(X)
White	40,869	46,261	49,451	52,243	53,934	100.0	100.0	100.0	100.0	100.0
Married couple [2]	36,212	41,049	42,969	44,751	45,529	88.7	88.7	86.9	85.7	84.4
Male householder [2]	1,100	1,048	1,270	1,441	1,621	2.6	2.3	2.6	2.8	3.0
Female householder [2]	[3]3,557	4,165	5,212	6,052	6,784	8.7	9.0	10.5	11.6	12.6
Black	[3]4,242	4,887	5,498	6,184	6,675	100.0	100.0	100.0	100.0	100.0
Married couple [2]	[3]3,117	3,323	3,346	3,433	3,446	73.6	68.0	60.9	55.5	51.6
Male householder [2]	[3]175	182	232	258	354	4.0	3.7	3.9	4.1	5.3
Female householder [2]	[3]950	1,382	1,940	2,495	2,874	22.4	28.3	35.3	40.3	43.1

(X) Not applicable.
1. Includes other races, not shown separately.
2. No spouse present.
3. Black and other races.
Source: Statistical Abstract of the United States, 1986.

147

Table 2
Years of School Completed, by Race, Spanish Origin, and Sex: 1960 to 1984

[Persons 25 years old and over. Persons of Spanish origin may be of any race.]

YEAR, RACE, SPANISH ORIGIN, AND SEX	Popula-tion (1,000)	PERCENT OF POPULATION COMPLETING—							Median school years completed
		Elementary school			High School		College		
		0-4 years	5-7 years	8 years	1-3 years	4 years	1-3 years	4 years or more	
1960, all races	99,438	8.3	13.8	17.5	19.2	24.6	8.8	7.7	10.6
White	89,581	6.7	12.8	18.1	19.3	25.8	9.3	8.1	10.9
Male	43,259	7.4	13.7	18.7	18.9	22.2	9.1	10.3	10.7
Female	46,322	6.0	11.9	17.8	19.6	29.2	9.5	6.0	11.2
Black	9,054	23.8	24.2	12.9	19.0	12.9	4.1	3.1	8.0
Male	4,240	28.3	23.9	12.3	17.3	11.3	4.1	2.8	7.7
Female	4,814	19.8	24.5	13.4	20.5	14.3	4.1	3.3	8.6
1970, all races	109,899	5.5	10.0	12.8	19.4	31.1	10.6	10.7	12.1
White	98,246	4.5	9.1	13.0	18.8	32.2	11.1	11.3	12.1
Male	46,527	4.8	9.7	13.3	18.2	28.5	11.1	14.4	12.1
Female	51,718	4.1	8.6	12.8	19.4	35.5	11.1	8.4	12.1
Black	10,375	14.6	18.7	10.5	24.8	21.2	5.9	4.4	9.8
Male	4,714	17.7	19.1	10.2	22.9	20.0	6.0	4.2	9.4
Female	5,661	12.0	18.3	10.8	26.4	22.2	5.8	4.6	10.1
Spanish origin	3,938	18.9	17.1	10.2	17.7	22.0	7.9	6.0	9.6
Male	1,923	18.3	16.3	10.0	17.5	20.9	9.2	7.8	9.9
Female	2,014	19.6	17.9	10.4	18.0	23.1	6.7	4.3	9.3
1980, all races	132,836	3.6	6.7	8.0	15.3	34.6	15.7	16.2	12.5

White	114,290	2.6	5.8	8.2	14.6	35.7	16.0	17.1	12.5
Male	53,941	2.8	6.0	8.0	13.6	31.8	16.4	21.3	12.5
Female	60,349	2.5	5.6	8.4	15.5	39.1	15.6	13.3	12.6
Black	13,195	8.2	11.7	7.1	21.8	29.3	13.5	8.4	12.0
Male	5,895	10.0	12.0	6.7	20.5	28.3	14.0	8.4	12.0
Female	7,300	6.7	11.6	7.3	22.9	30.0	13.2	7.6	12.0
Spanish origin	6,739	15.2	16.6	8.1	15.8	24.4	12.0	9.4	10.8
Male	3,247	1.52	16.2	7.7	15.5	22.6	13.4	6.0	11.1
Female	3,493	15.8	17.1	8.4	16.1	26.0	10.6		10.6
1984, all races	140,794	2.8	5.0	6.6	12.4	38.4	15.8	19.1	12.6
White	123,103	2.2	4.5	6.6	11.7	39.1	16.1	19.8	12.6
Male	58,476	2.3	4.7	6.6	11.1	35.1	16.3	23.9	12.7
Female	64,627	2.1	4.4	6.6	12.2	42.8	15.8	16.0	12.6
Black	14,369	7.0	8.7	6.7	19.0	34.3	13.8	10.4	12.2
Male	6,334	8.8	8.9	6.6	18.6	32.9	13.8	10.5	12.2
Female	8,035	5.7	8.6	6.8	19.3	35.4	13.9	10.4	12.3
Spanish origin	7,269	13.9	15.9	8.5	14.6	27.3	11.6	8.2	11.3
Male	3,388	13.6	15.6	8.1	14.1	26.2	12.9	9.5	11.7
Female	3,880	14.1	16.2	8.9	15.0	28.2	10.5	7.0	11.0

Source: Statistical Abstract of the United States, 1986.

Table 3

Civilian Labor Force and Participation Rates, by Race, Sex, and Age: 1960 to 1980

[Persons 16 years old and over. Labor force data are annual averages of minority figures. Rates are based on annual average civilian noninstitutional population of each specified group and represent proportion of each specified group in the civilian labor force.]

	CIVILIAN LABOR FORCE (millions)							PARTICIPATION RATES (percent)						
	1960	1965	1970	1975	1978	1979	1980	1960	1965	1970	1975	1978	1979	1980
Total	69.6	74.5	82.7	92.6	100.4	102.9	104.7	59.4	58.9	60.4	61.2	63.2	63.7	63.8
White	61.9	66.1	73.5	82.1	88.5	90.6	92.2	58.8	58.4	60.2	61.5	63.4	64.0	64.2
Male	41.7	43.4	46.0	49.9	52.3	53.1	53.6	83.4	80.8	80.0	78.7	78.6	78.6	78.3
Female	20.2	22.7	27.5	32.2	36.2	37.5	38.5	36.5	38.1	42.6	45.9	49.5	50.6	51.3
Black and other	7.7	8.3	9.2	10.5	12.0	12.3	12.5	64.5	62.9	61.8	59.3	61.8	61.8	61.2
Male	4.6	4.9	5.2	5.7	6.3	6.4	6.5	83.0	79.8	76.5	71.5	72.1	71.9	70.8
Female	3.1	3.5	4.0	4.8	5.7	5.9	6.0	48.2	48.6	49.5	49.2	53.3	53.5	53.4
Male	46.4	48.3	51.2	55.6	58.5	59.5	60.1	83.3	80.7	79.7	77.9	77.9	77.9	77.4
16-19 years	2.8	3.4	4.0	4.8	5.1	5.0	4.9	56.2	53.8	56.1	59.2	62.1	60.7	60.7
16-17 years	1.3	1.5	1.8	2.0	2.2	2.1	2.0	46.0	43.9	47.0	48.6	51.9	51.6	50.1
18-19 years	1.5	1.9	2.2	2.7	2.9	2.9	2.9	69.3	65.9	66.7	70.7	73.0	72.1	71.5
20-24 years	4.1	4.9	5.7	7.4	8.1	8.2	8.3	88.1	85.8	83.3	84.6	86.0	86.6	86.0
25-34 years	10.3	9.9	11.3	13.9	15.3	15.8	16.3	97.5	97.3	96.4	95.3	95.4	95.4	95.3
35-44 years	11.0	11.1	10.5	10.3	11.0	11.3	11.6	97.7	97.3	96.9	95.7	95.7	95.8	95.5
45-54 years	9.6	10.0	10.4	10.4	10.1	10.1	10.0	95.7	95.6	94.2	92.1	91.3	91.4	91.2
55-64 years	6.4	6.8	7.1	7.0	7.1	7.1	7.2	86.8	84.6	83.0	75.8	73.5	73.0	72.3
65 yr. and over	2.3	2.1	2.3	1.9	1.9	1.9	1.9	33.1	27.9	26.8	21.7	20.5	20.0	19.1
Female	23.2	26.2	31.5	37.0	41.9	43.4	44.5	37.7	39.3	43.3	46.3	50.0	51.0	51.6
16-19 years	2.1	2.5	3.2	4.0	4.5	4.5	4.3	39.3	38.0	44.0	49.2	53.9	54.5	53.1
16-17 years	.8	1.3	1.3	1.7	1.9	1.8	1.7	29.1	27.7	34.9	40.2	45.5	45.8	43.8
18-19 years	1.3	1.6	1.9	2.4	2.6	2.6	2.6	50.9	48.2	53.6	58.1	62.1	62.9	62.1
20-24 years	2.6	3.4	4.9	6.1	6.9	7.0	7.1	46.1	49.9	57.7	64.1	68.3	69.1	69.0
25-34 years	4.1	4.3	5.7	8.5	10.5	11.2	11.8	36.0	38.5	45.0	54.6	62.1	63.8	65.4
35-44 years	5.3	5.7	6.0	6.5	7.6	8.1	8.6	43.4	46.1	51.1	55.8	61.6	63.6	65.5
45-54 years	5.3	5.7	6.5	6.7	6.8	6.9	7.0	49.8	50.9	54.4	54.6	57.1	58.4	59.9
55-64 years	3.0	3.6	4.2	4.2	4.5	4.6	4.6	37.2	41.1	43.0	41.0	41.4	41.9	41.5
65 yr. and over	.9	1.0	1.1	1.0	1.1	1.1	1.1	10.8	10.0	9.7	8.3	8.4	8.3	8.1

Source: Statistical Abstract of the United States, 1981.

Table 4
Occupations of Employed Workers, Percentage Distribution, by Race: 1960 to 1980

[Civilians 16 years old and over, except percent. "N.e.c." means not elsewhere classified]

	WHITE					BLACK AND OTHER				
	1960	1970	1975	1979	1980	1960	1970	1975	1979	1980
Total employed (1,000)	58,850	70,182	75,713	86,025	86,380	6,927	8,445	9,070	10,920	10,890
Percent	100.0	100.0	100.0	100.0	100.0	100.0	100.0	100.0	100.0	100.0
White-collar workers	46.6	50.8	51.7	52.5	53.9	16.1	27.9	34.7	37.9	39.2
Professional, technical, and kindred[1]	12.1	14.8	15.5	15.9	16.5	4.8	9.1	11.4	12.2	12.7
Medical and other health	2.1	2.3	2.5	2.9	3.0	1.6	1.6	2.7	2.7	2.9
Teachers, except college	2.6	3.2	3.6	3.3	3.3	1.7	2.9	3.1	2.9	2.9
Managers and administrators, exc. farm	11.7	11.4	11.2	11.6	12.0	2.6	3.5	4.4	5.2	5.2
Salaried workers	5.9	8.4	9.0	9.6	9.9	.9	2.1	3.4	4.3	4.3
Self-employed	5.8	3.0	2.2	2.0	2.1	1.7	1.4	1.0	1.0	.9
Salesworkers	7.0	6.7	6.9	6.8	6.8	1.5	2.1	2.7	2.8	2.9
Retail trade	4.1	4.0	3.8	3.5	3.4	1.0	1.6	2.0	1.7	1.9
Clerical workers	15.7	18.0	18.1	18.2	18.6	7.3	13.2	15.7	17.7	18.4
Stenographers, typists, and secretaries	3.9	4.7	5.4	5.1	5.2	1.4	2.3	3.4	3.9	3.9
Blue-collar workers	36.2	34.5	32.4	32.6	31.1	40.1	42.2	37.4	36.7	35.8
Craft and kindred workers[1]	13.8	13.5	13.4	13.8	13.3	6.0	8.2	8.8	9.4	9.6
Carpenters	1.4	1.1	1.2	1.4	1.3	.4	.7	.6	.6	.6
Constr. craftworkers, exc. carpenters	2.7	2.5	2.7	2.8	2.7	1.6	1.8	2.1	2.3	2.4
Mechanics and repairers	3.2	3.7	3.6	3.7	3.5	1.7	2.6	2.1	2.4	2.5
Metalcraft workers, except mechanics	1.8	1.6	1.4	1.4	1.4	.6	.8	.8	1.9	1.0
Blue-collar supervisors, n.e.c.	1.9	2.0	1.7	1.9	1.8	.4	.9	1.0	.9	1.2
Operatives	17.9	17.0	14.6	14.4	13.5	20.4	23.7	20.0	19.9	19.4
Operatives, except transport	(NA)	(NA)	10.9	10.8	10.1	(NA)	(NA)	15.0	15.1	14.5
Transport equipment operatives	(NA)	(NA)	3.7	3.6	3.4	(NA)	(NA)	5.0	4.8	4.9
Nonfarm laborers	4.4	4.1	4.4	4.5	4.3	13.7	10.3	8.7	7.4	6.9
Service workers	9.9	10.7	12.3	12.0	12.1	31.7	26.0	25.8	23.2	23.1
Private household workers	1.7	1.3	1.0	.8	.8	14.2	7.7	4.9	3.3	3.2
Service workers, exc. private household	8.2	9.4	11.3	11.1	11.3	17.5	18.3	20.9	19.9	19.9
Farmworkers	7.4	4.0	3.6	2.9	2.9	12.1	3.9	2.6	2.2	1.8
Farmers and farm managers	4.3	2.4	2.0	1.6	1.7	3.2	1.0	.6	.3	.3
Farm laborers and supervisors	3.0	1.6	1.5	1.2	1.2	9.0	2.9	2.0	1.9	1.5

NA Not available.

1. Includes occupations not shown separately.

Source: Statistical Abstract of the United States, 1981.

Table 5
Minority Group Employment in the Federal Government, All Agencies, by Pay System: 1967 and 1974

[Covers full-time employment excluding Hawaii, Guam, Puerto Rico, and foreign nationals abroad]

PAY SYSTEM	November 30, 1967				May 31, 1974			
	Minority groups total	Percent of total Federal employment	Negroes	Spanish surnamed	Minority groups total	Percent of total Federal employment	Negroes	Spanish surnamed
All pay systems, total	496,672	18.9	390,842	68,945	510,061	21.0	390,361	78,972
General schedule and similar, total	173,951	13.7	133,626	21,450	230,126	17.0	171,658	33,125
GS 1-4 ($5,017-$9,358)	93,111	25.2	75,845	9,687	90,642	28.5	59,700	12,056
GS 5-8 ($8,055-$14,341)	52,448	15.0	40,494	6,688	87,062	21.1	68,413	11,377
GS 9-11 ($12,167-$19,072)	20,039	6.8	12,631	3,631	33,392	10.8	22,075	6,208
GS 12-18 ($17,497-$35,000)	8,353	3.3	4,658	1,444	19,030	6.0	11,470	3,484
Wage systems, total	166,506	27.9	121,829	32,024	138,389	29.2	99,208	29,120
Regular nonsupervisory	(NA)	(NA)	(NA)	(NA)	113,907	31.1	80,462	25,536
Regular leader					3,702	26.2	2,711	713
Regular supervisory					7,857	19.1	5,314	1,775
Other wage systems					12,923	24.5	10,721	1,096

	(1)	(2)	(3)	(4)	(5)	(6)	(7)	(8)
U.S. Postal Service, total[2]	151,602	21.7	132,011	14,776	137,537	24.6	116,621	16,139
Level 1-5[4]	141,512	23.5	123,632	13,626	114,801	26.1	97,765	13,413
Level 6-9	9,337	12.4	7,805	1,034	14,259	30.0	12,096	1,612
Level 10-12	606	4.0	467	87	944	11.2	754	104
Level 13-42	147	3.3	107	29	7,533	11.9	6,006	1,010
Other pay systems, total	4,613	8.1	3,376	695	4,009	8.7	2,874	588
Through $6,499	2,887	16.5	2,325	338	710	23.3	548	130
$6,500-$9,999	945	6.0	596	169	1,143	11.4	952	75
$10,000-$13,999	308	3.9	240	81	922	9.7	671	120
$14,000-$17,999	226	3.2	129	60	501	7.0	304	91
$18,000 and over	157	2.4	86	47	733	4.4	309	163

NA Not available.

1. Includes Negroes, American Indians, Orientals, and persons with Spanish surnames.
2. Pay rates as of Jan. 1, 1974 for general schedule. Each grade (except GS-18) includes several salary "steps." Range is from lowest to highest step of grades shown.
3. 1974 groupings; equivalent groupings for 1967 were PFSI-4, 5-8, 9-11, etc. Prior to November 30, 1972, postal data reported under Postal Field Service only; thereafter, also includes reports for Postal Headquarters.
4. Includes 4th class postmasters and rural carriers.

Source: Statistical Abstract of the United States, 1975.

Table 6
Federal Government Employment, by Race and Hispanic Origin, and by Pay System: 1982 and 1984

[As of Sept. 30. Covers total employment for only Executive Branch agencies participating in OPM's Central Personnel Data File. Excludes foreign nationals abroad and U.S. Postal Service]

PAY SYSTEM	1982					1984, prel.				
	Total employees (1,000)	Minority groups				Total employees (1,000)	Minority groups			
		Total[1] (1,000)	Percent of total	Black, non Hispanic (1,000)	Hispanic (1,000)		Total[1] (1,000)	Percent of total	Black, non Hispanic (1,000)	Hispanic (1,000)
All pay systems, total	2,008.5	484.0	24.1	311.1	90.0	2,023.3	502.9	24.9	317.9	95.6
General schedule and similar[2]	1,508.3	336.2	22.3	222.0	59.0	1,523.1	355.5	23.3	231.5	64.1
GS 1-4 ($8,676-$15,531)	303.6	101.9	33.6	71.0	16.1	291.0	103.0	35.4	71.6	16.7
GS 5-8 ($13,369-$23,838)	464.9	126.5	27.2	90.2	20.2	467.1	132.8	28.4	93.2	21.8
GS 9-12 ($20,256-$38,185)	530.0	87.6	16.5	50.1	18.7	552.3	97.8	17.7	55.4	21.3
GS 13-15 ($34,930-$57,500)	209.8	20.1	9.6	10.7	4.0	212.7	21.9	10.3	11.4	4.3
Executive, total	7.8	.6	7.2	.3	.1	7.9	.5	6.7	.3	.1
Wage systems	414.0	134.6	32.5	83.5	28.0	414.7	134.4	32.4	81.4	28.7
Other pay systems	69.3	10.1	14.6	3.7	2.3	74.1	11.4	15.4	3.9	2.4

1. Includes American Indians, Alaska natives, Asians, and Pacific Islanders, not shown separately.
2. Pay rates as of Oct. 1982 for general schedule. Each grade (except Executive) includes several salary steps. Range is from lowest to highest step of grades shown.

Source: Statistical Abstract of the United States, 1986.

154

Table 7
Federal Government Loans to All Small Businesses: 1970 to 1984

[For years ending June 30 except beginning 1977 ending Sept. 30. A small business must be independently owned and operated, must not be dominant in its particular industry, and must meet standards set by the Small Business Administration as to its annual receipts or number of employee]

LOANS APPROVED	Unit	1970-1964, avg.	1975	1976	1977	1978	1979	1980	1981	1982	1983	1984
Loans, all businesses	1,000	25.6	22.3	26.1	31.8	31.7	30.2	31.7	28.7	15.4	19.2	21.3
Minority-operated businesses	1,000	5.8	5.4	5.5	6.2	6.1	5.5	6.0	5.2	2.5	2.7	3.1
Percent of all businesses	Percent	23	24	21	19	19	18	19	18	16	14	15
Value of total loans	Mil. dol.	2,467	1,594	2,071	3,049	3,314	3,407	3,858	3,668	2,038	3,007	3,450
Loans to minority-operated businesses	Mil. dol.	318	229	262	352	402	428	470	454	238	295	383
Percent of all loans	Percent	13	14	13	12	12	13	12	12	12	10	11

Source: Statistical Abstract of the United States, 1986.

Table 8
Money Income of Families, Percentage Distribution by Income Level in Constant (1984) Dollars, by Race and Spanish Origin: 1960 to 1984

RACE AND SPANISH ORIGIN OF HOUSEHOLDER AND YEAR	Number of families (1,000)	PERCENT DISTRIBUTION OF FAMILIES, BY INCOME LEVEL								Median income (dol.)
		Under $5,000	$5,000–$9,999	$10,000–$14,999	$15,000–$19,999	$20,000–$24,999	$25,000–$34,999	$35,000–$49,999	$50,000 and over	
ALL FAMILIES										
1960	45,539	8.3	12.2	14.0	20.9	11.5	12.0	8.0	13.0	19,711
1965	48,509	5.7	10.6	12.0	17.6	10.6	12.2	9.2	22.0	22,903
1970	52,227	4.2	8.5	10.3	14.5	9.3	28.2	13.8	11.3	26,394
1975	56,245	3.7	9.2	10.9	11.2	11.8	26.9	13.8	12.5	26,476
1980	60,309	4.8	8.9	10.9	11.1	10.8	21.0	18.6	13.8	26,500
1981	61,019	5.1	9.4	11.5	11.3	11.3	19.8	18.1	13.3	25,569
1982	61,393	5.6	9.7	11.5	11.3	11.6	19.6	17.2	13.5	25,216
1983	62,015	5.5	9.7	11.1	11.4	11.1	19.3	17.7	14.1	25,594
1984	62,706	5.0	9.4	10.8	10.8	10.7	19.0	18.4	15.8	26,433
WHITE										
1960	41,123	6.8	11.2	13.4	21.5	11.9	12.5	8.4	14.2	20,465
1965	43,497	4.8	9.4	11.1	17.8	10.8	12.5	9.6	24.0	23,871
1970	46,535	3.5	7.6	9.5	14.3	9.3	29.3	14.5	12.1	27,381
1975	49,873	3.0	8.0	10.4	11.0	11.9	27.8	14.5	13.4	27,536
1980	52,710	3.8	7.6	10.3	11.1	11.0	21.8	19.5	14.8	27,611
1981	53,269	4.0	8.2	11.0	11.3	11.5	20.5	19.1	14.3	26,858
1982	53,407	4.4	8.4	11.0	11.4	11.8	20.3	18.2	14.6	26,475
1983	53,890	4.3	8.4	10.8	11.4	11.4	20.0	18.7	15.1	26,814
1984	54,400	3.8	8.1	10.3	10.7	11.0	19.8	19.4	16.9	27,686

BLACK

1960[1]	4,333	22.4	22.3	18.9	16.1	7.4	6.4	3.4	3.2	11,329
1965[1]	4,782	13.9	22.1	20.7	16.4	8.3	7.9	4.7	5.9	13,145
1970	4,928	10.6	17.8	16.2	16.5	9.3	19.0	7.0	3.6	16,796
1975	5,586	9.7	19.9	15.2	13.2	11.6	19.1	7.3	4.0	16,943
1980	6,317	13.0	19.1	15.4	12.2	9.8	14.7	10.9	4.9	15,976
1981	6,413	14.5	19.5	15.7	11.5	10.1	14.5	9.8	4.4	15,151
1982	6,530	15.8	19.8	15.4	11.0	10.2	14.5	9.5	3.6	14,633
1983	6,681	15.6	19.8	14.5	11.7	9.7	14.2	9.8	4.8	15,150
1984	6,778	14.8	19.2	14.9	12.3	9.4	13.1	10.5	5.8	15,432

SPANISH ORIGIN

1975	2,499	7.6	15.8	16.8	14.6	12.1	20.8	8.0	4.4	18,432
1980	3,235	9.0	15.2	16.1	14.0	11.3	17.0	11.8	5.7	18,550
1981	3,305	8.7	15.3	15.7	13.7	12.6	16.1	12.0	5.8	18,731
1982	3,369	9.4	18.0	15.7	13.8	11.6	15.4	10.9	5.3	17,462
1983	3,788	9.7	17.4	15.1	13.9	12.6	14.8	10.8	5.8	17,626
1984	3,939	9.7	15.7	15.0	11.7	12.1	16.7	12.3	6.7	18,833

1. For 1960 and 1965, Black and other races.
2. Persons of Spanish origin may be of any race.
Source: Statistical Abstract of the United States, 1986.

Table 9
Type of Family by Race and Median Income, 1970 to 1983 (current dollars)

Type	1970		1980		1983	
	Black	White	Black	White	Black	White
Married couple families	$ 7,186	$10,723	$18,593	$23,501	$21,040	$27,691
Husband and wife in paid Labor Force	9,721	12,543	22,795	27,238	26,389	32,569
Wife Not in paid Labor Force	5,961	9,531	12,419	19,430	13,821	22,359
Female Households (no husband present)	3,576	5,754	7,425	11,908	7,999	13,761
All families	6,279	10,236	12,674	21,904	14,506	25,757

Source: Prepared by the National Urban League Research Department from U.S. Bureau of the Census, *Current Population Reports*, Series P-60, No. 127, and 145, Money Income and Poverty Status of Families and Persons in the United States: 1980 and 1983.

Table 10
Persons Below Poverty Level, and Below 125 Percent of Poverty Level, by Family Status, Race, and Sex of Householder: 1959 to 1979

[Persons as of March of following year.]

FAMILY STATUS, RACE, AND SEX OF HOUSEHOLDER	NUMBER BELOW POVERTY LEVEL (millions)					NUMBER BELOW 125 PERCENT OF POVERTY LEVEL (millions)				
	1959	1966	1969	1975[1]	1979[1]	1959	1966	1969	1975[1]	1979[1]
All persons[2]	39.5	28.5	24.1	25.9	25.3	54.9	41.3	34.7	37.2	35.6
In families	34.6	23.8	19.2	20.8	19.4	49.3	35.6	28.6	30.1	27.3
Householder	8.3	5.8	5.0	5.5	5.3	11.8	8.6	7.2	8.0	7.6
Related children under 18 yr.	17.2	12.1	9.5	10.9	9.7	24.3	17.7	13.9	15.0	13.0
Children 5-17 yr.	(NA)	8.6	7.1	8.0	(NA)	(NA)	(NA)	3.3	11.0	(NA)
Other family members	9.0	5.9	4.7	4.5	4.3	13.2	9.3	7.3	7.2	6.7
Unrelated individuals	4.9	4.7	5.0	5.1	5.6	5.6	5.7	6.1	7.1	7.9
White	28.5	19.3	16.7	17.8	16.8	41.8	29.5	24.5	26.6	24.6
In families	24.4	15.4	12.6	13.8	12.2	37.2	24.7	19.5	20.9	18.0
Householder	6.2	4.1	3.6	3.8	3.5	9.2	6.5	5.4	5.8	5.2
Related children under 18 yr.	11.4	7.2	5.7	6.7	5.8	17.5	11.5	8.7	9.8	8.0
Other family members	6.9	4.1	3.4	3.2	2.9	10.5	6.8	5.4	5.3	4.7
Unrelated individuals	4.0	3.9	4.0	4.0	4.4	4.7	4.7	5.0	5.7	6.3
Black[3]	11.0	8.9	7.1	7.5	7.8	13.1	11.2	9.5	9.8	10.1
In families	10.1	8.1	6.2	6.5	6.6	12.1	10.4	8.5	8.6	8.6
Householder	2.1	1.6	1.4	1.5	1.7	2.6	2.1	1.9	2.0	2.2
Related children under 18 yr.	5.8	4.8	3.7	3.9	3.7	6.8	5.9	4.9	4.8	4.6
Other family members	2.2	1.7	1.2	1.1	1.3	2.7	2.3	1.8	1.7	1.8
Unrelated individuals	.9	.8	.9	1.0	1.1	1.0	.9	1.0	1.2	1.4
In families with female householder, no husband present	10.4	10.3	10.4	12.3	13.1	11.8	12.4	13.0	15.7	16.9
In families	7.0	6.9	6.9	8.8	9.1	8.0	8.3	8.6	10.9	11.3
Householder	1.9	1.7	1.8	2.4	2.6	2.2	2.1	2.3	3.1	3.2
Related children under 18 yr.	4.1	4.3	4.2	5.6	5.5	4.6	4.9	5.2	6.7	6.6
Other family members	1.0	.9	.8	.8	1.1	1.2	1.3	1.1	1.2	1.5
Unrelated individuals[4]	3.4	3.4	3.5	3.4	3.7	3.8	4.1	4.3	4.8	5.2
In all other families[5]	29.1	18.3	13.7	13.6	12.2	43.1	28.9	21.7	21.4	18.7
In families	27.5	16.9	12.3	11.9	10.3	41.3	27.2	19.9	19.2	16.0
Householder	6.4	4.1	3.2	3.0	2.7	9.6	6.5	5.0	4.9	4.3
Related children under 18 yr.	13.1	7.9	5.3	5.3	4.2	19.7	12.7	8.8	8.3	6.4
Other family members	8.1	5.0	3.9	3.6	3.3	12.1	8.0	6.1	6.0	5.2
Unrelated individuals	1.6	1.3	1.4	1.7	1.9	1.8	1.6	1.8	2.2	2.6

Table 10 (Continued)

FAMILY STATUS, RACE, AND SEX OF HOUSEHOLDER	PERCENT OF PERSONS BELOW POVERTY LEVEL					PERCENT OF PERSONS BELOW 125 PERCENT OF POVERTY LEVEL				
	1959	1966	1969	1975[1]	1979[1]	1959	1966	1969	1975[1]	1979[1]
All persons[2]	22.4	14.7	12.1	12.3	11.6	31.1	21.3	17.4	17.6	16.3
In families	20.8	13.1	10.4	10.9	10.1	29.7	19.6	15.4	15.8	14.3
Householder	18.5	11.8	9.7	9.7	9.1	26.2	17.6	14.3	14.2	13.0
Related children under 18 yr.	26.9	17.4	13.8	16.8	16.0	37.9	25.3	20.2	23.1	21.3
Children 5-17 yr.	(NA)	17.1	13.6	16.3	(NA)	(NA)	(NA)	6.3	22.4	(NA)
Other family members	15.9	9.5	7.2	6.4	6.0	21.9	14.9	11.3	10.3	9.4
Unrelated individuals	46.1	38.3	34.0	25.1	21.9	52.7	46.4	41.8	34.9	30.7
White	18.1	11.3	9.5	9.7	8.9	26.7	17.3	14.0	14.5	13.1
In families	16.5	9.7	7.8	8.3	7.4	25.2	15.5	12.0	12.6	10.9
Householder	15.2	9.3	7.7	7.7	6.8	22.6	14.6	11.7	11.7	10.2
Related children under 18 yr.	20.6	12.1	9.7	12.5	11.4	31.6	19.2	14.9	18.1	15.9
Other family members	13.3	7.4	5.8	5.2	4.6	20.4	12.2	9.2	8.6	7.4
Unrelated individuals	44.1	36.1	32.1	26.8	19.7	50.8	44.4	40.0	32.5	28.6
Black[3]	56.2	41.8	32.2	31.3	30.9	66.8	53.0	43.2	40.6	39.7
In families	56.0	40.9	30.9	30.1	29.9	67.0	52.4	42.2	39.5	38.8
Householder	50.4	35.5	27.9	27.1	27.6	61.0	45.9	37.9	36.1	35.9
Related children under 18 yr.	66.7	50.6	39.6	41.4	40.7	78.0	62.8	52.7	51.2	50.8
Other family members	42.5	29.4	20.0	16.9	17.9	53.4	40.4	29.5	26.0	25.6
Unrelated individuals	57.4	54.4	46.7	42.1	36.8	64.0	61.6	53.9	51.1	45.0
In families with female householder, no husband present	50.2	41.0	38.4	34.6	31.9	57.1	49.6	47.8	44.4	41.2
In families	40.4	39.8	38.2	37.5	34.8	56.2	48.3	48.0	46.3	43.1
Householder	42.6	33.1	32.7	32.5	30.2	49.7	41.1	41.5	41.0	38.0
Related children under 18 yr.	72.2	58.2	54.4	52.7	48.6	79.4	67.4	66.2	62.8	58.0
Other family members	24.0	18.6	17.5	15.0	16.4	29.8	26.6	25.0	21.8	23.4
Unrelated individuals[4]	52.1	43.5	38.7	28.9	26.0	59.1	52.3	47.5	40.6	37.0
In all other families[3]	18.7	10.8	8.0	7.8	6.9	27.7	16.1	11.9	11.5	9.7
In families	18.2	10.3	7.4	7.1	6.2	27.3	17.1	12.6	12.2	10.6
Householder	15.8	9.3	6.9	6.2	5.5	28.6	14.8	10.9	10.1	8.7
Related children under 18 yr.	22.4	12.6	8.6	9.8	8.5	33.8	20.4	14.4	15.3	12.9
Other family members	15.3	8.7	6.4	5.7	5.0	22.8	13.9	10.2	9.3	8.0
Unrelated individuals[5]	36.8	29.3	26.2	19.9	16.9	42.8	36.2	32.4	26.8	22.9

NA Not Available.

1. Beginning 1975, not strictly comparable with prior years due to revised procedures.
2. Beginning 1966, includes races not shown separately. For 1979, includes members of unrelated subfamilies not shown separately. For earlier years unrelated subfamily members are included in "the families" category.
3. For 1959, Black and other races.
4. For persons in families, sex of family householder; for unrelated individuals, sex of individual.
5. Includes male unrelated individuals.

Source: Statistical Abstract of the United States, 1981.

Table 11
Ever Married Persons 25–54 Years Old Who Were Divorced or Separated at Time of Survey by Race and Sex: 1960–1981

	Percent Divorced			Percent Separated		
	Total[1]	White	Black	Total[1]	White	Black
1960						
Male	2.4	2.4	3.1[2]	2.1	1.4	8.2[2]
Female	3.8	3.4	6.5[2]	2.8	1.7	12.4[2]
1970						
Male	3.3	3.1	5.5	1.8	1.1	9.4
Female	5.2	5.0	7.7	3.3	1.8	16.3
1975						
Male	5.4	5.2	8.5	2.6	1.6	12.4
Female	7.6	7.1	12.4	4.4	2.8	18.6
1980						
Male	8.2	7.9	12.6	3.0	2.3	10.4
Female	11.0	10.5	16.5	4.5	2.9	18.7
1981						
Male	9.0	7.9	12.6	3.0	2.3	10.4
Female	11.7	11.0	18.3	4.9	3.2	19.3

1. Includes other races not shown separately.
2. Blacks and other races.
Source: U.S. Bureau of the Census, Current Population Reports, Series P-20 No. 372 and earlier reports.

Table 12
Child Support and Alimony, Selected Characteristics of Women: 1983

[Women as of Spring 1984. Child support data are for women with own children under 21 years of age present from an absent father. Alimony data are for ever-divorced and currently separated women. Covers civilian noninstitutional population. Based on Current Population Survey.]

RECIPIENCY STATUS OF WOMEN	Unit	Total[1]	CURRENT MARITAL STATUS				RACE		Span-ish ori-gin[4]	AGE		
			Divor-ced	Mar-ried[2]	Sin-gle[3]	Sepa-rated	White	Black		18 to 29 years	30 to 39 years	40 years and over
CHILD SUPPORT												
All women, total	1,000	8,690	3,204	2,129	1,854	1,451	6,183	2,341	790	3,077	3,316	2,298
Payments awarded[5]	1,000	5,015	2,443	1,613	328	593	4,137	788	323	1,341	2,275	1,399
Percent of total	Percent	57.7	76.2	75.8	17.7	40.9	66.9	33.7	40.9	43.6	68.6	60.9
Due child support payment in 1983	1,000	3,995	2,092	1,226	219	434	3,389	534	252	1,071	1,947	976
Received payment	1,000	3,037	1,598	881	166	378	2,614	370	158	781	1,527	730
Percent of total	Percent	34.9	49.9	41.4	9.0	26.1	42.3	15.8	20.0	25.4	46.0	31.8
Percent of due	Percent	76.0	76.4	71.9	75.8	87.1	77.4	69.3	62.7	72.9	78.4	74.8
Did not receive payment	1,000	958	494	345	53	55	774	164	94	291	420	246
Payments not awarded	1,000	3,675	761	516	1,526	858	2,045	1,553	467	1,735	1,041	899
Mean money income:												
Women received payments	Dollars	13,132	14,986	11,602	7,257	11,207	13,534	10,188	10,067	9,142	13,545	16,534
Mean child support	Dollars	2,341	2,491	2,164	1,132	2,682	2,475	1,465	1,839	1,723	2,356	2,968
Women did not receive payments	Dollars	8,433	9,635	6,936	(B)	(B)	8,383	8,578	10,438	5,654	9,961	9,106
Women not awarded payments	Dollars	7,389	10,611	7,774	5,366	7,971	8,068	6,615	5,885	5,013	9,310	9,752

	Units											
Women with incomes below the poverty level in 1983, total	1,000	2,898	925	187	1,048	726	1,577	1,256	394	1,465	928	506
Payments awarded[5]	1,000	1,231	632	120	177	297	828	375	116	511	504	217
Received payments in 1983	1,000	568	287	45	77	158	403	153	53	226	267	75
Mean income from child support	Dollars	1,425	1,548	(B)	926	1,502	1,528	1,158	(B)	1,293	1,462	1,692
Did not receive payment	1,000	348	228	45	42	31	250	90	23	147	139	62
Payments not awarded	1,000	1,667	293	66	871	428	750	882	278	954	424	288
ALIMONY												
All women, total	1,000	17,122	7,404	6,178	(X)	2,631	14,250	2,573	1,103	2,958	5,062	9,103
Payments awarded[5]	1,000	2,382	1,143	853	(X)	268	2,198	183	132	193	537	1,852
Received payments in 1983	1,000	608	415	45	(X)	146	538	65	26	58	199	351
Mean income from alimony	Dollars	3,976	4,450	(B)	(X)	3,233	4,292	(B)	(B)	(B)	2,457	5,332
Did not receive payment	1,000	183	114	45	(X)	22	171	10	20	32	55	96
Payments not awarded	1,000	14,741	6,261	5,324	(X)	2,363	12,052	2,410	971	2,765	4,525	7,451
Women with incomes below the poverty level in 1983, total	1,000	3,765	1,839	500	(X)	1,171	2,635	1,050	413	976	1,117	1,672
Payments awarded	1,000	348	206	44	(X)	71	306	36	35	49	87	211
Payments not awarded	1,000	3,417	1,633	457	(X)	1,101	2,329	1,014	377	927	1,030	1,461

B Base less than 75,000. X Not applicable.

1. Includes other items, not shown separately.
2. Remarried women whose previous marriage ended in divorce.
3. Never-married women.
4. Persons of Spanish origin may be of any race.
5. Includes women who were not supposed to receive payments in 1983, not shown separately.

Source: Statistical Abstract of the United States, 1986.

Table 13

Housing Units

Occupied Housing Units, Tenure, and Population per Occupied Unit, by Race of Household Head and by Residence: 1900 to 1973

[In thousands, except percent. Prior to 1960, excludes Alaska and Hawaii. Tenure allocated for housing units which did not report. Minus sign (–) denotes decrease.]

YEAR, RACE, AND RESIDENCE	OCCUPIED UNITS[1]					PERCENT INCREASE OVER PRECEDING CENSUS		Popula-tion per occupied unit[2]
	Total	Owner occupied		Renter Occupied		Total occupied units	Total popula-tion	
		Number	Percent	Number	Percent			
TOTAL								
1900	15,964	7,455	46.7	8,509	53.3	25.8	20.7	4.8
1910	20,256	9,301	45.9	10,954	54.1	26.9	21.0	4.5
1920	24,352	11,114	45.6	13,238	54.4	20.2	14.9	4.3
1930	29,905	14,280	47.8	15,624	52.2	22.8	16.1	4.1
1940	34,855	15,196	43.6	19,659	56.4	16.6	7.2	3.8
1950	42,826	23,560	55.0	19,266	45.0	22.9	14.5	3.4
1960	53,024	32,797	61.9	20,227	38.1	23.4	18.5	3.3
1970	63,450	39,885	62.9	23,565	37.1	19.7	13.3	3.1
1973	69,337	44,653	64.4	24,684	35.6	9.3	(NA)	(NA)
RACE								
White:								
1900	14,064	7,007	49.8	7,057	50.2	25.0	21.2	4.8
1910	(NA)	(NA)	(NA)	(NA)	(NA)	(NA)	22.3	(NA)
1920	21,826	10,511	48.2	11,315	51.8	(NA)	16.0	4.3
1930	26,983	13,544	50.2	13,439	49.8	23.6	16.3	4.1

1940	31,561	14,418	45.7	17,143	54.3	17.0	7.2	3.7
1950	39,044	22,241	57.0	16,803	43.0	23.7	14.1	3.3
1960	47,880	30,823	64.4	17,057	35.6	22.5	17.5	(NA)
1970	56,529	36,979	65.4	19,551	34.6	18.1	11.9	(NA)
1973	61,463	41,239	67.1	20,224	32.9	8.7	(NA)	(NA)

Negro and other:

1900	1,900	448	23.6	1,452	76.4	32.4	17.1	4.8
1910	(NA)	(NA)	(NA)	(NA)	(NA)	(NA)	11.5	(NA)
1920	2,526	603	23.9	1,923	76.1	(NA)	6.3	4.3
1930	2,922	737	25.2	2,185	74.8	15.7	14.7	4.3
1940	3,293	778	23.6	2,516	76.4	12.7	7.7	4.1
1950	3,783	1,319	34.9	2,464	65.1	14.9	17.1	3.9
1960	5,144	1,974	38.4	3,171	61.6	33.0	26.7	(NA)
1970	6,920	2,907	42.0	4,014	58.0	34.5	24.3	(NA)
1973	7,874	3,414	43.4	4,460	56.6	13.8	(NA)	(NA)

NA Not applicable

1. Statistics on the number of occupied units are essentially comparable although identified by various terms—the term "family" applies to figures for 1930 and earlier; "occupied dwelling unit," 1940 and 1950; and "occupied housing unit," 1960, 1970 and 1973. For 1910 and 1920, includes the small number of quasi-families; 1900 and 1930 present private families only. From 1950 to 1970, population in occupied housing units was determined by dividing population in housing units by number of occupied housing units.

2. Not comparable with data for earlier censuses because of a basic change in definition of farm residence. For conditions used in 1960 and 1970.

Source: Statistical Abstract of the United States, 1975.

Table 14
Suicide Rates, by Sex, Race, and Age Group: 1970 to 1978

[Rates per 100,000 population in specified group. Excludes deaths of nonresidents of U.S.]

AGE	MALE								FEMALE							
	White				Black				White				Black			
	1970	1975	1977	1978	1970	1975	1977	1978	1970	1975	1977	1978	1970	1975	1977	1978
All ages [1]	18.0	20.1	21.4	20.2	8.0	10.0	10.7	10.8	7.1	7.4	7.3	6.9	2.6	2.7	3.0	2.8
5–14 years	.5	.8	1.0	.7	.1	.1	.3	.3	.1	.2	.2	.2	.2	.1	.2	.2
15–24 years	13.9	19.6	22.9	20.8	10.5	12.9	13.3	13.4	4.2	4.9	5.5	5.0	3.8	3.3	3.8	2.7
25–34 years	19.9	24.4	26.7	25.8	19.2	24.3	26.3	24.4	9.0	8.9	9.3	8.5	5.7	5.6	6.2	5.6
35–44 years	23.3	24.5	24.7	22.5	12.6	16.0	14.8	16.9	13.0	12.6	11.2	10.9	3.7	3.9	4.8	4.6
45–54 years	29.5	29.7	27.3	24.7	13.8	12.1	11.5	13.8	13.5	13.8	13.6	12.1	3.7	4.0	4.0	4.2
55–64 years	35.0	32.1	30.9	29.3	10.6	10.8	12.6	10.2	12.3	11.7	11.2	10.3	2.0	3.5	3.5	3.2
65 and over	41.1	39.4	41.3	40.8	8.7	11.3	11.1	11.7	8.5	8.5	8.3	7.9	2.6	2.3	1.6	2.3

1. Includes other age groups not shown separately.

Source: Statistical Abstract of the United States, 1981.

166

Table 15
Aid to Families with Dependent Children (AFDC) Recipient Characteristics

Percentage Increase of Types of Families by Race, 1967–1979

	White	Black
Total U.S. families	15.7	31.0
U.S. families with children[1]	7.1	32.5
U.S. female-headed families with children[1]	90.1	108.4
AFDC families	162.0	164.5

1. This is calculated using 1968 proportions to estimate 1967 breakdown by race.
The Census Bureau published data on families with own children by race in 1967; but not families with related children
Source: U.S. Social Security Administration, Office of Research and Statistics, 1982, unpublished data.

Table 16
Aid to Families with Dependent Children (AFDC), Percentage Distribution of Recipient Families and Children, by Characteristics: 1975 to 1979

[Refers to federally-aided State programs providing aid to needy children deprived of parental care or support.]

FAMILIES	1975	1977	1979
Recipient families (1,000)	3,420	3,523	3,428
PERCENT DISTRIBUTION			
Metropolitan areas[1]	78.5	77.1	77.8
Nonmetropolitan areas[2]	21.5	22.9	22.2
White	50.2	52.6	51.7
Black	44.3	43.0	43.9
American Indian and other[2]	5.5	4.4	4.4
Families with 1 child	37.9	40.3	42.5
Families with 2 children	26.0	27.3	28.0
Families with 3 children	16.1	16.1	15.5
Families with 4 or 5 children	15.0	12.7	11.4
Families with 6 or more children	5.0	3.6	2.5
Years as recipient[3]			
Under 1 year	27.7	30.8	28.5
1-3 years	27.3	29.1	28.2
4-5 years	18.8	15.4	15.4
6-10 years	19.3	18.5	19.9
Over 10 years	6.3	5.4	7.1

CHILDREN	1975	1977	1979
Recipient children (1,000)	8,121	7,836	7,230
PERCENT DISTRIBUTION			
Basis for eligibility:			
Father is—			
Deceased	3.7	2.6	2.2
Incapacitated	7.7	5.9	5.3
Unemployed	3.7	5.0	4.1
Absent from home:			
Divorced	19.4	21.4	20.3
Separated[4]	28.6	25.5	24.4
Not married to mother	31.0	33.8	37.8
Other	4.3	4.1	4.4
Mother is absent, not father	1.6	1.6	1.5
Age:			
Under 6, including unborn	34.6	35.1	36.5
6-11	33.7	33.9	33.0
12-17	28.5	27.6	27.1
18-20	2.4	2.6	2.7
Unknown	.8	.9	.9

1. Refers to 243 standard metropolitan statistical areas as designated in 1970 census publications.
2. Includes unknown or not reported.
3. Excludes unknown or not reported.
4. Includes legally and nonlegally separated.

Source: Statistical Abstract of the United States, 1981.

Table 17
United States Statistical Report on Medical Care, Recipients and Services: 1975

TYPE OF MEDICAL CARE OR SERVICE	WHITE, NOT HISP ORIGIN	BLACK, NOT HISP ORIGIN	AMER INDIAN OR ALASK NATIVE	ASIAN OR PAC ISLE	HISPANIC	UNKNOWN
Unduplicated Total	8,384,300	0	0	0	0	11,936,069
IP Hospital Services	1,458,739	0	0	0	0	1,837,094
Mental Hospital Services for the Aged	36,857	0	0	0	0	30,423
SNF/ICF MH Services for the Aged	0	0	0	0	0	0
IP PSYC Services for Age 21 and under	0	0	0	0	0	0
ICF Services for the Mentally Retarded	52,070	0	0	0	0	16,636
ICF Services - All Other	483,633	0	0	0	0	198,368
SNF Services	306,170	0	0	0	0	323,704
Physicians' Services	5,931,974	0	0	0	0	8,025,615
Dental Services	1,673,317	0	0	0	0	2,175,586
Other Practitioners' Services	972,909	0	0	0	0	1,700,034
Outpatient Hospital Services	2,978,283	0	0	0	0	4,440,438
Clinic Services	340,244	0	0	0	0	746,086
Home Health Services	136,367	0	0	0	0	206,387
Family Planning Services	480,312	0	0	0	0	736,247
Lab and X-ray Services	1,379,396	0	0	0	0	3,113,131
Prescribed Drugs	5,549,482	0	0	0	0	7,478,436
Early and Periodic Screening	0	0	0	0	0	0
Rural Health Clinic Services	0	0	0	0	0	0
Other Care	1,113,856	0	0	0	0	1,209,153

Source: Department of Health and Human Services - 1985, unpublished data.

Table 18
United States Statistical Report on Medical Care, Recipients and Services: 1983

TYPE OF MEDICAL CARE OR SERVICE	WHITE, NOT HISP ORIGIN	BLACK, NOT HISP ORIGIN	AMER INDIAN OR ALASK NATIVE	ASIAN OR PAC ISLE	HISPANIC	UNKNOWN
Unduplicated Total	11,129,942	7,215,640	300,362	191,244	1,098,794	0
IP Hospital Services	3,609,339	2,437	125	59	354	0
Mental Hospital Services for the Aged	33,921	15,299	79	38	112	0
SNF/ICF MH Services for the Aged	2,307	475	15	3	37	0
IP PSYC Services for Age 21 and Under	18,601	7,305	882	58	458	0
ICF Services for the Mentally Retarded	128,163	19,884	826	356	1,807	0
ICF Services - All Other	696,708	81,629	5,060	2,261	7,599	0
SNF Service	507,425	55,551	3,466	3,587	3,514	0
Physicians' Services	7,851,840	5,074,013	147,055	136,988	846,062	0
Dental Services	2,690,696	1,820,111	52,821	69,861	305,707	0
Other Practitioners' Services	1,971,552	1,064,395	47,209	18,229	204,859	0
Outpatient Hospital Services	4,462,553	3,351,462	94,780	58,516	488,078	0
Clinic Services	869,933	737,953	28,215	21,075	103,246	0
Home Health Services	285,129	118,678	2,875	6,138	8,908	0
Family Planning Services	692,935	741,418	12,645	9,428	80,922	0
Lab and X-ray Services	2,206,985	1,827,425	24,441	37,941	364,735	0
Prescribed Drugs	7,772,235	4,860,379	170,563	118,522	802,013	0
Early and Periodic Screening	1,007,779	927,658	94,662	16,585	133,841	0
Rural Health Clinic Services	52,884	17,070	2,018	1,764	3,431	0
Other Care	1,660,980	797,055	42,104	17,107	93,780	0

Source: Department of Health and Human Services, 1985; unpublished data.

Table 19
United States Statistical Report on Medical Care, Recipients, Payments, and Services: 1975

TYPE OF MEDICAL CARE OR SERVICE	WHITE, NOT HISP ORIGIN	BLACK, NOT HISP ORIGIN	AMER INDIAN OR ALASK NATIVE	ASIAN OR PAC ISLE	HISPANIC	UNKNOWN
Grand Total	$7,468,981,960	$0	$0	$0	$0	$4,658,040,592
IP Hospital Services	$1,857,369,777	$0	$0	$0	$0	$1,476,892,950
Mental Hospital Serv for the Aged	$268,743,922	$0	$0	$0	$0	$136,064,115
SNF/ICF MH Service for the Aged	$0				$0	$0
IP PSYC Serv for Age 21 and Under	$0	$0	$0	$0	$0	$0
ICF Serv for the Mentally Retarded	$296,480,380	$0	$0	$0	$0	$83,990,828
ICF Services – All Other	$1,534,677,475	$0	$0	$0	$0	$350,282,803
SNF Services	$1,363,742,293	$0	$0	$0	$0	$1,070,460,415
Physicians' Services	$715,031,887	$0	$0	$0	$0	$482,319,948
Dental Services	$180,573,213	$0	$0	$0	$0	$157,551,639
Other Practitioners' Services	$65,553,421	$0	$0	$0	$0	$61,646,274
Outpatient Hospital Services	$191,935,398	$0	$0	$0	$0	$180,190,921
Clinic Services	$203,451,953	$0	$0	$0	$0	$185,500,748
Home Health Services	$37,510,396	$0	$0	$0	$0	$32,502,899
Family Planning Services	$24,842,306	$0	$0	$0	$0	$42,220,990
Lab and X-ray Services	$49,078,729	$0	$0	$0	$0	$71,901,086
Prescribed Drugs	$538,301,522	$0	$0	$0	$0	$254,466,495
Early and Periodic Screening	$0	$0	$0	$0	$0	$0
Rural Health Clinic Services	$0	$0	$0	$0	$0	$0
Other Care	$141,689,288	$0	$0	$0	$0	$72,048,481

Source: Department of Health and Human Services, 1985, unpublished data.

171

Table 20
United States Statistical Report on Medical Care, Recipients, Payments, and Services: 1983

TYPE OF MEDICAL CARE OR SERVICE	WHITE, NOT HISP ORIGIN	BLACK, NOT HISP ORIGIN	AMER INDIAN OR ALASK NATIVE	ASIAN OR PAC ISLE	HISPANIC	UNKNOWN
Grant Total	$22,666,280,824	$8,043,495,846	$402,469,999	$217,961,086	$898,020,014	$0
IP Hospital Services	$4,813,525,440	$3,305,429,876	$181,664,313	$68,779,772	$386,635,934	$0
Mental Hospital Serv for the Aged	$477,545,707	$77,350,690	$711,715	$374,155	$907,117	$0
SNF/ICF MH Services for the Aged	$27,124,459	$4,085,587	$217,853	$5,876	$137,880	$0
IP PSYC Serv for Age 21 and Under	$234,208,288	$97,591,700	$3,491,477	$956,449	$7,462,579	$0
ICF Serv for the Mentally Retarded	$3,433,716,788	$575,085,688	$19,039,994	$8,261,345	$42,735,756	$0
ICF Services - All Other	$4,625,110,409	$643,129,477	$38,061,377	$28,405,430	$45,861,166	$0
SNF Services	$4,053,532,900	$467,705,347	$33,628,370	$41,732,525	$24,384,060	$0
Physicians' Services	$1,243,210,104	$744,956,793	$33,192,710	$24,515,115	$128,683,662	$0
Dental Services	$260,722,258	$158,945,251	$5,755,594	$9,686,383	$31,962,157	$0
Other Practitioners' Services	$151,513,751	$56,355,083	$6,218,816	$1,506,686	$10,560,660	$0
Outpatient Hospital Services	$736,143,566	$628,001,901	$23,653,527	$10,277,487	$71,166,066	$0
Clinic Services	$259,240,391	$194,478,716	$4,346,558	$2,948,839	$17,894,377	$0
Home Health Services	$381,289,830	$196,394,134	$5,856,795	$3,957,241	$9,672,532	$0
Family Planning Services	$70,228,191	$73,169,205	$2,103,474	$1,391,459	$9,078,551	$0
Lab and X-ray Services	$89,899,624	$78,721,333	$1,004,386	$1,352,459	$15,766,856	$0
Prescribed Drugs	$1,194,590,266	$486,629,176	$15,200,109	$9,355,673	$65,071,946	$0
Early and Periodic Screening	$60,351,474	$32,912,377	$17,442,094	$925,243	$4,093,936	$0
Rural Health Clinic Services	$4,022,532	$1,041,357	$101,523	$101,507	$217,614	$0
Other Care	$549,900,846	$224,512,155	$10,779,314	$3,427,442	$25,727,165	$0

Source: Department of Health and Human Services, 1985, unpublished data.

172

Table 21
Selected WIN Activity by Characteristics of Registrants: 1976

CHARACTERISTICS OF APPLICANTS	REGISTRANTS		ENTERED EMPLOYMENT			TAX CREDITS AUTHORIZED	EMP AFT REG OFF AFDC	EMP VOL NOT OFF AFDC	NEVER AFDC RECIPIENT	DEREGISTRATIONS			
	CUMULATIVE TOTAL	ON HAND END OF PERIOD	TOTAL	PLACED	OBTAINED EMPLOYMENT					EXEMPT	SANCTIONED	OFF AFDC OTHER	TOTAL
Ethnic Group	1740085	1535091	62633	21890	41536	7883	29945	1690	17152	35101	6190	123002	212303
White	928519	797556	42677	13390	29816	5278	21956	1073	11686	18003	3456	80189	135856
Black	705054	640982	17665	7573	10318	2411	6729	540	4760	14622	2252	37603	66276
American Indian	11046	9275	475	193	289	51	242	31	143	393	64	986	1852
Other	38680	34987	1071	356	731	97	549	29	269	738	180	1988	3745
INA	56786	52291	745	369	382	46	469	17	294	1344	238	2176	4535

Source: Prepared by author from WIN Program Management Information Report, 1976. National Report. #MA5-101.

Table 22
Selected WIN Activity by Characteristics of Registrants: 1983

CHARACTERISTICS OF APPLICANTS	REGISTRANTS		ENTERED EMPLOYMENT	TAX CREDITS AUTHORIZED	EMP AFT REG OFF AFDC	EMP VOL NOT OFF AFDC	NEVER AFDC RECIPIENT	DEREGISTRATIONS				
	CUMULATIVE TOTAL	ON HAND END OF PERIOD						EXEMPT	SANCTIONED INITIAL	SANCTIONED SUBSEQUENT	OFF AFDC OTHER	TOTAL
Total	1325879	946027	130769	10746	69714	2989	36198	54281	8444	66	275104	436660
White (not Hispanic)	581606	382972	74468	5243	43672	1518	20897	28346	4284	33	133416	226283
Black (not Hispanic)	418915	322028	31787	3822	15027	1150	7964	15311	2895	29	76431	116358
Hispanic	227716	165508	18396	1257	8213	209	5308	7328	971	2	48613	69292
American Indian & Alaskan Native	9778	6221	1111	85	583	47	302	695	147	1	2326	3995
Asian & Pacific Isl.	67122	54699	3785	304	1585	39	1326	1537	111	1	9601	13970
INA	20300	14275	1161	33	635	21	385	1052	35	0	4638	6631

Source: Prepared by author from WIN Program Management Information Report, 1983. National Report.

Table 23
Occupational Category of Employment Entered by Characteristic of WIN Registrants: 1976

CHARACTERISTIC	TOTAL	PROF TECHN MANAGER	CLER- ICAL	SALES	DOMES- TIC	OTHER SERVICE	FARM FOREST FISHING	PROC- ESSING	MACHINE TRADES	BENCH WORK	STRUC- TURAL	MOTOR FREIGHT TRANSP	OTHER
Ethnic Group	66259	3867	9761	3649	2193	17370	991	2510	3693	5624	4917	2970	8713
White	45135	2456	6519	2731	1026	10615	839	1760	2972	3613	4166	2444	5990
Black	18721	1251	2931	822	1085	6166	102	647	595	1695	595	453	2380
American Indian	499	50	71	19	18	135	7	20	19	44	42	19	55
Other	1129	64	149	51	30	259	30	48	61	133	73	38	193
INA	775	47	90	26	34	196	13	35	46	139	39	15	95

Source: Prepared by author from the WIN Program Management Information Report, 1976. National Report #MA5-105.

Table 24
Occupational Category of Employment Entered by Characteristic of WIN Registrants: 1983

CHARACTERISTIC	TOTAL	PROF TECHN MANAGER	CLER- ICAL	SALES	DOMES- TIC	OTHER SERVICE	FARM FOREST FISHING	PROC- ESSING	MACHINE TRADES	BENCH WORK	STRUC- TURAL	MOTOR FREIGHT TRANSP	OTHER
Race/Ethnic	149619	8922	24715	6650	5411	37031	5483	4393	6507	9246	11923	5743	21663
White (not Hispanic)	84574	4685	12855	4396	2768	19680	2433	2336	4298	4421	8550	4037	14120
Black (not Hispanic)	30652	2828	7526	1347	1705	13665	370	766	748	2057	911	699	4030
Hispanic	21327	765	3253	708	701	4184	2293	1058	1032	1946	1950	826	2611
American Indian & Alaskan Native	1423	196	168	29	57	335	78	60	47	60	114	53	226
Asian & Pacific Isl.	4255	317	501	103	124	794	286	132	356	667	321	97	557
INA	1327	130	331	67	50	352	21	41	30	93	75	30	107

Source: Prepared by author from the WIN Program Management Information Report, 1976. National Report.

Table 25
Starting Wage by Characteristics of WIN Registrants: 1976

CHARACTERISTICS	TOTAL	STARTING WAGE									AVERAGE	OTHER
		UNDER $2.10	$2.10-$2.29	$2.30-$2.49	$2.50-$2.99	$3.00-$3.49	$3.50-$3.99	$4.00-$4.49	$4.50-$4.99	$5.00 & OVER		
Ethnic Group	66259	3997	5471	16535	14291	9206	4932	3486	1725	5503	3.05	1112
White	45135	2672	3041	10090	9663	6780	3687	2695	1307	4300	3.13	690
Black	18721	1063	2207	5940	4122	2091	1059	675	354	1024	2.91	187
American Indian	499	25	47	135	119	58	38	22	12	35	3.21	8
Other	1129	37	45	253	258	203	104	67	42	97	3.24	23
INA	775	201	131	117	128	66	44	27	10	47	3.15	4

Source: Prepared by author from the WIN Program Management Information Report, 1976. National Report #MA5-104.

Table 26
Starting Wage by Characteristics of WIN Registrants: 1983

CHARACTERISTICS	TOTAL	STARTING WAGE					AVERAGE	OTHER
		UNDER $3.35	$3.35-$3.99	$4.00-$4.99	$5.00-$5.99	$6.00 & OVER		
TOTAL	149619	3914	70426	29947	18189	22462	4.53	4701
Race/Ethnic								
White (not Hispanic)	84574	2875	36515	17092	10989	13629	4.61	3474
Black (not Hispanic)	36652	631	21928	6134	3233	4129	4.21	597
Hispanic	21827	319	9074	4983	2944	3508	4.73	499
American Indian & Alaskan Native	1423	25	538	315	156	337	5.16	42
Asian & Pacific Isl.	4255	36	1785	1134	632	599	4.65	69
INA	1327	26	545	285	198	254	4.75	19

Source: Prepared by author from the WIN Program Management Information Report, 1976. National Report.

Table 27
Low-Rent Public Housing: Tenant Occupancy in Projects Past Initial Occupancy Stage, by Total, Minority Group Categories and State: June 30, 1972

	Total units available	Total units occupied by tenants	Occupied by minority groups - percent of tenant occupied					
			White	Black	American Indian	Spanish American	Oriental	Other Minorities
Total	978,614	954,073	43	49	1	7	1	*
Alabama	36,727	35,405	41	59	*	*	*	*
Alaska	915	873	36	6	20	*	*	37
Arizona	4,726	4,668	20	23	23	33	*	*
Arkansas	10,769	10,253	58	42	*	*	--	--
California	58,380	57,372	36	39	1	21	3	1
Colorado	5,546	5,484	41	16	1	42	*	--
Connecticut	15,418	15,012	45	45	*	10	*	*
Delaware	2,111	2,041	27	73	--	*	*	--
District of Columbia	11,131	10,510	2	98	--	*	*	*
Florida	31,271	30,435	34	61	*	5	*	*
Georgia	45,730	44,209	34	66	*	*	*	*
Hawaii	4,730	4,698	20	1	*	7	39	33
Idaho	801	798	90	1	6	3	*	--
Illinois	67,765	66,114	38	61	*	1	*	*
Indiana	12,789	12,358	49	50	*	1	*	--
Iowa	2,294	2,272	88	11	1	1	*	--
Kansas	5,109	4,868	63	35	1	1	*	--
Kentucky	19,298	19,046	61	39	--	*	*	*
Louisiana	25,822	25,332	21	79	*	--	--	*
Maine	2,051	2,022	99	1	*	--	--	--
Maryland	15,763	15,653	22	78	*	*	*	*
Massachusetts	31,207	30,307	71	24	*	4	*	*
Michigan	22,421	21,829	43	56	*	1	*	*
Minnesota	17,514	17,043	88	8	4	1	--	--
Mississippi	9,398	9,069	36	63	*	*	*	--

Missouri	15,763	14,665	40	59	*	1	*	*
Montana	1,430	1,395	58	*	41	L	*	-
Nebraska	8,035	7,871	75	22	2	*	*	*
Nevada	3,059	3,012	50	38	7	8	-	-
New Hampshire	3,355	3,341	98	1	-	*	-	-
New Jersey	43,662	42,758	47	47	*	6	*	*
New Mexico	3,123	3,056	34	7	27	32	-	1
New York	100,739	99,699	34	47	*	19	1	-
North Carolina	25,661	25,303	23	76	1	*	-	*
North Dakota	1,751	1,739	70	-	29	*	*	*
Ohio	42,761	41,638	42	58	*	1	*	*
Oklahoma	9,261	8,955	46	34	19	1	*	*
Oregon	7,787	7,686	87	11	1	1	*	*
Pennsylvania	62,863	61,076	46	52	*	3	*	*
Rhode Island	9,114	8,342	84	15	*	*	1	-
South Carolina	9,005	8,733	31	69	-	*	*	*
South Dakota	1,877	1,737	32	*	68	-	-	-
Tennessee	32,905	32,244	45	55	*	*	*	*
Texas	46,184	44,139	33	38	*	28	*	*
Utah	202	202	41	5	43	11	-	-
Vermont	863	810	99	*	-	-	-	-
Virginia	16,410	16,225	16	84	*	*	*	*
Washington	15,031	14,053	82	12	2	2	1	1
West Virginia	4,092	4,052	79	21	-	*	-	-
Wisconsin	9,238	8,994	82	14	3	*	*	*
Wyoming	282	276	53	9	14	23	1	-
Puerto Rico	41,724	41,662	NA	NA	NA	NA	NA	NA
Virgin Islands	2,501	2,489	NA	NA	NA	NA	NA	NA
Quam	250	250	4	-	1	1	13	82

*Less than 0.5 percent.

NA Not Applicable

Source: 1972 Statistical Yearbook, U.S. Department of Housing and Urban Development, Superintendent of Documents, U.S. Government Printing Office, Washington, D.C.

Table 28

Low-Income Housing: Tenant Occupancy in Projects Past Initial Occupancy Stage, by Total, Minority Group Category and State: June 30, 1978

State	Total Units occupied by tenants	Percent of tenant occupied units[a]					
		White/non minority	Negro/ Black	American Indian	Spanish American	Oriental	Other Minorities
Total	1,100,614	38.4	47.1	1.5	12.2	.5	.5
Alabama	39,152	36.5	63.4	*	*	*	*
Alaska	1,019	28.1	7.1	18.3	1.8	*	43.1
Arizona	6,230	14.1	18.7	32.3	34.6	1.8	.1
Arkansas	12,902	57.7	41.8	.1	.1	.3	.1
California	57,947	32.3	37.3	.9	25.2	3.5	.8
Colorado	7,003	40.4	15.1	.7	40.9	2.0	.9
Connecticut	16,879	43.5	43.8	.1	12.4	.1	.1
Delaware	2,500	24.2	75.0	-	.8	*	-
District of Columbia	11,059	1.2	98.6	-	*	.1	*
Florida	35,284	26.1	64.3	.3	8.1	.1	1.1
Georgia	45,580	29.2	70.4	.1	*	.1	.1
Hawaii	4,374	14.6	.5	.2	6.1	41.1	37.6
Idaho	933	87.6	1.2	7.1	3.6	.2	.3
Illinois	70,392	36.4	62.1	.1	1.0	.2	.3
Indiana	15,550	46.1	51.9	.1	1.5	.1	.5
Iowa	3,418	88.1	10.9	.1	.8	.1	.1
Kansas	6,911	68.2	31.7	1.0	.9	.1	.2
Kentucky	20,939	60.9	38.9	*	*	.1	.1
Louisiana	28,289	18.0	81.9	*	*	*	*
Maine	3,253	98.8	.7	.3	*	.1	.1
Maryland	18,545	25.3	74.2	.1	.4	.1	-
Massachusetts	33,419	70.8	21.3	.3	6.0	.1	1.5
Michigan	22,715	41.6	56.8	.5	.8	.	.3
Minnesota	20,122	85.4	9.3	3.8	1.1	.1	.4
Mississippi	11,926	32.9	66.3	.3	*	.1	.4
Missouri	17,761	47.6	51.1	.1	.4	.6	-
Montana	1,583	59.4	.1	39.7	.5	.2	-
Nebraska	8,462	73.9	22.2	3.0	.6	.1	.2
Nevada	3,408	38.4	37.9	1.41	8.9	.5	.2
New Hampshire	3,920	98.1	1.1	-	.6	.1	-

New Jersey	44,253	43.7	49.6	*	6.4	.1	.3
New Mexico	5,692	13.1	4.3	44.7	43.3	*	.2
New York	121,613	28.7	49.1	.1	21.6	.4	.1
North Carolina	33,449	21.5	77.2	1.6	*	*	.1
North Dakota	3,099	82.3	.1	17.3	*	.2	.1
Ohio	49,341	41.3	58.0	*	.6	*	*
Oklahoma	13,245	49.9	24.1	25.4	.4	.1	.2
Oregon	6,411	83.1	10.9	1.6	3.4	.7	.3
Pennsylvania	70,918	45.9	50.3	*	3.6	*	*
Rhode Island	9,092	83.6	13.5	*	2.7	.1	*
South Carolina	11,071	24.7	75.2	*	*	*	*
South Dakota	3,430	48.1	.1	51.6	.1	.1	*
Tennessee	36,558	43.3	56.6	*	*	*	*
Texas	52,370	31.3	32.4	.4	35.0	.9	.1
Utah	946	76.1	4.7	9.2	9.8	–	.2
Vermont	2,206	99.5	.5	–	–	–	*
Virginia	17,536	13.4	86.5	*	*	.1	*
Washington	14,600	78.3	12.7	3.1	2.7	2.2	1.0
West Virginia	5,340	79.4	20.1	*	*	*	.4
Wisconsin	10,937	77.7	15.8	5.7	.6	.1	.1
Wyoming	541	73.9	7.6	7.2	10.9	.4	*
Guam	345	2.9	–	–	.3	16.5	80.3
Puerto Rico	50,423	–	–	–	100.0	–	–
Virgin Islands	2,723	.7	80.8	–	18.4	–	–

aBased on units in projects reporting by minority group category.
*Less than 0.05 percent

Source: 1979 Statistical Yearbook, U.S. Department of Housing and Urban Development, Superintendent of Documents, U.S. Government Printing Office, Washington, D.C.

BIBLIOGRAPHY

Alexander, Bill. "The Black Church and Community Empowerment." In Robert L. Woodson, ed. *On the Road to Economic Freedom: An Agenda for Black Progress* (Washington, D.C.: The National Center for Neighborhood Enterprise, 1987), pp. 45–69.

Alexander, Chauncey, and Weber, David. "Social Welfare: Historical Dates." *Encyclopedia of Social Work* 17 (1977): 1497–1503.

"America's Underclass, Broken Lives: A Nation Apart." *U.S. News and World Report* (March 17, 1986): 18–21.

Anderson, Martin. *Welfare*. Stanford, California: Hoover Press, 1982.

Anderson, Talmadge. "Black Enterpreneurship and Concepts Toward Economic Coexistence." *Western Journal of Black Studies* 6 (Summer, 1982) 2: 80–88.

Axinn, June, and Levin, Herman. *Social Welfare*. New York: Dodd, Mead and Company, 1975.

Bahr, Stephen. "The Effects of Welfare on Marital Stability and Remarriage." *Journal of Marriage and the Family* 41 (1979): 553–650.

Bane, Mary Jo. *Economic Influence on Divorce and Remarriage*. Cambridge, Massachusetts: Center for the Study of Public Policy, 1975.

Barol, Bill. "The Eighties Are Over." *Newsweek* (January 4, 1988): 40–48.

Bell, Carolyn. *The Economics of the Ghetto*. New York: Pegasus, 1970.

Bell, Derrick A. *Race, Racism and American Law*. Boston: Little, Brown, and Company, 1980.

Berlage, Gai and Egelman, William. *Experience with Sociology*. Reading, Massachusetts: Addison-Wesley, 1983.

Berry, Mary Francis and Blassingame, John. *Long Memory: The Black Experience in America*. New York: Oxford University Press, 1982.

Billingsley, Andrew. *Black Families in White America*. Englewood Cliffs, New Jersey: Prentice-Hall, 1968.

Billingsley, Andrew and Billingsley, Amy. "Negro Family Life in America." *Social Service Review* 39 (September, 1965): 310–319.

Billingsley, Andrew and Giovannoni, Jeanne. *Children of the Storm*. New York: Harcourt, Brace, Jovanovich, 1972.

Blackwell, James E. "Persistence and Change in Intergroup Relations: The Crisis Upon Us." *Social Problems* 29 (1982) 4: 325–346.

Blassingame, John W. *The Slave Community*. New York: Oxford University Press, 1972.

Boykin, Wade A. "The Academic Performance of Afro-American Children," in Janet T. Spence, ed., *Achievement and Achievement Motives* (San Francisco: W. H. Freeman and Company, 1983), pp. 324–371.

Boykin, Wade A., and Toms, Forrest D. "Black Child Socialization: A Conceptual Framework." In Harriette McAdoo and John McAdoo, eds. *Black Children* (Beverly Hills, California: Sage Publications, 1985), pp. 33–51.

Brown, Tony. "The Freedom Philosophy." *Tony Brown's Journal* (October, 1985): 3–8.

"City May Order Housing for Poor." *Columbus Dispatch*. (March 28, 1986), p. 1.

Cobb, Sidney. "Social Support as a Moderator of Life Stress." *Psychosomatic Medicine* 38 (1976): 300–314.

Coleman, Milton. "Reagan's 'Rising Tide' Is Sinking Blacks." *The National Leader* (February, 1984), p. 1.

Compton, Beulah Roberts. *Introduction to Social Welfare and Social Work*. Homewood, Illinois: 1980.

Cooke-Vaughn, Dennys. "The Economic Status of Black America—Is There A Recovery?." In *The State of Black America*. Washington, D.C.: National Urban League (1984): 10.

"Court to Congress: You Cut Budget." *USA Today* (July 8, 1986): 1.

Cross, Theodore. *The Black Power Imperative*. New York: Faulkner Books, 1984.

Darity, William A. Jr. and Myers, Samuel L. Jr., "Does Welfare Dependency Cause Female Headship? The Case of the Black Family," *Journal of Marriage and the Family* 46 (November, 1984): 766–767.

DiMatteo, M. R. and Hays, R. "Social Support and Serious Illness." In Benjamin Gottlieb, ed. *Social Networks and Social Support*. Beverly Hills, California: Sage, 1981.

Drake, Clayton S. "The Social and Economic Status of the Negro in the United States." In T. Parsons and K. B. Clark, eds. *The Negro American*. Boston: Beacon, 1965.

Dubois, W. E. Burghardt. "The Function of the Negro Church." In Hart M. Nelsen, Raytha L. Yokley, and Anne K. Nelsen, eds., *The Black Church in America* (New York: Basic Books), pp. 77–81.

Duncan, Greg J. and Saul D. Hoffman. "A Reconsideration of the Economic Consequences of Marital Disruption." *Demography* 22 (November, 1985): 493–495.

Edelman, Marian Wright. " 'The Sea Is So Wide and My Boat Is So Small': Problems Facing Black Children Today." In Hariett Mcadoo and John McAdoo, eds. *Black Children*. Beverly Hills, California: Sage (1985), pp. 72–82.

Ehrenreich, Barbara, and Stallard, Karin. "The Nouveau Poor." *Ms.* 11 (August, 1982): 217–224.

Elkins, Stanley. *Slavery: A Problem in American Institutional and Intellectual Life*. New York: Grosset and Dunlap, 1963.

Emerson, Richard M. "Power-Dependence Relations." *American Sociological Review* 27 (1962): 31–41.

"Employment and Training Reporter: 1982 Employment and Training Report to the President: Selected Tables." Washington, D.C.: *The Bureau of National Affairs* 14 (February 9, 1983) 22: 670–671.

Evans, William L. *Race, Fear and Housing in a Typical American Community*. National Urban League, 1946.

Feshbach, Muriel. "Dynamics in the AFDC Caseload 1967-Present." Department of Health and Human Services (unpublished report, 1982).

Fischer, Ann; Beasley, Joseph; and Harter, Carl. "The Occurrence of the Extended Family of Procreation: A Developmental Approach to Negro Family Structure." *Journal of Marriage and the Family* (May, 1968): 291–300.

Franklin, John Hope. *From Slavery to Freedom: A History of American Negroes*. New York: Alford A. Knopf, 1948.

Frazier, E. Franklin. *The Free Negro Family*. Nashville: Fisk University Press, 1932.

———. *The Negro Family in Chicago*. Chicago: University of Chicago Press, 1932.

———. *The Negro Family in the United States*. Chicago: University of Chicago Press, 1939.

Furstenberg, Frank; Hershberg, Theodore; and Modell, John. "The Origin of the Female-Headed Black Family: The Impact of the Urban Experience." *Journal of Interdisciplinary History* 5 (Spring, 1975): 211–233.

Gilder, George. *Wealth and Poverty*. New York: Basic Books, 1981.

Glasgow, Douglas. *The Black Underclass*. New York: Vintage Books, 1981.

Gouldner, Alvin Ward. "The Norm of Reciprocity: A Preliminary Statement." *American Sociological Review* 25 (1960): 161–178.

Grier, William, and Cobbs, Price. *Black Rage*. New York: Bantam Books, 1968.

Gurin, Gerald; Veroff, Joseph; and Feld, Sheila. *Americans View Their Mental Health*. New York: Basic Books, 1960.

Gutman, Herbert. *The Black Family in Slavery and Freedom, 1750–1925*. New York: Pantheon Books, 1976.

Guzzardi, Walter Jr. "Who Will Care for the Poor?" *Fortune* (February, 1982): 34–42.

Hampton, Robert L. "Institutional Decimation, Marital Exchange, and Disruption in Black Families." *Western Journal of Black Studies* 4 (Summer, 1980): 134–135.

Handel, Gerald. *Social Welfare in Western Society*. New York: Random House, 1982.

Hannan, Michael T. and Tuma, Nancy Brandon. "Income and Marital Events: Evidence from an Income Maintenance Experiment." *American Journal of Sociology* 82 (May, 1977): 1186–1211.

Hare, Nathan. "The Frustrated Masculinity of the Negro Male." *Negro Digest* (August, 1964): 5–9.

Hare, Nathan, and Hare, Julia. "Black Women, 1970." *Transaction* (November, 1970): 66–67.

Hayes, Floyd W. "The Political Economy, Reagonomics, and Blacks." *Western Journal of Black Studies* 6 (1982): 90.

Herskovits, Melville. *The Myth of the Negro Past*. Boston: Beacon, 1970.

Hill, Robert. *The Strengths of Black Families*. New York: Emerson Hall, 1972.

———. *Economic Policies and Black Progress: Myths and Realities*. Washington, D.C.: National Urban League, 1981.

———. "Self-help Groups in the African–American Community: Current Organization and Service." University of North Carolina School of Social Work, University of North Carolina at Chapel Hill. Unpublished paper.

———. "The Black Family: Building on Strengths." In Robert L. Woodson, ed., *On the Road to Economic Freedom: An Agenda for Black Progress*. Washington, D.C.: The National Center for Neighborhood Enterprise, 1987, pp. 71–92.

———. *The Impact of AFDC-UP on Black Families: Report for the Black Family Resource Center*. Baltimore, Maryland: Baltimore Urban League, April 23, 1987.

Honig, Marjorie. "AFDC Income, Recipient Rates, and Family Dissolution." *Journal of Human Resources* 9 (Summer, 1974): 302–322.

Hoover, Theressa. "Black Women and the Churches: Triple Jeopardy." In Alice Hagemen, ed. *Sexist Religion and Women in the Church*. New York: Association Press, 1974, pp. 63–76.

Hopkins, Thomas J. "The Role of Community Agencies as Viewed by Black Fathers." *Journal of Orthopsychiatry* 42 (1972): 508–516.

Jencks, Christopher. "Divorced Mothers Unite!" *Psychology Today* 16 (November, 1982): 73.

Jewell, K. Sue. "An Analysis of the Visual Development of a Stereotype: The Media's Portrayal of Mammy and Aunt Jemima as Symbols of Black Womanhood," Dissertation. The Ohio State University, 1976.

———. "The Changing Character of Black Families: The Effects of Differential Social and Economic Gains," *Journal of Social and Behavioral Sciences* 33 (1988): 143–154.

———. "Black Male/Female Conflict: Internalization of Negative Definitions Transmitted Through Imagery," *The Western Journal of Black Studies* 7 (Spring 1983): 43–48.

———. "Use of Social Welfare Programs and the Disintegration of the Black Nuclear Family." *Western Journal of Black Studies* 8 (Winter, 1984): 192–198.

———. "Will the Real Black, Afro-American, Mixed, Colored, Negro Please Stand Up? Impact of the Black Social Movement, Twenty Years Later," *Journal of Black Studies* 16 (September 1985): 57–75.

Joe, Tom, and Rogers, Cheryl. *By the Few for the Few: The Reagan Welfare Legacy*. Lexington, Massachusetts: Lexington Books, 1986.

Joe, Tom, and Yu, Peter. *The "Flip" Side of Black Families Headed by Women: The Economic Status of Black Men*. Washington, D.C.: The Center for the Study of Social Policy, 1984.

Johnson, Wayne. *The Social Services: An Introduction*. Itasca, Illinois: F. E. Peacock Publishers, 1982.

Kramer, Morton, and Zane, Nolan. "Projected Needs for Mental Health Services." In Stanley Sue and Thom Moore, eds. *The Pluralistic Society: A Community Mental Health Perspective*. New York: Human Sciences Press, 1984, pp. 47–76.

Landsburgh, Therese W. "Child Welfare: Day Care of Children." *Encyclopedia of Social Work* (Washington, D.C.: National Association of Social Workers, 1977. 17th issue: 138.

Leavy, Walter. "Is the Black Male an Endangered Species?" *Ebony* (June 1983): 41–46.

Lefley, Harriet P., and Bestman, Evalina W. "Community Mental Health and Minorities: A Multi-Ethnic Approach." In Stanley Sue and Thom Moore, eds. *The Pluralistic Society: A Community Mental Health Perspective*. New York: Human Sciences Press, 1984, pp. 116–148.

Levitan, Sar A., and Johnson, Clifford M. *Beyond the Safety Net: Reviving the Promise of Opportunity in America*. Cambridge, Massachusetts: Ballinger Publishing Company, 1984.

Levy, Leo, and Rowitz, Louis. *The Ecology of Mental Disorders*. New York: Behavioral Publications, 1973.

"Life Below the Poverty Line." *Newsweek* (April 5, 1982): 25.

Lincoln, C. Eric. "Black Studies and Cultural Continuity." *Black Scholar* (October, 1978): 12–18.

MacDonald, J. Fred. *Blacks and White T.V.:Afro-Americans in Television Since 1948*. Chicago: Nelson-Hall, 1983.

Maguire, Lambert. *Understanding Social Networks*. Beverly Hills, California: Sage, 1983.

Manpower Information Service. "Economically Disadvantaged Make Up Bulk of Fiscal '76 Title I Clients." Division of the Bureau of National Affairs, Inc. 8 (September, 1976) 1: 8–9, 23–24.

Marable, Manning, "Reaganism, Racism, and Reaction: Black Political Realignment in the 1980's." *Black Scholar* (Fall, 1982): 2–15.

Martin, Thad. "The Black Church: Precinct of the Black Soul." *Ebony* (August, 1984): 154–158.

McAdoo, Harriette Pipes. "Black Mothers and the Extended Family Support Network." In La Frances Rodgers-Rose, ed. *The Black Woman*. Beverly Hills, California: Sage Publications, 1982, pp. 125–144.

———. "Patterns of Upward Mobility in Black Families." In Harriette Pipes McAdoo, ed. *Black Families*. Beverly Hills, California: Sage, 1981.

McCray, Carrie Allen. "The Black Woman and Family Roles." In La Frances Rodgers-Rose, ed. *The Black Woman*. Beverly Hills, California: Sage Publications, 1982, pp. 67–78.

McElvaine, Robert. *The Great Depression: America, 1929–1941*. New York: Times Books, 1984.

McGhee, James D. "The Black Family Today and Tomorrow." *The State of Black America*. New York: National Urban League, 1985: 1–15.

Mead, Lawrence. *Beyond Entitlement*. New York: The Free Press, 1986.

Merton, Robert K. "The Unanticipated Consequences of Purposive Social Action." *American Sociological Review* 1 (1936): 894–904.

Miller, Seymour Michael. "The American Lower Classes: A Typological Approach." In Arthur B. Shostak and William Gomberg, eds. *Blue Collar World*. Englewood Cliffs, New Jersey: Prentice-Hall, 1964.

Moles, Oliver C. "Marital Dissolution and Public Assistance Payments: Variation Among American States." *Journal of Social Issues* 32 (Winter, 1976): 87–101.

Mott, Frank L. and Moore, Sylvia F. "The Causes of Marital Disruption Among Young American Women: An Interdisciplinary Perspective." *Journal of Marriage and the Family* 41 (May, 1979): 355–365.

Moynihan, Daniel P. *Family and Nation*. New York: Harcourt Brace, Jovanovich Publishers, 1987.

————. *The Negro Family: The Case for National Action*. Washington, D.C.: U.S. Government Printing Office, 1965.

Naisbitt, John. *Megatrends: Ten Directions Transforming Our Lives*. New York: Warner Books, Inc., 1982.

"1984 *Black Enterprise*'s Top 100 Black Businesses." *Black Enterprise* (June, 1985): 87–105.

Nobles, Wade. "Africanity: Its Role in Black Families." The *Black Scholar* 9 (June, 1974): 10–17.

"One Giant Step for Washington." *U.S. News and World Report* (December 23, 1985): 18–19.

Parsons, Talcott. "Age and Sex in the Structure of the United States." *American Sociological Review* 7 (1942).

Parsons, Talcott, and Bales, Robert. *Family, Socialization and the Interaction Process*. Glencoe, Illinois: Free Press, 1955.

Pattison, E.; Francisco, D.; Wood, P.; Frazier, H.; and Crowder, J. "A Psychosocial Kinship Model for Family Therapy." *American Journal of Psychiatry* 132 (1975): 1246–1251.

Pinkney, Alphonso. *The Myth of Black Progress*. New York: Cambridge University Press, 1984.

Piven, Frances, and Cloward, Richard. *Regulating the Poor: The Functions of Public Welfare*. New York: Vintage, 1971.

Pollack, E. S. "Monitoring A Comprehensive Mental Health Program." In L. M. Roberts; N. S. Greenfield; and M. H. Miller, eds. *Comprehensive Mental Health: The Challenge of Evaluations*. Madison, Wisconsin: University of Wisconsin Press, 1968.

Rainwater, Lee. *Family Design*. Chicago: AVC, 1965.

Rainwater, Lee, and Yancey, William. *The Moynihan Report and the Politics of Controversy*. Cambridge: M.I.T. Press, 1967.

"Reagan's Polarized America." *Newsweek* (April 5, 1982): 17–18.

Rodgers-Rose, La Frances. *The Family Woman*. Beverly Hills, California: Sage, 1981.

Rodman, Hyman "Family and Social Pathology in the Ghetto." *Science* 161 (1968), pp. 756–762.

Ross, Heather L., and Sawhill, Isabel V. *Time of Transition: The Growth of Families Headed by Women*. Washington, D.C.: The Urban Institute, 1975.

Roth, Dee; Bean, Jerry; Lust, Nancy; and Saveanu, Trian. *Homelessness in Ohio: A Study of People in Need*. Columbus, Ohio: The Ohio Department of Mental Health, 1985.

Rothman, David J. *The Discovery of the Asylum*. Boston, Massachusetts: Little, Brown and Company, 1971.

Scanzoni, John. *The Black Family in Modern Society: Patterns of Stability and Security*. Chicago: University of Chicago Press, 1977.

————. "Black Parental Values and Expectations of Children's Occupational and Educational Success: Theoretical Implications." In Harriette McAdoo and John McAdoo, eds. *Black Children*. Beverly Hills, California: Sage Publications, 1985, pp. 113–122.

"Senate, 93–3, Votes Welfare Revision Mandating Work," *The New York Times* (June 17, 1988): A-1.

Sowell, Thomas. *The Economics and Politics of Race*. New York: William Morrow and
    Company, 1983.
Spanier, Graham and Glick, Paul. "Mate Selection Differentials Between Blacks and
    Whites in the United States." *Social Forces* 58 (March, 1980): 707–725.
Spratlen, Thaddeus H. "The Continuing Factor of Black Economic Inequity in the United
    States." *Western Journal of Black Studies* 6 (Summer, 1982): 73–88.
Stack, Carol. *All Our Kin: Strategies for Survival in a Black Community*. New York:
    Harper and Row, 1974.
Staples, Robert. "The Black Professional Woman: Career Success and Interpersonal
    Failure." In *Black Working Women: Direction Toward a Humanistic Context for
    Social Science Research*. Berkeley, California: Center for the Study, Education
    and Advancement of Women (1981): 197–210.
———. "Family Life in the 21st Century: An Analysis of Old Forms, Current Trends
    and Future Scenarios." In Ida Martinson et al., eds. *Family Nursing*. (Englewood
    Cliffs, New Jersey: Prentice Hall, 1988), in press.
———. *Introduction to Black Sociology*. New York: McGraw-Hill, 1976.
———. "The Myth of the Black Matriarchy." *Black Scholar* (June, 1970): 2–9.
———. *The World of Black Singles: Changing Patterns of Male-Female Relations*.
    Westport, Connecticut: Greenwood Press, 1981.
"Still More Billions for Food Stamps." *U.S. News and World Report* (May, 1980): 7.
Sudarkasa, Niara. "Interpreting the African Heritage in Afro-American Family Orga-
    nization." In Harriette Pipes McAdoo, ed. *Black Families*, Beverly Hills, Cali-
    fornia: Sage Publications, 1981, pp. 37–53.
Swinton, David. "Economic Status of Blacks 1985." *The State of Black America*. Na-
    tional Urban League, 1986.
Taylor, William. "Access to Economic Opportunity: Lessons Since Brown." In Leslie
    W. Dunbar, ed. *Minority Report: What Has Happened to Blacks, Hispanics,
    American Indians and Other Minorities in the Eighties*. New York: Pantheon
    Books, 1984.
Tolsdorf, Christopher. "Social Networks, Support and Coping: An Exploratory Study."
    Family Process 15 (1976): 407–417.
Tucker, William. "Kindness Is Killing the Black Family." *This World* (January, 1985):
    7.
United States Bureau of the Census. *America's Black Population: 1970 to 1982. A
    Statistical View*. Special Publication, P10/POP 83–1. Washington, D.C.: U.S.
    Government Printing Office, 1983.
United States Bureau of the Census. *Current Population Reports*. Series P–20, No. 388.
    Washington, D.C.: U.S. Government Printing Office, 1984.
United States Bureau of the Census. *The Social and Economic Status of the Black
    Population in the United States: An Historical View, 1790–1978*. Series P–23,
    No. 80. Washington, D.C.: U.S. Goverment Printing Office, 1979.
United States Bureau of the Census. *Statistical Abstract of the United States. National
    Data Book and Guide to Sources*. Washington, D.C.: U.S. Goverment Printing
    Office, 1984.
U.S. Department of Health and Human Services." Statistical Report on Medical Care:
    Recipients, Payments, and Services." Health Care Financing Administration,
    1985 (unpublished).

U.S. Department of Health, Education and Welfare. *Findings of the 1973 AFDC Study: Park I.* Washington, D.C.: National Center for Social Statistics, 1974.

U.S. Department of Labor. *WIN Handbook.* No. 318. Washington, D.C.: U.S. Government Printing Office, 1984.

U.S. Social Security Administration. *Aid to Families With Dependent Children. Social Security Bulletin. Annual Statistical Supplement.* Washington, D.C.: Department of Health and Human Services, 1982.

Verbrugge, Lois M. "Marital Status and Health." *Journal of Marriage and the Family* 41 (May, 1979): 267–285.

Weitzman, Lenore. "The Economics of Divorce: Social and Economic Consequences of Property, Alimony and Child Support Awards." *UCLA Law Review* 28 (1981):1228.

"What Must Be Done About Children Having Children?" *Ebony.* (March, 1985): 76.

Williams, J. Allen, Jr., and Stockton, Robert. "Black Family Structures and Functions: An Emprical Examination of Some Suggestions Made by Billingsley." *Journal of Marriage and the Family* 35 (February, 1973): 39–49.

Williams, Walter E. *The State Against Blacks.* New York: McGraw-Hill, 1982.

Wolkon, George H.; Moruwaki, Sharon; Mandel, David; Archuleta, Jeraldine; Bunje, Pamela; and Zimmerman, Sandra. "Ethnicity and Social Class in the Delivery of Services: Analysis of a Child Guidance Clinic." *American Journal of Public Health* 64 (1974): 709–712.

Woodson, Robert L. "A Legacy of Entrepreneurship." In Robert L. Woodson, ed. *On the Road to Economic Freedom: An Agenda for Black Progress.* Washington, D.C.: National Center for Neighborhood Enterprise, 1987, pp. 1–26.

Zastrow, Charles. *Introduction to Social Welfare Institutions: Social Problems, Services and Current Issues.* Homewood, Illinois: Dorsey Press, 1982.

INDEX

About the Author

K. SUE JEWELL received her B.A. and M.A. degrees from Kent State University, and her Ph.D. from the Ohio State University. She is a sociologist and assistant professor at the Ohio State University. Over the past five years, she has published articles in the areas of the black family, cultural images of black women, the socialization of black children, and social policy. She previously conducted extensive research and evaluation in community mental health.